THE BLUEPRINT

THE BIBLE FOR BECOMING A SUCCESSFUL PERFORMING ARTIST IN THE DIGITAL AGE

FRANK DEMILT

Blue Heron Book Works, LLC

Allentown, Pennsylvania

ISBN:978-1-7354019-4-2

www.blueheronbookworks.com
www.frankdemilt.com
Cover image by Will Brunner @wgbrunner_design
Cover design by Angie Zumbrano

Praise for *The Blueprint* …

This is the most informative step-by-step guide on how to achieve success in the music industry. What makes this book unique is the covering of the total process by starting in the studio, no other book is showing you that.
Michael Cameron, Grammy/Emmy Nominated Music Publisher

As a working artist myself, I find *The Blueprint* refreshingly honest when it comes to today's music industry. A must read for any young or professional artist. The illustrations are well done, and it comes with a wealth of knowledge and guidance. It truly is a blueprint.
Barry Bee, saxophonist, performed with Prince, Sting, Ray Charles, Herbie Hancock, George Benson, & Larry Graham

Your book is very good, you've covered all of the bases in detail.
Ritch Esra, Music Registry

The new bible for what every new artist needs in the music business.
Ynvs DJ S-Nice

I see this book as a must read!! Very detailed with important facts and information for those who have serious interest in the music business.
Eric White, Grammy and Emmy award nominated music publisher

I definitely agree with the premise that the recording industry has kind of fragmented - artists are expected to produce fully completed works on their own AND establish a following before being of any interest to a label. There is definitely a need for a consolidated document like this. All the tools needed (+ specific examples), techniques, production steps in a logical order - really, really awesome references. I also like the mixture of ideas that clearly stem from professional experience, blended with the author's subjective opinion. I'm a fan of this book!
Aaron Rourk, composer and musician

Your new book is a great read and covers all the bases.
Rick Goudzwaard, M.A., ACC - Artist Development Coach

For the Creators

Contents

ACKNOWLEDGMENTS

Before starting, I feel it is important to write a few words of thanks to the people who have helped me in writing this book, inspired me to write this book, and helped me along my journey in the music industry.

Thank you to my mentor Michael Cameron. You have groomed me into the music professional I am today. You gave me a chance after one phone call in 2016, and we have been working together ever since. A one-word answer of, "Yes," to your question, "Do you know Pro Tools," is all that it took for you to give a struggling newbie engineer a home to learn and grow. Your teachings and methodology (however crazy it may have been) was the inspiration for this book. As you always preach, "One song, one opportunity, or one person can change your life," and if it wasn't for your sentiment of, "Everybody had an issue with Frank. I never had an issue with Frank. We understand each other and that's why he's still here," I wouldn't be in the position I am today.

Thank you to Eric White, Kim and the rest of the team at Water Music Publishing/Sloppy Vinyl. What we have been able to build and accomplish over the last few years has provided me with the opportunity to learn so many different aspects of the industry and trusting in me every step of the way has been paramount in my growth in the music industry.

Thank you to my parents. You have always supported me and my dreams of working in the music industry. You gave me the greatest gift in life, the opportunity to pursue my passion with unwavering encouragement. It hasn't always been easy, there have been some bumps along the road, but no matter how bad things seemed you never doubted that I would succeed. That unconditional love and support is what gave me the strength to keep going and the mindset to never give up and believe that I would succeed. I can't thank you enough for everything that you have done and continue to do for me.

Thank you to Alex. You showed up at one of the lowest and darkest times in my life. You immediately brought an energy with you that lightened up my life. You showed me there was a brighter side and lifted me up from where I was. You provided me with unmatched love, happiness, security, and peace of mind. No matter how bad things got you were always there with a smile on your face and words of encouragement. The effect you have had on my life is one that I never thought a single person could have on me. You gave me the greatest gift I have ever received. You showed me love, happiness, peace, and most importantly you showed me who I could truly be. Thank you from the bottom of my heart. Forever & Always, Infinity.

INTRODUCTION

I have spent the last decade working with Grammy Award-winning artists and producers, Grammy and Emmy Award-nominated music publishers, and executives responsible for tens of millions of records sold in multiple positions including: intern, studio runner, recording engineer, mixing engineer, head engineer, studio manager, studio head, A&R, artist manager and music publisher. Working in these positions I have come to the major realization that artist development is a dying art form. This sentiment is shared by the executives I have worked with who have stated, "Artist development no longer happens. Talent no longer matters. If an artist doesn't have the numbers, a non-artist with a million followers will get signed faster than the most talented singer with a mere thousand followers."

Because of the advancement of technology, the ubiquity of social media, and the rise of the DIY era of music, major record labels no longer spend the time and money to build an artist from the ground up. Labels are looking for artists that have an already established fan base, hundreds of thousands of monthly listeners on streaming platforms, millions of social media followers, and multiple songs on major curated playlists. Talent has become a secondary attribute, replaced by numbers and analytics.

Nowadays, major labels no longer expend their resources on undeveloped talent. In the past, major record labels were on a worldwide search for promising talent. They would put tens of thousands of dollars into the development process, hoping to create the next musical sensation. This rigorous artist development program would span the course of months or sometimes years and would include: media training, vocal coaching, songwriting, song structure, show rehearsal, choreography, branding, image and, in more recent years, social media/content creation.

While there are independent labels, production companies, and publishing companies that still invest in artist development, even these labels and companies are looking at numbers more so than talent. An independent label is looking for emerging artists that have not yet reached their tipping point. Production companies are looking for the next big producer. Publishing companies are on the prowl for songwriters and producers that have multiple placements on major artists.

While this is great for established artists, writers, and producers, where does it leave the hundreds of thousands of up-and-coming artists? It leaves these artists in the cold to figure out the music industry for themselves. New and emerging talent has to decipher the formula for creating great music, how to release/promote their music, and how to grow/maintain a fan base on their own.

As easy as some of those answers seem on the surface, the results are the tough part. You can easily promote your music through the multitude of social media channels. However, with over three billion active monthly users across all platforms, and billions of more posts in that same time frame, how does a new artist stand a chance to make an impact? How is a new artist supposed to get noticed?

Because of the ever-changing nature of the music industry, there is no "One Size Fits all" for breaking into this industry. I would be remiss to say *The Blueprint* serves as an end all be all. Rather this book serves as a guide to take you through the process from recording your first song to getting signed and it finishes with how to sustain your career.

Every artist is in a unique position, comes from a unique background, and has their own starting point, all of which ultimately affects this process. One major artist originally came out as a teenager under her real name. Her team realized she wasn't fully ready and took her back into development before she reemerged years later to become a Grammy Award winning artist. Another was in development with a top independent label for over two years before her first album release (which went platinum). The artist development process takes years when done properly. As the cliché goes, "It's a marathon not a sprint."

Chapter 1   THE EQUIPMENT

The right equipment and understanding the nuances of recording is the difference between someone listening to your song or discarding it after a few bars. In recording there are many things to consider.

But before you can consider anything, you have to know what equipment is needed for the music creation process to be done effectively. Here is a list of the equipment you will need to get started on your recording:

- Digital Audio Workstation (DAW - recording/editing audio computer software program)
- Audio Interface
- Studio Monitors
- Microphone
- Headphones
- Cables
- Mic Stand
- Pop Filter
- Computer

Choosing the correct DAW to use comes with a few caveats. First, it's going to depend on the computer you have. Second, which operating system you're running. Last, how powerful your computer is (meaning the amount of RAM and internal cores the computer has). Pro Tools, Fruity Loops (FL Studios), Logic, and Ableton are your top DAW options (Luna, a new competitor, is gaining recognition as well). Each DAW has its own strengths and weaknesses, but they are all comparable. Even Garageband, the free MAC software program, provides a decent alternative if you can't afford one of the other programs.

Pro Tools is the industry standard, used in every major music studio in the world. However, Pro Tools has the steepest learning curve. This program is best used for recording and mixing as its setup, design, and functionality were created specifically for these purposes.

Logic and Fruity Loops (FL Studios) are mainly used by producers. Some producers and engineers will argue that Logic gives you more flexibility and a better workflow compared to Pro Tools in terms of recording, editing, and production, but this is a personal preference. The same debate applies to Logic and FL Studios regarding music production.

Ableton is better used for DJs performing a live show. However, more producers are swearing by it, and using this DAW for their production. For live show editing, Ableton provides a quick and easy workflow for manipulating sounds and MIDI (musical instrument digital interface) compared to the other DAWs. Allowing you complete editing in real time with a seamless workflow is why this DAW is preferred by DJs compared to Pro Tools, Logic, or FL Studios.

Most of these programs offer a trial period of around seven days to decide if you want to purchase. Seven days won't be enough time to understand the full functionality of each program, but it will allow you enough time to see what the program has to offer. If you're an artist looking to record vocals, Pro Tools, Logic, or Ableton are going to be your best options. Logic or Ableton are going to initially be easier to use than Pro Tools, but as someone who has used each of these programs, I am partial to Pro Tools (the program I started with) because being the "industry standard" you're going to have to know how to use this DAW when working with other people in the studio. Not everyone uses the other DAWs, but all studios and engineers use Pro Tools when tracking and mixing. For production, Logic or FL Studios are going to be the go-to options. If you're going to be performing more live shows as a DJ, Ableton is the right choice.

Once you've chosen your software, it's time to select equipment. Starting with the interface and microphone, Focusrite or Mbox are going to be the most affordable options. These interfaces and microphones can either be bought separately, or as a combination including the interface, a microphone, cables, and a set of headphones. For your first in-home studio, I recommend purchasing them as a combination, because it's less expensive, offers guaranteed compatibility and technical support. Two bundle options to consider are:

The Presonus AudioBox iTwo recording bundle:[i]

- Bus powered USB audio interface for true portability (USB cable included)
- M7 condenser microphone (mic cable included)
- Studio One Artist DAW software
- Capture Duo iPad app

Focusrite's Scarlett 2i2 3rd generation recording bundle:[ii]

- Ableton Live Lite Music Making Software
- Pro Tools First Focusrite Creative Pack
- Focusrite Red 2 & Red 3 Plug-in Suite
- XLN Audio Addictive Keys Virtual Instruments
- Softube Time & Tone Bundle
- Access to Focusrite Plug-In Collective
- Free three-month Splice Sounds Subscription

These interfaces are easy to use as they have only an input (volume) control for the microphone and the rest of the settings will come from the DAW. When I purchased my studio bundle, I chose the Scarlett 2i2 because of the extra software plug-in features for Pro Tools. Like the DAW choice, this will be a preference based on your needs. I suggest reading reviews and watching YouTube videos on each of these interfaces to see which one entices you the most.

Choosing the right microphone will depend on what you're recording, the room you're recording in, and how you want the audio to sound. Each microphone has a distinct polar pattern that determines how sound is recorded into the microphone. There are three different polar patterns a microphone can have:

- Cardioid, meaning audio will only be picked up from the front of the microphone.
- Figure eight, meaning audio will be picked up from both the front and back of the microphone.
- Omni, meaning audio will be picked up from all sides of the microphone.

Polar Patterns

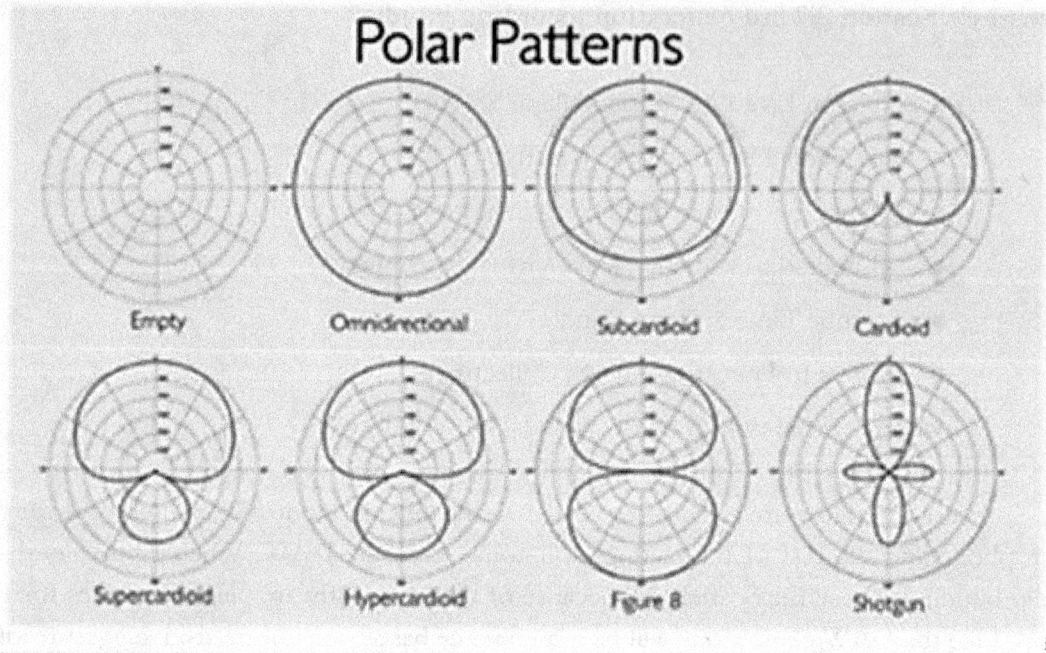

Empty · Omnidirectional · Subcardoid · Cardoid · Supercardoid · Hypercardoid · Figure 8 · Shotgun

iii

These pick-up patterns and the mechanics inside the microphone are important because each voice and instrument has different frequencies that the microphone will pick up differently. Some microphones will add more high frequencies creating a thinner sound, and some will add more low frequencies creating a fuller sound.

If you're a vocalist with a strong low vocal tone like Issac Hayes and the microphone you're recording with has a fuller, low frequency sound, your vocal could turn out muddy. Conversely, if you have a high-pitched vocal tone like Tones and I and the microphone you're using enhances the high frequencies, your vocal could sound harsh and brittle. Therefore, most artists have a specific microphone they will always record with, because they know this microphone will create the optimal recording for their voice.

There are three different types of microphones you can choose from:

- Dynamic Microphone
- Ribbon Microphone
- Condenser Microphone

A dynamic microphone has a thin membrane attached to a coil. These two pieces are surrounded by a magnet, so when the microphone picks up sound, the membrane and coil move and create an electromagnetic signal that can be transferred to your sound system. Not only are dynamic microphones usually the most affordable, they're also durable and because of their durability, they're the most common choice for live sound. Unfortunately, they aren't considered to be as accurate as the other microphones, because of their wide frequency range and high sensitivity.[iv]

Ribbon microphones are considered to be the most authentic sounding as they are the oldest form of microphone technology. Their construction is very simple and often built by hand because the components are so delicate. Ribbon microphones contain a very thin piece of corrugated tin foil placed between two high powered, permanently charged magnets. The resulting electrical signal then goes through a transformer that increases the power to a usable level for amplification, as they need a lot of gain (or level) for a usable signal. Because of their fragile nature, ribbon microphones are easy to damage, in fact the foil that makes up a ribbon microphone can disintegrate if rubbed between your fingers, and some ribbon microphones can be damaged if you accidentally apply phantom power to the microphone. Ribbon microphones can be more expensive than their counterparts, but they offer a great sounding recording.[v]

Condenser microphones are a nice middle ground between ribbon and dynamic microphones, and you'll typically see them being used in a recording studio setting. Condenser microphones are relatively durable, but not as durable as dynamic microphones. However, newer solid state condenser microphones are comparable to the most durable dynamic microphones. Condenser microphones create sound with an electrically charged plate next to a solid capacitor placed inside the microphone capsule. When sound enters the microphone, the diaphragm moves and the backplate stays still. The changing distance between the two plates creates an electrical signal which is a recreation of the original sound source. Condenser microphones need a power source of either phantom power or batteries to strengthen the signal. Phantom Power is when Direct Current (DC) is delivered to microphones requiring electric power to drive active circuitry. A battery located inside the microphone can provide the power, or (most commonly) the pre-amp/mixer is delivered to the condenser microphone via the microphone cable. The worldwide standard for phantom power is 11 to 52 volts of DC, and your pre-amp will typically have a button labelled 48v, which allows you to turn phantom power on/off. Some older mixers and cheaper audio interfaces may not have phantom power. If this is the case an external phantom power supply can be added between the condenser microphone and the pre-amp.[vi]

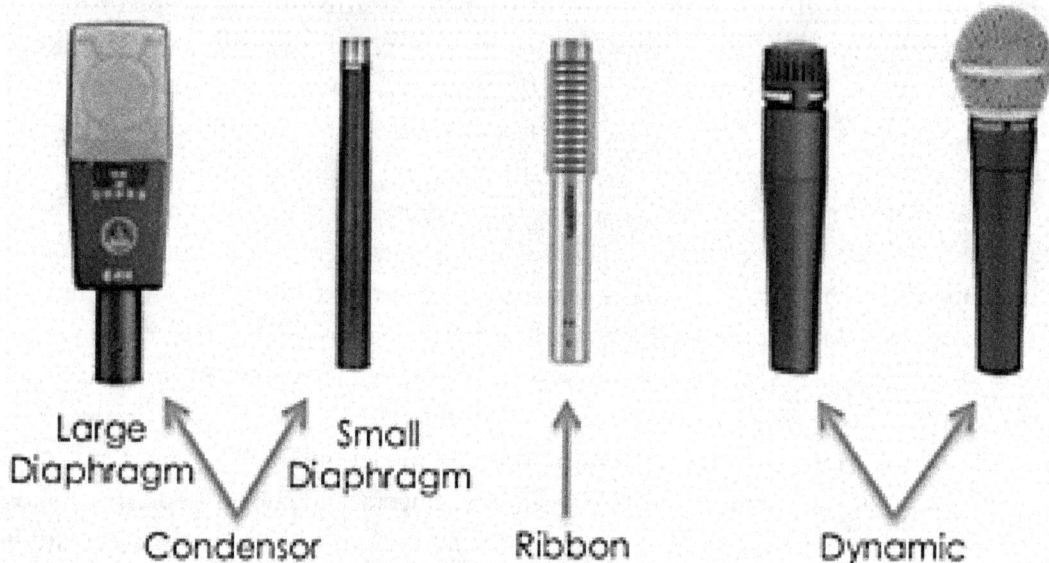

Large Diaphragm — Small Diaphragm — Condensor — Ribbon — Dynamic

Tonal problems and proximity effect can be more prevalent in lower-priced microphones. In singers with lower registers, like crooners, proximity effect (when the lower frequencies become exaggerated) can occur if they are standing too close to the microphone when recording. For other vocal styles, it can make them come across as muddy and indistinct. You'll want to listen for plosive sounds like "p," "ck," or "t," as in lower-quality equipment these sounds may create a severe popping noise. To remedy this, you must use a pop filter in front of your microphone to ease the harshness that comes from pronouncing these letters. Various commercial nylon and metal mesh pop shields are available, but you can create your own using a nylon stocking material stretched over a suitable hoop. The pop filter should be about two inches away from the microphone (use your fist as a measuring tool), and the singer should be about six inches away from the pop filter. If you're too close to the microphone when recording you can sound muffled and are more likely to clip or distort. If your vocals are distorting or clipping (meaning the input level on your vocals are too high) you cannot fix this in post-production. You will have to re-record the vocals completely.

Last, look for consistency, as some companies will have better quality control than others. It's important to do your research and see if the microphone model you're buying performs consistently well. Since most artist start out just recording vocals, here are a few of the "classic" vocal microphones I recommend:

- **BLUEBIRD SL**

Bluebird SL delivers pristine, highly versatile sound that makes every detail of your performance come to life. With a high-pass filter and -20dB pad, Bluebird SL is ideal for capturing standout vocal performances, expressing the true tone of guitars, piano and more with extended upper clarity, smooth mids and rich lows. Next stop, top-flight sound.[vii]

- **SHURE SM27**

Cardioid large diaphragm condenser microphone delivers exceptional stage and studio performance applications. Features include a preamplifier for transparency, switchable low-frequency filter, and a -15dB switchable attenuator for SPL versatility.[viii]

Courtesy of sE Electronics

- **sE X1 S:**

X1 S utilizes a hand-made condenser capsule, meticulously constructed and tuned in sE's capsule room by technicians with decades of experience. The redesigned electronics of the X1 S take its performance to a whole new level, giving it the highest dynamic range in its class. Its internal redesign also allows for improved sensitivity, dramatically increased SPL handling (up to 160dB), and a huge reduction in self-noise. The -10 dB and -20 dB pad switches provide extended dynamic range, enabling a wide range of applications and close-mic techniques for even the loudest instruments. Think super-heavy electric guitars, fortissimo brass instruments, and heavy-footed kick drums. Selectable at either 80Hz or 160Hz, these two filters help eliminate low-frequency rumble or footfall noise, as well as help compensate for excessive bass (proximity effect) with close-mic techniques.[ix]

A helpful piece of equipment to assist with a cleaner recording is a microphone shock mount. This isn't mandatory, but it helps eliminate low-frequency vibrations coming up from the floor and is especially helpful on wooden floors. Some microphones come with a shock mount, but if not, inexpensive generic mounts are available for most microphones.

The next piece of equipment you will need is a set of headphones. There are two different types of headphones you can choose from:

- Closed-back headphones
- Open-back headphones

While open-back headphones are considered more of a luxury for your first studio, closed-back headphones are a necessity. The difference between open-back and closed-back headphones is the amount of noise that is let through the back of the headphones. Closed-back headphones let in very little sound and are sound isolating to a certain extent. Open back headphones allow you to hear natural room noise. While open-back headphones are good for mixing, unless you have a trained ear these headphones are not necessarily something you should use. I prefer to use closed-back headphones because they block out most if not all other sound, which for me is great when mixing so I am not hearing outside noise which could affect the sound of my mix. A general rule to remember:

- Closed-back headphones are for tracking
- Open-back headphones are for mixing

A few headphone options are:

SENNHEISER HD280 – SENNHEISER ELECTRONIC CORPORATION – SENNHEISER.COM

SHURE SRH440 – "©SHURE INCORPORATED. ALL RIGHTS RESERVED.

AKG – K240 STUDIO

AUDIO TECHNICA ATH – M20x

My two preferences of headphones are either of the AKG models. The K240 Studios are ones I have used in studios for years because they block out all background sound and music bleed and are comfortable to wear for long periods of time. The same holds true with the ATH-M20x model which are my everyday headphones. I wear these to critically listen to music on my phone or laptop because of the great sound quality they offer.

The last piece of equipment needed to complete your in-home studio are a set of monitors. Depending on your set-up these may not be necessary, but they are extremely helpful if you are planning on doing the entire creation process by yourself. A good pair of headphones can get you relatively far, but a set of monitors will take your music quality to the next level. Be mindful of your room's acoustic set-up, as this can drastically affect the sound from the monitors.

When purchasing studio monitors you have to understand you need *monitors not speakers*. Monitors provide you with a flatter more natural frequency response. Your mix sounds like exactly what you're hearing, where speakers give you an inaccurate depiction of what your mix sounds like. There are a few different physical aspects you need to consider when deciding on your studio monitors:

- **ROOM SIZE:** Based on your room size, there are two different types of monitors to consider:

1. **Near field monitors:** These are designed to be 4-5 feet away from where you sit. This makes them ideal for home studios or bedroom studios that may not have proper acoustic treatment, as a shorter distance will reduce the reflections of the audio.[x]

2. **Far field/soffit monitors:** These are mounted on high stands or built into the music studio's back wall. They are ideal for large studios treated with acoustic panels. The main purpose of far field monitors is for checking the low end of the mix.[xi]

- **ACTIVE VS PASSIVE MONITORS**
    1. **Active monitors:** These monitors have a built-in amplifier. The amplifiers in active monitors are matched specifically to the power needs of the monitors.
    2. **Passive monitors:** These monitors will need to be plugged into an external amplifier.

- **TWEETERS AND WOOFERS**

    1. **Tweeter:** This handles all the higher frequencies, from 2kHz-20kHz.

    2. **Woofer:** This handles the lower frequencies, from 40Hz-5kHz. The larger the size of your woofer, the better it will handle the lower frequencies.

With a better understanding of what types of monitors will best fit your studio needs, what are some of your monitor options? A few studio monitors to consider are:

1.   KRK ROKIT 5 G4:

   The KRK Rokit 5 G4's feature matching Kevlar drivers, onboard equalization (EQ) with a visual screen, and a scientifically designed enclosure. They ensure the sonic quality is the same regardless of the frequencies playing, thus keeping your ears from fatiguing quickly allowing you to work longer. KRK Rokits are sturdy and have been built with very high-quality materials, which also translates to providing a better, more accurate sound. These studio monitors have a frequency response range of 43Hz-40kHz.[xii]

2. JBL 305P MkII:

The active amplified 305Ps boast a 5-inch woofer, and a frequency response rate of 49Hz-20kHz. These studio monitors have EQ controls on the back, so you can adjust low and high frequencies to get the most out of the monitors based on the acoustic treatment of your room and provide rich low end and clear top end without adding coloration. The port on the back of each monitor is tailored specifically for low-end frequencies with Slipstream technology to ensure that low frequencies will not overload the woofers. The sweet spot of the monitors is broad, so no matter where you are in the room you will get a very accurate representation of your mix.[xiii]

3. YAMAHA NS-10:

I have an affinity for the Rokit KRKs because they are the very first studio monitor, I ever purchased and used in my home studio. I have also used them in almost every other studio I have worked in to some capacity so when I am mixing, I know exactly how a mix should sound on these speakers. My other go to would be the Yamaha HS-10 monitors because of the sound and frequency range they provide. I have been using a set of these speakers for the last five years when mixing songs and, because of their heavy mid-range frequency response, I know that if I can make the low end of the mix sound good on these it will translate to any speaker system.

Deciding which equipment to outfit your studio with is comparable to interior designing your house. You could have the most beautifully structured house, but if the furniture you pick doesn't accent the room, the beauty of the house is lost. Choosing the right equipment for your room will be the difference in creating amazing quality music and sounding like a novice.

When deciding which equipment to buy, at first you need to know your budget. Most artists at the beginning of their careers don't necessarily have an immense budget to work with. But if price is of no concern, splurge for the top-of-the-line equipment which will provide the best quality sound for your music. The quality will still be affected by your recording room and your knowledge of the equipment. If you are on a budget, it's better to get the best bang for your buck than to get the most expensive equipment. Remember, it won't matter how good the equipment is if the person using the equipment doesn't know how to use it. Music is not a case of "The builder is only as good as the tools they have." It's quite the opposite.

If you're on a budget and looking to outfit your recording studio needs, the equipment you will absolutely need is:

- **Microphone:** One of the dynamic condenser microphones I mentioned above will suffice and will provide a good quality recording for a relatively low price.

- **Headphones:** I would suggest either the Behringer HPM1000 or the TASCAM TH-02 as these two closed-back headphones have a great sound quality and comfortability for their price points.

- **Interface:** For your first interface, there a few different options. However, as I mentioned above, my preference is the Scarlett. This interface is easy to use, connects to any computer with a USB port, and is compatible with both PC and MAC.

- **XLR Cable:** This cable is what connects your microphone to the interface. The price for these cables will vary depending on length, however, for your first set-up a short cable of 3-6 feet will suffice and be your cheapest option.

- **Mic Stand:** This stand is so you don't have to hold the microphone while recording. For the needs of your first equipment purchase, this stand doesn't have to be elaborate, and just about any stand will do.

NEUMANN TLM 102 – SENNHEISER ELECTRONIC CORPORATION
SENNHEISER.COM

NEUMANN U87 – SENNHEISER ELECTRONIC CORPORATION
SENNHEISER.COM

TOWNSEND LAB SPHERE L22 – UNIVERSAL AUDIO

RØDE NTI-A

COURTESY RØDE MICROPHONES

As mentioned before, most of this equipment can be purchased as part of a bundle, but this will restrict you're buying options to one manufacturer. Choosing to purchase the equipment separately can be slightly pricier but will give you a wider variety of manufacturers and designers.

Now, if budget is of no concern and you're looking to purchase the best equipment possible then the equipment you should be looking for will consist of a wider range:

- **Microphone:** If you're looking to purchase an incredible microphone, a few options are pictured above (still remembering that each microphone works better on certain voices than others).

- **Headphones:** Honestly, one set of headphones will probably be enough, but if you're not worried about price, why not splurge and purchase both closed-back and open-back headphones. If this is your choice get the Audio-Technica ATH-M50x closed-back headphones for recording and the Sennheiser HD 600 open-back headphones for mixing.

- **Monitors:** You're going to want at least one set of monitors to provide a better gauge on how your mix sounds, but you could also choose to purchase two separate sets of monitors, one for near-field listening and one for far-field listening. If you're creating an in-home studio, far-field monitors are not necessary, so a single pair of studio monitors will suffice. A great set of speakers to buy would be the Yamaha HS5.

- **Interface:** When it comes to great interfaces Universal Audio (UAD) makes some of the best audio interfaces, bar-none. Your best choice of UAD interfaces is going to be the Apollo. They make a few different models of the Apollo interface that are all equally incredible, the only difference being the number of inputs and outputs each one has:

  - Apollo Twin X Duo 10x6
  - Apollo Twin X Quad 10x6
  - Apollo x4 12x18
  - Apollo x6 16x22
  - Apollo x8 18x24
  - Apollo x8p 16x22
  - Apollo x16 18x20

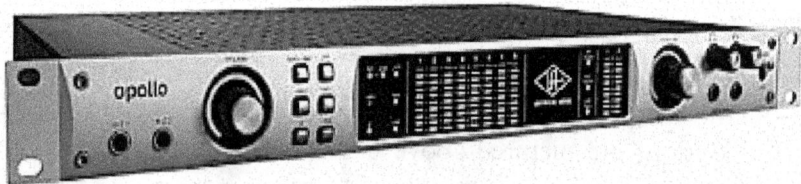

UNIVERSAL AUDIO

With all of that being said, the same can be true with top-of-the-line interfaces. As I mentioned with budget interfaces, they can be purchased in a bundle or individually. If you would rather purchase a bundle to get everything at once, instead of purchasing the equipment individually, here are some great options:

- **Townsend Labs Sphere L22 and Apollo Twin X Quad bundle:**[xiv] This bundle provides you with the Apollo interface, XLR cable, microphone stand, pop filter and the Townsend Microphone Modeling System. This microphone comes with a software that emulates the best microphones available. It allows you to create a combination of multiple microphones thus creating your own unique sound it also allows you to choose how much of each microphone sound you want and where you want to place the microphone. Possibly the best part, is that you're able to change all of these settings after the recording is complete. This is one of the best bundles you can buy.

- **Manley Reference Cardioid Microphone & Shelford Channel Bundle:**[xv] This bundle provides you with one of the best cardioid microphones available. Manley microphones are used by some of the top studios, top engineers, and world-renowned singers. Coupled with a Shelford channel strip and XLR cable, this bundle provides you with an incredible quality and flexibility to manipulate your voice through the channel to create the optimal recording.

I would lean towards the Apollo interface and bundle if you are looking to go a little higher end. In using the Apollo interface for a few years now, I can attest to the sound quality, flexibility and power it gives you when both recording and mixing. In the same bundle, the Townsend microphone gives you emulations of the best microphones in the world.

Whether on a budget or not, bundles are the way to go to begin your journey in becoming an artist. Providing you with all of the necessary equipment to get you started is a luxury that passing up would be ill-advised.

Chapter 2   THE RECORDING PROCESS

The recording process is arguably the most important step in starting your music career. The listener will decide within the first bar if they want to continue listening to your songs. A song with great sound quality can make the listener continue listening even if they don't know who the artist is. Whereas bad sound quality can turn the listener off before your song begins.

As an audio engineer myself, I have a unique perspective on listening to music. Apart from listening as a fan and consumer, I listen to each song in a technical aspect, dissecting each part. How the vocals sound, how the instruments sound, where the vocals are sitting in the mix, the efx used, the structure of the beat, the structure of the song, the lyrics, and how the artist flows and sits in the pocket. The average consumer listening to music won't listen this intently, but subconsciously their listening experience will be affected by these aspects.

Before we go through the intricacies of how to properly record a song, it's best for you to understand the full process your music will go through beginning to end.

1. You record your music. If you can afford it, you hire a producer and/or recording engineer to guide you through the recording process. If you can't afford it, you produce the song yourself.
2. You then send your song to a mixing engineer. During the mixing stage, the engineer raises or lowers the levels of each track so they have their own place in the mix. The engineer communicates with you as they work on the mix to ensure you approve how it sounds.
3. You send the mix to a mastering engineer. The mastering engineer's job is to listen to the final mix and adjust the overall volume of the song and add any post-production eft or additional compression. This readies the song for commercial release and makes it more appealing to listeners.

So, where do you begin? What are the best settings for your voice? How do you know if your levels are correct? How do you set up your recording session in your DAW?

The first step in recording is creating your recording session. Each DAW has a set of pre-made templates for different recording styles, and if you're new to the recording process, I would suggest finding which template is the most suitable for your music style and begin there.

These pre-made templates are constructed by the makers of each DAW and equipped with the necessary tracks and routing for a seamless recording.

Creating your own recording template is also an option, but this can be complicated if you're new to recording. If you create your own session, you will start with a blank slate that allows you to add any track you like and as many as you like. The issue is the intricacy that goes into creating your own session. You will need "audio tracks" to record each of your vocal takes, "auxiliary tracks" used for controlling multiple tracks at one time, "efx tracks" for your desired vocal efx, and a "master track" to control the overall volume of your session. Ensuring these tracks are set up properly can be difficult when you're just starting out but creating your own session can be beneficial as it will allow you complete control over your workflow. It took me close to five years to perfect my recording and mixing templates, and to this day as I continue to learn new methods and new plugins are released, I am constantly changing and updating my templates. Here is how you would set up your recording session:

1. **Create Your Tracks:** When you create your tracks there will be a few options you can choose from:
    a. **Audio Track:** These tracks allow you to record any type of audio into your DAW.
    b. **Auxiliary Track:** These tracks allow you to have control over multiple tracks on a single track. This can be audio tracks, other auxiliary tracks, or a combination of both.
    c. **Master Track:** This is the track that will control all tracks in the session.

2. **Name Your Tracks:** It's important to name all of your created tracks so you can easily identify which track is which, as every created track will initially be titled with the type of track followed by a number.

3. **Color Code Your Tracks:** Making all similar tracks the same color allows for further identification of each track. Make all vocal tracks one color, instruments another color, auxiliary tracks a third color, and so on.

4. **Route Your Tracks:** This is how you will control multiple tracks with one track. If you look at the picture below, at the top there is a section labeled, "I/O" which means In and Out. This indicates where the track is receiving a signal from and where that signal is being sent out to. The input needs to be set on audio tracks to your microphone

input, on auxiliary tracks it will be a "bus." A bus allows you to send signals to and from other auxiliary tracks while not interfering with other auxiliary track signals. For example: you have a group of audio tracks containing vocals that you want to send an auxiliary track labeled "Vocals" so you can manipulate all of your vocals through this auxiliary track. First, you will set the input (the first light grey rectangle under the "I/O") to the "bus" of your choice. Next, you will set the output (the second light grey rectangle under the "I/O") of all the vocal tracks you want to send to this auxiliary track to the "bus" you chose for the input of your "Vocals" auxiliary track. If done properly all the selected vocal tracks will now send their signal to this auxiliary track, allowing you to affect the sound of all these vocal tracks at once through this auxiliary track.

The picture below is of the "mix window" in Avid Pro Tools. This is to give you a better understanding of what I have explained above. The in/out (I/O) referred to above is at the top of the picture. The names and colors of your tracks are at the bottom. Minus the names associated with each track below, this is what a track will look like once created in the Avid Pro Tools DAW.

AVID PRO TOOLS

Once you have all of your tracks created, labeled, color coded, and routed correctly, you can begin testing each track to ensure they are sending and receiving signal properly, enabling you to start recording.

The second step is to set your input volume on your interface to a level so that your audio is not distorting or peaking. You can check this by looking at the levels in the DAW, making sure you are in the green and not in the red at the top of the meter. If you look at the above picture, you will see a meter is associated with every track. These meters show you how much volume each track is receiving and sending out. If the track is at a good level, the meter will be green; if the track is at a slightly high level the meter will be yellow; and if the track is too high, the meter will be red. While visual cues are good, use your ears, they are your best friends in this process. How else do you listen to music? You can tell if your vocals are clipping or distorting because they will sound crunchy and unclear.

Video tutorials on YouTube (YouTube University) are a good place to go for help if you're having issues when recording. Channels such as Pensado's Place, RecordingRevolution, and Produce Like A Pro, (all of which I used when starting my career 10 years ago as an engineer) offer top tier video tutorials that can assist you in all aspects of creating music. If you're looking for a more personal mentor approach, you can join one of our artist groups on www.frankdemilt.com and/or become part of our monthly book club. Through these groups you become part of our artist development community allowing you to interact with other artists, receive personalized one-on-one coaching, and overall assistance in every aspect of your artist development journey. It is important to have two types of mentors. Your first mentor should someone in your field you look up to, even if you don't have a personal connection, whose work you both admire and strive to emulate. Your second mentor should be someone you can connect with for questions and guidance.

Lastly, before recording, set the volume of the beat you're using. Depending on where you got the beat from you will have to lower the level of the beat to hear yourself recording. DO NOT TURN YOUR VOCALS UP SO YOU CAN HEAR THEM OVER THE BEAT WHEN THE BEAT IS AT 0 DB! This will cause your vocals to distort immediately and will make it impossible to blend the beat and your vocals properly when mixing. A rule of thumb I learned in one of my first internships is turn the beat down to -10db. This will differ for each beat. Using this level mark will create more headroom (overall level before hitting 0db) in your recording, allowing for a better sound quality during the mixing process.

Now think about the room you will be recording in. A room with soft furnishings (bedroom or living room) is preferable compared to a room with hard surfaces or windows (kitchens). When you're recording vocals, you want the room to have the least number of reflective surfaces for these reasons:

- Natural reverberation (reverb), room resonances and reflections are detrimental to vocal recordings because this noticeable reverb makes it difficult to blend artificial reverb plug-ins when mixing.
- Reverb effects the vocals place in the mix which makes them more difficult to hear in the mix. The vocals are the main part of your song. You want them to be front and center.
- Natural reverb effects the accuracy of pitch correction.
- Applying dynamic processing to the vocals during the mix will make any natural reverb more noticeable.

However, if a room is too dead, meaning there is too much sound absorption, the sound recordings will sound unnatural. The ideal recording room has a balance of sound absorption and reflective surfaces as this will create a natural sounding recording while eliminating unwanted reflections.

Reflective walls, ceilings, and furniture are a common problem in home studios as these fixtures tend to corrupt your vocal sound. To alleviate some of these issues, you can hang a duvet behind the person recording, as this will eliminate any reflections coming from behind your head that the microphone would otherwise pick up. To reduce the microphone picking up sound from the sides, you can hang two duvet covers in the form a 'V' then stand with your back facing the apex. These home-made acoustic treatments are effective at high and mid-range frequencies, but their efficiency falls off at low-frequencies. They are adequate for vocal ranges but doubling up the thickness or using a heavy winter-grade duvet will improve the efficiency in the low-end. Adding a rug or carpet on the floor, and a foam panel above the microphone will also help tremendously. As a last fix, you can shield the rear of the microphone with a piece of acoustic foam. Think of setting up for your recording like you're trying to take a great vacation picture. A budget camera can give you a fantastic picture if what is in front of the lens looks good. But if the lighting is bad, and the angle is incorrect, even the most expensive editing equipment won't fix the picture.

Now think about the distance of the microphone from your mouth, as this will relate to the perceived character of the recording. Being close to the microphone (a distance of two to four inches) produces a tight, warm, breathy detailed recording. However, being this close to the microphone will also enunciate all the sounds of the mouth (lip smacks, sounds from the tongue, throat and saliva), and create greater vocal pops and sibilance ("esses" and "whistling sounds" in the high-end vocal frequency). On the other hand, standing about ten to sixteen inches from the microphone when recording will produce a more natural, open, and less "in your face" vocal, and it is less likely to suffer from excessive sibilance. However, being this far from the microphone will add more natural room sounds to your recording, which are not always desired. A typical working distance that produces the best results is around six-ten inches. This distance will allow for the least amount of natural room sound, less emphasis on mouth sounds, and create a more even recording. Ultimately, it's up to you to decide what sounds better for your recoding. If you're unsure try test recording with the microphone in different positions to see what sounds the best. A few of the different microphone positions to experiment with are:

- Closer to the nose which accentuate nasality but reduces mouth pops and sibilance frequencies.
- Closer to the throat which produces a deeper and darker sound.

Next, decide a placement for the microphone in the recording room. There are two rules to take into account:

- Avoid the direct center of the room.
- Avoid placing the microphone directly next to reflective surfaces and walls.

Considering these rules, the best placement for your microphone is just off the center of the room. Most people don't realize how important this step is. Microphone choice combined with position is 80% of your vocal sound and finding the best position for the microphone takes some experimentation. All singers are different, and this step will be easier for some artists than for others. Skip either of these steps, and your vocal is going to be harder to mix.

The last step of the pre-production process is deciding if you want to record with efx on your voice, or if you want to record dry. If you record with efx on your voice, your options include: reverb, delays, equalization, compression, and a myriad of other plug-in options that allow for digital audio manipulation. If you use plug-ins on your recording track, you will hear a difference in your voice according to what plug-ins you add. I prefer to record dry, using only light compression for dynamic control, as this gives me more leeway in post-production. I know many engineers who record with EQ and compression on the vocals (normally from outboard gear) but this is the preference of the engineer and artist. One thing to consider if you do record your vocals with EQ, compression and/or efx on your vocals, is that once recorded, you can no longer change these efx and you would have to re-record the entire vocal if you want to change how they sound. This is only the case if you're recording through an outboard gear chain. If you're recording into your DAW, you can take the efx off after the recording channel and not affect the overall sound. Each plug-in has various presets created by professional engineers and using these presets will give you a good baseline on where to start in the post-production process.

Once the pre-production process is complete, the first vocal you're going to record is the lead vocal. This is going to be the main vocal of your track. You want this vocal to be clear, strong, have feeling and be believable. This is the vocal that the rest of your vocal takes will be based on. If you're mumbling, the audience won't be able to sing along because they won't be able to understand what you're saying. If your lead lacks feeling, or believability, you won't keep your listeners' attention, and your performance will be forgettable. Your lead vocal is the most important part of your song. A good lead can propel a song to great heights. A bad lead can make a song crash and burn.

Stacks and backing tracks are used to emphasize certain words and phrases throughout the song. With rappers, stacks (recording a copy of the lead in the same vocal tone) are used in a technique called "In and Out." This means that the last word or few words of each phrase will be recorded one or two more times to emphasize what is being said. An older recording technique used in rap is stacking the entire lead vocal to create more presence in the lead vocal. For singers using this technique, the "In and Out" will not be in the same tone but rather a harmony note. For the hook with both rappers and singers, there will be at least two stacks of the lead vocal panned hard left and right to create a surrounding effect giving the impression of a wider vocal. Not every song needs this technique, and you will make this decision depending on the style of the song. If you want to stack the lead vocal, it's best to do it live. You may have enough spare takes from compiling your lead vocal that you can build this vocal stack without re-recording, but this may cause more correction effort in post-production. If you're unable to closely match the lead vocal recording, you have the option of compiling different takes and aligning them to match the lead. As a last resort you can use digital processing. However, mechanical methods never sound like live takes.

In the early days of recording, artists and engineers attempted a process of a short tape delay using a spare tape recorder to create a 'fake' double-track which they called Automatic Double-Tracking (ADT). Nowadays, there are plug-ins that simplify this process through pitch and time variation instead of using a physical tape machine. This allows you to create an excellent result by copying the lead vocal to a new track, then digitally processing it with a pitch correction plug-in to create a subtle pitch difference between the original and the copy. Then if you add a delay of 60-100ms to the copied vocal track, you can create the illusion that there are two different vocal sections.

Whether you are a rapper, a singer, or somewhere in between, harmonies and background vocals are an essential part of the song. These vocals emphasize and support your lead, giving the listener different vocal tones that change their listening experience throughout the song. In the simplest style of vocal harmony, the main vocal melody is supported by a single backup vocal line, either at a pitch that's above or below the main vocal line, often in thirds or sixths which fit in with the song's chord progression. In more complex vocal harmony arrangements, different backup singers may sing two or three other notes at the same time as each of the main melody notes, mostly with consonant thirds, sixths, and fifths (although dissonant notes may be used as short passing notes). As a singer when recording these harmony notes, you will want to stack or double each harmony note, so when it's time to mix the song, you can pan each note hard left and right to create a bigger and wider sounding vocal mix. I've worked with singers who sing the same harmony notes up to four times to create a fuller vocal harmony sound. Harmonies are not used on every line, and in most cases the number of harmonies grows as the song builds. A basic rule to follow is to use harmonies sparingly in the first verse, add a few more harmonies in the first hook (along with stacking tracks), possibly add more harmonies in verse two, build on the harmony structure from the first hook in the second hook, have a few harmonies in the bridge, and finally end with the final hook having a full assortment of harmonies.

Your last type of vocals are ad-libs. Singers will use vocal runs like "ohs and ahs," or humming as their ad-libs throughout the song. Sometimes ad-libs won't appear until the end of the song as a way to create a vocal climax by adding another vocal layer before the song ends. In most R&B songs you will hear the singer add what sounds like another lead vocal track to the last hook and outro singing different lines than the lead vocal or echoing the lead vocal. This is where the singer shows off their vocal range and ability to the fullest extent.

In most rap songs today, you will hear the rappers saying different words or vocal sounds in the background that are not associated with the lead or stacked vocals. These are their ad-libs. Some artists use ad-libs effectively (Migos or Eminem) while others use them so much that you can no longer hear the lead. The key to a good ad-lib track is being creative, giving the listener another layer to keep their ear intrigued by what they are listening to. Ad-libs are not always necessary as they can clutter the track taking away from the lead vocal. However, more often than not artists (especially rap artists) will insist on recording a few ad-lib tracks. I generally allow the artist to record as many ad-lib tracks as they want, because this way I have a variety of ad-libs to pick from for the final mix. This can be tedious but it's better to have vocals and not need them than to not have vocals and have to have the artist come back.

Once you have compiled the best vocal take and cleaned up any unwanted noise, what's next? If pitch is still a problem, you can use Antares Auto-Tune or a similar pitch correction plug-in to automatically force the vocal pitch to the nearest note or semitone. The first song to use Auto-Tune was Cher's "Believe." It happened 36 seconds into the song, on the phrase "I can't break through." This effect reappeared in the next verse, on the phrase "So sad that you're leaving." This pitch correction technology was created so a singer's notes and pitch could be placed exactly where they need to be and not sound irregular to the listeners' ear. Nowadays, the technology has become a sound of its own. Artists today are using the technology to hide their singing abilities, and as an effect to create a more melodic sounding vocal performance. Beginning with T-Pain, who has been on record saying that he first began using Auto-Tune to manipulate his voice to use it more as an instrument and bend his voice in unnatural ways, Auto-Tune has become popularized in the music industry in a different way than it was intended.

That said, artificial pitch-correction can create problems if a lot of vibratos is used or if the singer scoops up to notes. I find it's best to get the notes and pitch right during the recording, then use pitch-correction to hold the singer in place rather than completely change the vocal sound, as this results in a more natural sound. Where more drastic correction is needed, you can use Melodyne. This is a pitch correction plug-in that allows you to fine-tune individual notes in a graphic environment.

Once all the vocals are recorded and pitch-corrected, you can begin to add light efx to clean up the vocals before proceeding to post-production. This light efx and vocal clean-up is called a "Rough Mix." A rough mix is constructed to give the mixing engineer an idea of the final sound you're going for. During the rough mix, you (or your recording engineer) will clean up the vocals so all takes can be clearly heard. Start the rough mix with EQ.

First, use a low-pass filter to clean up subsonic audio and breath rumble, then remove frequencies in the 150-400Hz range to clean up boxiness, while boosting at 8kHz to add 'air' and sizzle to the vocal sound. This is always the first EQ steps that I use because too much low-end rumble causes muddiness in your track. The human ear can only hear frequencies as low as 20Hz. However, most sound systems don't register frequencies that low during playback, so rolling off the low-end frequencies with a high-pass filter is beneficial to eliminate unneeded and unheard frequencies. Ultimately, EQ is subtracting frequencies that are affecting the vocal sound, while enhancing other frequencies that are lacking in the vocal recording. The goal of the EQing process is to create a big and full sounding vocal that sits well in the mix and stands out in front of the instruments. Keep in mind that cutting too many frequencies will change the sound of the vocal, while enhancing too many frequencies will exaggerate some vocal imperfections.

Keeping the vocal level even is done with a compressor, aiming for around 6-8dB of gain reduction (overall volume) on the loudest points in the track, and the optimal attack and release settings depend on the compressor or plug-in used (using a ratio of between 2:1 and 6:1). When unsure how to set these, look at some presets and see what values are used. If compression alone isn't enough to tame the dynamics, use mix automation to bring up any words or syllables getting lost or to drop the level of those that stand out. A rule of thumb is to go through your vocal recording and level out each syllable, each word, and each phrase before using compression, as this will allow for steadier and even compression. If you find it hard to judge how loud the vocals should be, try listening to the track in different settings and through different speakers, as this will give you an idea of how your mix is translating. From this perspective, the vocal should be audible above the backing track, but not so loud that it doesn't sound like the same performance. If in doubt, play a commercial record as a reference.

Once the EQ and compression is set, a basic reverb and delay can be added to give presence to the vocal. Reverb and delay are a question of taste. For most classic vocal sounds, I prefer a plate reverb emulation, as these don't add any room sound on the vocal. Combining the plate reverb with a secondary short or small reverb creates a great ambiance bed for your vocals. By balancing these two types of reverbs, you can create anything from a tight in-your-face vocal to a long-drawn-out ballad sounding vocal. When I am mixing, I like to use a slower attack on the plate reverb and/or add a pre-delay to keep this plate reverb sound separated from the short or small reverb sound. Vocal plate reverbs are generally short and don't need to be longer than 2 seconds. Also, just like when you're EQing vocals, rolling off frequencies below 200Hz on the reverb provides a cleaner sound. Putting a subtle delay before the plate reverb can also produce a pleasant effect, provided the music has space to allow the effect to breathe.

With the variety of plug-ins and efx available to you, there is no right or wrong choice and everything is preference. How you want your vocals and track to sound is going to determine how much of each plug-in you use. At this point in the creation process, you don't want to add so many efx that it's hard to hear the vocals, but you also don't want to not add efx, as this will create a flat vocal sound and will leave the final sound of the track up to interpreting by the mixing engineer.

As an artist, you hear all the time about "Going to the studio." What does this mean? When an artist says they are going to the studio, they are going to work with professional audio engineers at a professional music recording studio to achieve professional quality sound. It's great that the advancement in technology allows you to record and mix music from your bedroom, but that doesn't always give you the best sound quality. There are famous exceptions to the "going to the studio" rule. Young Thug recorded his entire album, "Jeffery," in his basement. Billie Eilish records everything with her brother in their living room. I have worked with an engineer who recorded Akon in a hotel room. Keep in mind these artists are working with professional engineers with top-of-the-line audio equipment, then sending the songs to professional mixing engineers. Young Thug sent his project to Alex Tumay, an award-winning engineer. Akon had his song mixed by Serge Tsai, the Head engineer at Platinum Sound Studios in New York and a Grammy Winner. Billie Eilish's brother is a professional recording engineer and music producer. These professionals have decades of experience in recording and mixing music, affording them the ability to create a great sound quality with any recording. Who you work with is a major factor in the final sound of the track?

At this point you are probably thinking to yourself, "If I can spend a few hundred dollars to get all the equipment I need to record and mix my music in my room, why would I ever consider spending hundreds more to go to a professional studio to record one song?" While for an up-and-coming artist on a shoestring budget, your financial logic might make sense, here your music and career logic make little sense. A professional engineer in a professional studio can give you expertise that you can't get on your own when you're just starting out. Speaking for myself, I've put in years at school to learn the audio and recording trade, and I have years of training working in studios, using the equipment, and interacting with different artists. These years of experience gave me the knowledge and technique to write *The Blueprint*. Below are a few pros and cons of both the in-home studio and the professional studio:

Pros & Cons of A Home Studio:

PROS:
- **CONVENIENCE:** Create whenever you want to.
- **AFFORDABILITY:** One-time expenses to purchase all of the equipment.
- **ACCESSIBILITY:** Open access studio, scheduling is never an issue.
- **MEETING PLACE:** Private studios can help facilitate meetings and collaborations with fellow artists, allowing you to control the setting without having to rely on others.
- **LEVERAGE:** Provides a competitive advantage as you can use your home studio to provide value to others in order to cultivate better connections.

CONS:

- **NO NETWORKING:** Will not facilitate in-person networking opportunities as it's in your private home.
- **TAKES TIME TO BUILD:** It may take time to acquire all of the gear and proper outfitting needed for an ideal working environment.
- **DISTRACTIONS:** Other people in your home can be distractions and pull you away from your creative work.

Pros & Cons of A Professional Studio:

PROS:

- **SETTING:** Professional studio settings with high musical aesthetics can help inspire and enhance creative moments.
- **NETWORKING:** Being at a studio can help facilitate more professional networking opportunities amongst engineers, producers, songwriters, artists and labels..
- **QUALITY:** Recording room, a qualified engineer, and sound quality, coupled with high-end equipment is usually a recipe for better quality music.

CONS:

- **COST:** Long term higher cost as you are usually billed per hour of studio time, starting at $50+ per hour.
- **SCHEDULING:** Booking studio time will always depend on studio availability. Busy studios may not have any time for your sessions, or you may have to book well in advance.
- **BUILDING CHEMISTRY:** You will likely be working with an engineer from that studio, and it takes time to build chemistry and become familiarized with each other's sound and taste.

It's true, professional studios can be expensive, and having to work around their schedule may not always be conducive to how you want to work. Most times you cannot walk into a professional studio on a whim at 4 PM on Friday afternoon and get a session. You're going to have to work with them and their schedule to get your session. The convenience of having your own set up to record how and when you desire is appealing, but there are a multitude of major learning curves that come with it. You not only have to perfect yourself as the artist but also have to perfect your skills at recording, using the equipment, using the software, and understanding the post-production process too. All of which the professional engineer and the professional studio already have experience and knowledge of.

Chapter 3   THE POST-PRODUCTION PROCESS

Before going further let me say this, ***it's important to master your song***. Mastering makes your song comparable to all other released songs, with a consistent sound when played across all streaming platforms. But as a new artist who may or may not have the budget, you can get away with not mastering your songs, ***for now anyway***.

Just like recording, there are two options when looking to get your song mixed. You can do it yourself or you can send your session to a mixing engineer. If you send it to a mixing engineer, it's important to find the right one. Each engineer can mix for multiple genres, but most specialize in a specific genre. I specialize in R&B and Hip-Hop. The other engineer I work with specializes in Metal. I listen to Hip-Hop and R&B more than other genres. I work with more of these artists when recording. It's my wheelhouse because I know what these tracks are supposed to sound like when finished. There are two ways you can send your sessions to the mixing engineer:

1. Your vocals over a 2-track (an MP3 version of the beat you used).
2. Sending them the full tracked out stems (each instrument is separated on its own track).

If you just have the two-track, that's ok as most new artists don't have access to the full tracked out stems. A two-track makes the engineer's job a little easier as they don't have to worry about mixing each individual instrument and can focus solely on the sound of your vocals. I prefer getting the stems, as this gives me more control over how the entire song sounds, and I can manipulate each element to fit more cohesively. It's important to note that tracked-out stems create more work for the engineer and will cost more money. A mix can cost anywhere from $20 up to thousands of dollars for the top mixing engineers. Be careful though, getting a $20 mix may not produce the best sound, but if you're on a budget and this is all you can afford, spend the $20 to get an engineer to do the mix, especially if you don't understand the mixing process.

For many artists, mixing is the first time you hand your song to someone else. Since mixing is so important to the final sound of your song, handing it over to a professional mixing engineer is a solid investment but can also be a gamble. You're putting your work in the hands of someone else, hoping they correctly interpret your creative vision. Giving up creative control can be nerve-racking because you may or may not like the final mix. If you like the mix, great. If not, you could be stuck with the mix they sent back. If you're lucky, you may get a few revisions of the mix, but most likely only three before you have to pay extra to fix what you don't like. This can be frustrating if you don't get the sound, you wanted and you're out of revisions and/or money, because you're now stuck with the mix and face the choice of releasing the song as is or scrapping the song completely. This is a tough position. I have had countless artists come to me and say they had an engineer screw up a song and could never release it. All that time you spent recording that song is now for nothing more than practice, and a lesson learned to not use that engineer again.

What if you do the mix yourself? You feel confident enough that you can get the job done or don't want to worry about sending your music to an unknown person who doesn't have the same sonic vision as you. You feel if you mix your songs yourself, not only will you be saving money, but you will have full creative control over what the song sounds like. If this is your choice, I will applaud you for your confidence, but there are some things to know before diving headfirst into mixing the song yourself.

Before starting the mix, you might have to restructure the recording session in your DAW to be mixed. Your session should already be quasi-setup from your recording, but for mixing, the session setup is more detailed. This is exponentially more important if you're sending the session to an engineer. I can't tell you how many times I've had a mixing engineer tell me they won't start on the mix until they get the session sent to them correctly. Sometimes, the engineer will send the session back to the artist and won't do the mix because the session wasn't set up properly. That being said, there is no "correct way" to set up a session as each engineer has their own specific way to set up mixing sessions. But there are some general rules. If you don't know where to start for session setup similar to recording, most DAWs provide templates that can get you started. For example, Pro Tools offers a basic 'Rock' session template that includes pre-made tracks for: Drums, Bass, Organ, Guitar, Audio Recording, Click Track, Pre-routed Headphone Mix, Reverb Return, Delay Return, Chorus return, etc.

Pro Tools also offers other pre-made templates for a variety of music genres, but if you don't see what you're looking for, you can create your own template from scratch. If you followed the steps in the last chapter to create your own recording session, you can use this as a starting point for your mixing session as the basic setup is the same. The only difference between the two will be the number of auxiliary tracks. Your mixing session will have more because of the need for more efx and more intricate control.

Next, if you haven't already (and I don't know why you wouldn't have), label your tracks cohesively. Believe me, if you go back to this session two months later, you'll have no idea where the accent hi-hat is if the track is labeled as 'Audio track 48.' If you record a 'piano' do yourself a favor and label the track 'piano.' Improper track names add unnecessary set-up to your mixing session. Once your tracks are properly named you should color code your track groups (which should have been done already). For example, make all of your drum tracks shades yellow, vocal tracks shades blue, all your guitars shade green, and so on. Most engineers have specific colors for their tracks in every session, so just by seeing the track color they know what the instrument is. For me, I always make the drum tracks descending shades of yellow or orange, starting with the kicks being yellow and descending in shade for the snares, hi-hats, toms, shakers, and the rest of percussion. The rest of the instruments are shades of pink, the bass is brown, the vocals are shades of purple and blue, and the efx tracks are green. Taking two minutes to color code your tracks will save hours of searching later. There are no right or wrong color choices, these are strictly a preference, but it is extremely helpful in the long run when looking for specific groups and instruments.

Now that your session is set up, it's time to mix. The mixing process will continue from the rough mix I touched on in Chapter Two. The key to a good mix starts with the balance. This means leveling out the volume of each individual track in your session. As I spoke about in the previous chapter, if you're using a two-track, set the volume of the two-track around -10db. This will provide you with enough headroom to properly balance your vocals to the instrumental without distorting. When balancing your vocals, your lead should be the loudest, the stacks will be tucked underneath to provide an extra layer, the harmonies will surround the lead panned left and right, and the ad-libs will be the lowest in volume and panned left and right, and in certain cases middle. A rule of thumb, all of your vocals when played together should peak around -3db.

In most cases, the vocals are the key component of your song, and you want them to be featured front and center. In mixing lead vocals, there are four general areas (not that there aren't more) that will enhance your lead vocal sound:

- Clean up the low-end as much as possible. I've found cutting as high as 200Hz has cleared up the low-end rumble in a vocal mix. Using a high-pass filter, sweep the filter parameter until you find the spot that clears out the low-end and puts your vocal out front. This will not only clean up the direct low-end, but also knock out any low-end room noise that's sneaking into the microphone.
- Carve out space for the vocals. This is done with small frequency cuts in the instruments where you hear they are fighting for space with the vocals.
- Get the vocal to be present above your music and background vocals. This can be done by focusing on the middle/high-end frequencies (2-9 kHz and 5-15 kHz range).

- Smooth out the vocal by EQing the mid-range. This is where you create vocal clarity without effecting the heart of the vocal sound. You want your vocal to have presence without sounding muffled or tinny. You want the vocal to be present in the mix so it maintains emotion and feeling.

The Vocal Mixing Formula

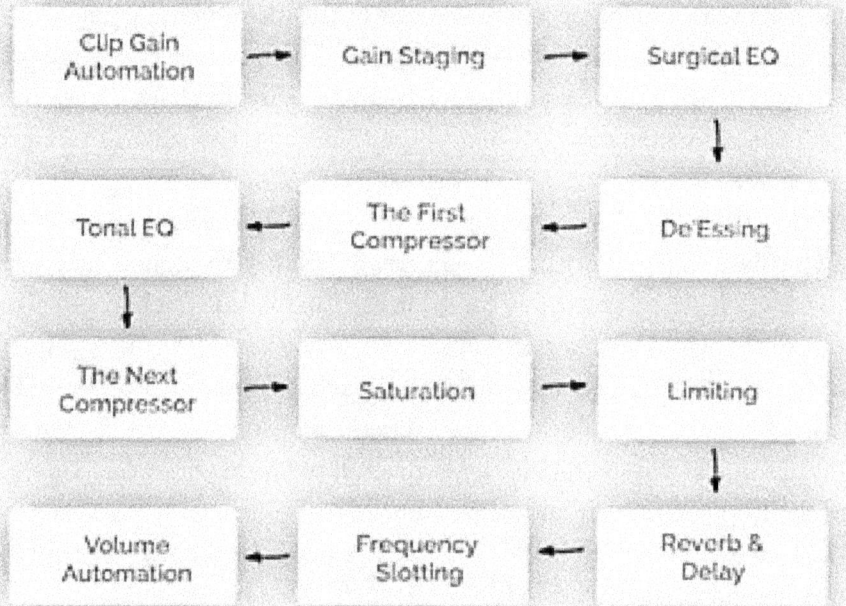

Clip Gain Automation	→	Gain Staging	→	Surgical EQ
Tonal EQ	←	The First Compressor	←	De'Essing
The Next Compressor	→	Saturation	→	Limiting
Volume Automation	←	Frequency Slotting	←	Reverb & Delay

xvi

Gain staging is the first step in the post-production/mixing process. Not every word or note will be sung at the same volume level in the performance. It is important to go through each syllable and note in the vocals and correctly match the volume to the rest of the track. This is especially important because if the listener can't hear or understand certain words it can be a huge deterrence for them to continue listening to the rest of the song. Always remember, the first line of the song is the most important, this is what draws the listener into wanting to hear the rest.

EQ is the next step in the mixing process and is used to subtract problem frequencies and extenuate other frequencies to make sounds cut through the mix. Asking "What is the best EQ" is equivalent to asking, "What's the best spice for cooking?" Finding the best EQ comes from sculpting the vocals so the leads and backgrounds each have their own space. The "best" mix comes from listening to all of the session's sonic elements and creating frequency spaces for each sound.

EQing is a science and is done with a combination of small precision changes and broad strokes. With that being said, there are a few basics for equalization:

- EQ the dominant frequencies.
- Cut for uniqueness. Instead of boosting frequencies, cut frequency bands.
- When EQing, cut first, boost second.
- Don't attempt to create something that isn't there. You can only work with the elements you have.
- There is no fix for a bad vocal recording. If there are multiple singers and one is having a hard time, don't be afraid to hide their voice behind the others. If you can, bury it.

When doctors are operating on a patient, they try to cut out the smallest amount of tissue. You should follow a similar thought process when working with problem frequencies. Only remove those you hear as troublesome. If too much of a frequency is removed it becomes audibly noticeable to the listener. It's best to use a wide boost in similar frequency ranges so the listener doesn't notice. My favorite way to begin the EQing process is to engage a High-Pass Filter (HPF). I start around 120Hz as a baseline and have moved the HPF as high as 200Hz. You might need to set it higher later in the mixing process because the low-end frequencies of your vocals are cluttering the sonic frequency range of your kick drum and bass.

EQing vocals is a process that can only be judged with your ears, not your eyes. The fundamental frequencies of the human voice when singing can go from around 80Hz-1,100Hz, and have harmonic frequencies that can extend up to the 10,000Hz. The human voice has key frequency ranges that create each person's vocal tone characteristics. For example, the 100Hz-300Hz range effects clarity and can make a vocal sound thin when taken away. Whereas the10-20kHz frequency can cause a harsh and brittle sounding vocal. Every singing voice is different, so you have to find that frequency spot on an individual basis. Remember, it's better to cut first and boost second. You can cover the stain on your shirt with a jacket, but the stain is still there. Here are some frequency ranges and their characteristics:

- 100 Hz–300 Hz: Clarity / Thin (Good for cutting these frequencies)
- 100 Hz–400 Hz: Thickness
- 100 Hz–600 Hz: Body / Warmth
- 100 Hz–700 Hz: Muddiness (Good for cutting)
- 400 Hz–1,100 Hz: Honky / Nasal

- 900 Hz–4,000 Hz: Intelligibility
- 1,000 Hz–8,000 Hz: Presence
- 1,500 Hz–7,000 Hz: Sibilance (Start in the 3,000 to 5,000 Hz range)
- 2,000 Hz–9,000 Hz: Clarity (Compared to the 100 to 300 range for cutting, this is good for boosting)
- 5,000 Hz–15,000 Hz: Sparkle
- 10,000 Hz–20,000 Hz: Air / Breathiness[xvii]

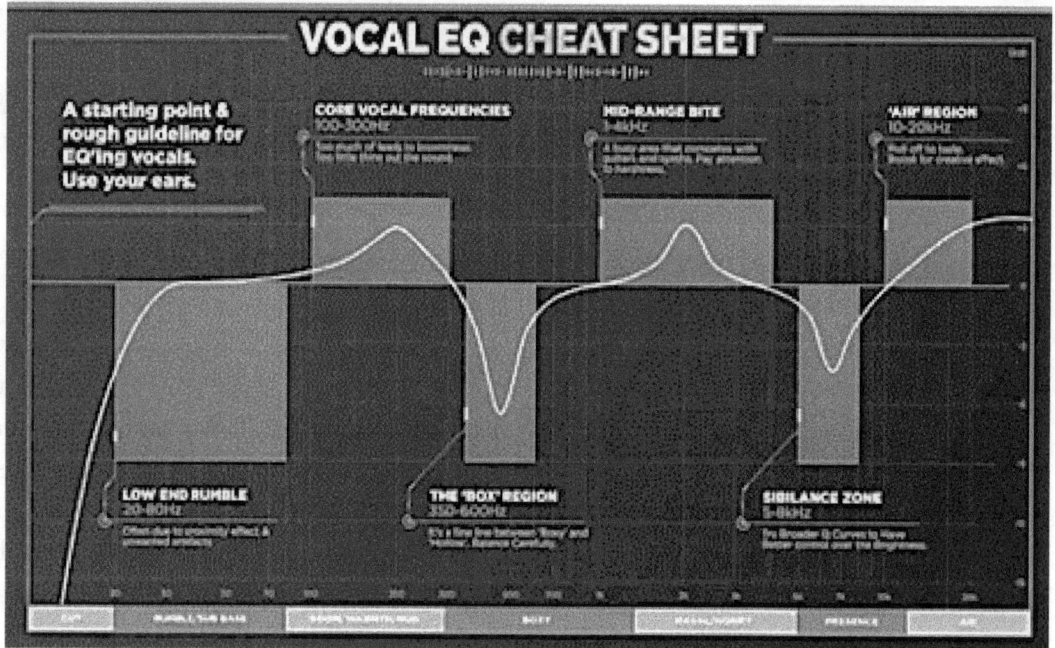

Sometimes the fix to your vocal frequency problem lies beyond the above ranges. For example, cutting in the 1,500Hz-2,000Hz range fixes the nasal sound. Or your vocal could be too harsh with heavy sibilance, so you need to tame the high-end frequencies by cutting them or using a low-pass filter to take them out completely. A technique I learned from Ty Dolla Sign's producer is that all his vocals use a low-pass filter to take away all frequencies above 15kHz. This way they don't sound too harsh, resulting in a fuller rounder sound. This is all preference and is dictated by the vocalist and music genre. Use your ears and commercial records as reference points to steer you in the right direction. When you have finished the EQing process and have your vocals shaped the way you want, dynamic control (compression) is next.

Compression is one of the hardest concepts and techniques to understand in mixing. Audio compression is the process of taming a sound's dynamic range by setting volume limitations on how much of a frequency is let through. Compressors boost the quiet sections and lower the louder sections to provide an overall consistent sound. The compressors ratio setting determines how much the compressor is working. The higher the compressor's ratio, the more the compressor affects the sound's dynamic range. Dynamics refer to the space between the loudest parts of a sound to the quietest part.

I'm sure you have heard dynamics in music is a good thing, so you're probably thinking why you would want to tame the dynamics. Dynamics are good, but you want a consistent sound level in your mix. This means if a sound is too loud, it'll stand out. Conversely, if the sound is too quiet, it'll get lost in your mix. Be careful using too much compression on a certain sound or your mix as a whole. Only using compression to balance levels leads to a flat sounding mix. Finding a good balance of compression requires listening, learning, and constant adaptation.

Each compressor has its own unique sound that it gives the incoming signal even before changing any settings. Each compressor has settings that include threshold, attack, release, input and output. The threshold is the level the compressor works at, meaning that until the incoming signal reaches the db threshold, the compressor won't activate. The input is the level of the sound going into the compressor, and the output is the level of the sound coming out of the compressor. With vocals these two are usually correlated as the higher the input, the lower the output and vice versa. This happens because if the level is louder coming in, the level needs to be lower coming out to balance the overall level. The Attack and Release settings on the compressor determine the reaction time of changes in the input signal of the compressor's gain-reduction. Attack dictates how fast the compressor reacts in reducing gain, while release dictates how fast the gain reduction resets. Be careful though, because too much compression will make it hard to hear and you'll literally have a squashed sound.

Dynamic sounds have a wide range between the quietest and loudest parts of the sound. For example, a snare hit has a fast and short peak (wide dynamic range), compared to an organ note that maintains the same level after its initial key hit (a less dynamic sound). Dynamics also exist within a vocal performance, such as the singer singing softer during the verse, then belting during the chorus. These dynamic swings can make it difficult to fit everything together in a mix. Therefore, consider these basic compressor settings:

- **ATTACK:** 30 ms (Quick to activate).
- **RELEASE:** 300 ms (Slow to release).
- **RATIO:** 3:1 (2:1 – 4:1) Applied significantly enough you don't have to make manual fader changes.

- **SOFT-KNEE SETTING:** Subtle change when compression begins being applied.[xix]

RATIO	LIGHT	MODERATE	HEAVY
	2:1	4:1	8:1
ATTACK	FAST/ SHORT	MEDIUM	SLOW/ LONG
	1-5ms	5-10ms	10-20ms
RELEASE	FAST/ SHORT	MEDIUM	SLOW/ LONG
	1-10ms	10-50ms	60-100ms [xx]

In the words of Steve Dennis, "Use compression to smooth out a vocal, but not so much that you suck the life and dynamics out of it."

There are a variety of different compressors, and each engineer will use these compressors in a different order depending on the need of the vocal (or sound). Some of the different compressors are:

DE-ESSER – WAVES AUDIO – WAVE.COM

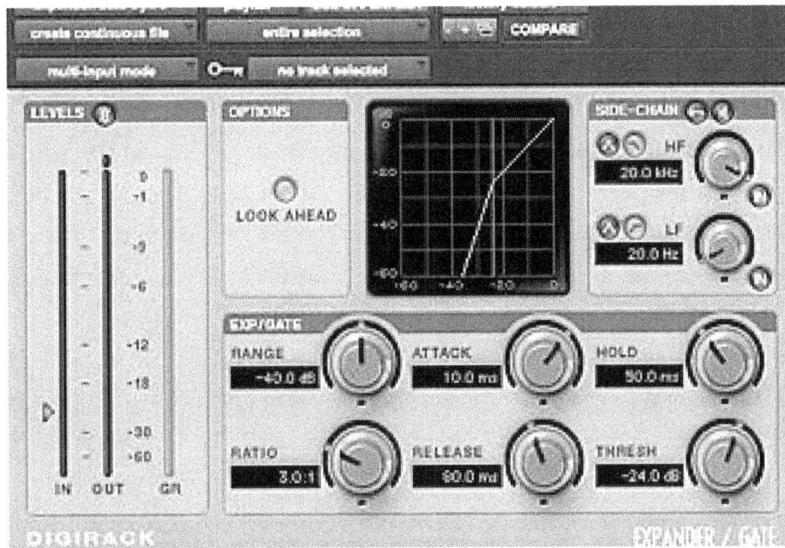

GATE/EXPANDER – AVID PRO TOOLS

AUDIO COMPRESSOR – UNIVERSAL AUDIO

Personally, I like to de-ess first, unless there is unwanted background noise, in which case gating is my first step. Gating is a way you can clean up the audio being picked up by the microphone when you aren't singing. Gating enables you to set a volume threshold where any sound that doesn't reach the specified threshold gets cut from the channel. Yes, you'll hear them a bit when singing, but every little bit helps.

De-essing is used to get rid of harsh sounding esses that come out when recording. Sometimes this can be accomplished through the EQing process, but sometimes the vocal sibilance needs extra taming. With two different settings, one similar to a low-pass filter and the other similar to an EQ band, the De-esser will only compress the specific frequency range you set it for, allowing you to compress only the problem frequencies and nothing else.

A caveat to keep in mind is sometimes it's better to use a gate and/or a De-esser before EQing your vocals. This will occur when you want to cancel out excess noise, harshness/sibilance before shaping your vocals. This can be beneficial because if you begin to EQ with this excess noise, harshness, and sibilance, the EQing process can be compromised, creating an undesired sound by extenuating the unwanted frequencies. If you choose to EQ before gating and De-essing, you will then eliminate and compress frequencies that you have shaped with EQ.

Now that you have your EQ and compressors set, it's time to add efx. The sound you're going for will dictate which and how much efx you should use. Take The Weeknd for example, most of his vocal tracks have a lot of efx because that is the sound, he is going for to create an ambiance in his tracks. If you listen to most rap tracks, the vocals have a minor efx on them, because the focus is on the lyrics and efx can take away from the upfrontness of the vocals. That being said, all vocals have reverb and delay on them regardless of the style or genre. As a beginner, I recommend using one of the presets given to you by the plug-ins and determine which one sounds the best for the vocals and your desired sound.

There is an overwhelming amount of plug-in efx you can use to manipulate your vocals. Reverb and delay are just the tip of the iceberg but are considered the most essential. Why? Reverb and delay are natural occurring sounding efx that we hear when any person speaks to us. Using these efx can be simple or complex. Used correctly, nobody may notice they are there, and you can create a pleasing sonic experience. Used incorrectly, you can clutter the entire mix, jumbling multiple sounds together causing an unenjoyable listening experience.

Reverb is the reflection of sound within an environment which is heard after the initial sound is broadcast. The first sound reflection is considered an echo. After that, the remaining sounds are called reverberation and last until the energy of the sound waves dissipates.[xxi] In music terms, reverb is an effect used to create depth, add emotion, and soften sounds within the song. By using reverb, you're altering the voice's unique sound and affecting the timbre. Reverb can do great wonders to your mix, but it can also hinder it greatly. Reverb can clutter up a mix if not used correctly. Too much reverb creates a sound swell which can cover up the complimenting instruments and vocals in the song. There are three common types of reverbs, room, hall, and plate:

- **ROOM REVERB** is a short time period of reverb that adds the characteristics of a small room. It adds a little depth and a little space.[xxii]

- **HALL REVERB** carries a larger fuller sound that lasts a longer period of time and carries more reflection. The smallest of halls is still bigger than the largest of rooms.[xxiii]

- **PLATE REVERB** does not emulate any specific space. Plate reverb is created through sound vibrating a metal plate at the end of a tube. This metal plate vibrates rapidly, therefore carrying a lot of early reflection. A benefit of plate reverb is it gives the thicker sound you might associate with a hall reverb but for a shorter period of time.[xxiv]

You're probably asking yourself, "Which type of reverb should I use?" Much like I spoke about for EQ and compression, there is no correct answer. Beyond just these basic reverbs, you can control a variety of settings within the reverb. Use your ear for selecting the right reverb for the track and setting the right reverb time. When I'm mixing, I tailor the reverb I use to the song. I usually start with a room or plate reverb and build from there.

Reverb plug-ins and consoles have settings for selecting the frequency ranges you want the reverb to be added. For example, on the reverb I use on my vocal chain, I roll off all frequencies below 200Hz and above 5kHz, which enables me to get a clear tone from the reverb. These extreme low and high frequencies could be exaggerated in the vocal you were attempting to eliminate through EQs.

Delay is another naturally occurring incidence when speaking. Sometimes described as an echo, delay develops as sound waves bounce off surfaces in varying lengths of time before arriving at your ear. For example:

- <20 ms (milliseconds): Produces timbre changes and can cause comb filtering problems.[xxv]
- 20-60 ms: The time in which doubling is easily perceived.[xxvi]
- 60-100 ms: More of a distant echo and can sound funky when sounds start echoing off of the walls.[xxvii]
- >100 ms: The time in which people register a sound to echo.[xxviii]

Vocal delay has its place in music and on vocals. However, the right amount of delay is a personal and stylistic preference. Too much delay can be jarring to the listener as they will be hearing sound in the background well after the initial sound has ended. For me, I build off of a basic quarter note delay. This quarter note delay is the basic preset in most delay plug-ins and is a great starting point for any singer in any genre of song. When deciding on the correct delay, consider these two things:

- Fill empty gaps in the song.
- Produce depth.

Mixing background and ad-lib vocals differs from the lead vocals. You want the lead to stand out from the rest, as this is the main vocal of the song. Your backgrounds (or stacks) are there to support your lead. These vocals don't need to be fully heard, but they should be audible. The stacks should have a tighter compression and a different EQ setting as to not interfere with the lead. The ad-libs are vocal efx that should be separated from all other vocals of the song. They need to be heard but should never overpower other vocals in the song. I like to put a telephone efx on the ad-libs to separate them so they can be heard but not interfere. All engineers and artists have a unique perspective on how ad-libs should sound, and this is usually an artist's preference. With Migos, their ad-libs sound like their leads but have an accent that doesn't interfere with what they are saying. Eminem uses ad-libs as vocal effects to complete the story. When you listen to an Eminem song (especially earlier in his career) his ad-libs were vocal sounds, much like a sound board emphasizing what he was saying. Some artists don't use ad-libs at all in certain songs because they are unnecessary and would be an adherence rather than an enhancement to the song. Be careful with ad-libs, too many can take away from the lead and make the song cluttered and busy, too few can create too much space in the song if your lead vocals have a lot of breaks. Here are seven methods to use when mixing background vocals:

1. **VOLUME CONTROL:** The background vocals should support the lead, not overpower it. However, there are times when they can be the main vocal part of the song.
2. **ROLL OFF HIGH-END FREQUENCIES:** You want the background vocals to be a single unified sound that is blended well.
3. **TAME THE LOW-END:** Use a low-pass filter to control the low-end frequencies in the vocals so they don't compete with the low-end frequencies of the instruments.
4. **BLEND THE VOCALS TOGETHER:** Blend the background vocals together to create a unified sound where no singer or note is sticking out above the rest.
5. **COMPRESS:** You don't want one background vocalist or harmony note sticking out above the rest. If this is the case, use a higher compression ratio to even them out.
6. **USE REVERB FOR SEPARATION AND BLENDING:** Separate the lead vocal from the background vocals by using two different types of reverbs: one on the leads and a second on the backgrounds. A good starting place is to use shorter reverbs on

the leads while using a longer reverb on the backgrounds. You can streamline your mixing process by grouping each set of vocals to an "AUX Track" and applying the reverb there.

7. **ACTIVELY MIX:** Group similar vocal recordings together and route them to a single fader. For example, send all of your background vocals to a single "AUX Track," as this will allow you to control the sound and volume of all of the background vocals with one channel.

Mixing your background vocals to fit in the track with your lead can be tricky. If the backgrounds are too loud, you won't be able to hear the lead, and nobody will sing along with the song. Mixing them too low and the beautiful harmonies and emphasized phrases are no longer heard. Think of backgrounds and harmonies as vocal ear candy, a way to give the listener something different to listen to instead of just the lead vocal for four-five minutes. Charlie Wilson uses backgrounds and ad-libs to enhance his tracks, so much so that his "Oh-we" ad-lib is a world-renowned trademark of his songs, and if you are lucky enough to get this ad-lib when doing a feature with him, you know you have a hit song. Once your vocals are set in the mix, it's time to move to the instruments.

Before moving on to mixing the instruments, it's important to note when beginning to mix that the balance (the volume of each individual track) is the most crucial aspect of a mix. Every mixing engineer has their own workflow process, meaning some will start mixing the instruments first before the vocals, while others will mix vocals first. From there each engineer has a preference as to which instrument group and which specific instrument they will start with. I like to start with the vocals because they are the most important part of the song. If the vocals can't be heard, what will the listener sing along to? After the vocals, I like to begin with the drums because this is the backbone of the track.

When I am building the balance of my mix I always start with the drums and specifically the kick and snare. These are going to be the driving factors of your track and if they aren't at the right volume the rest of your track won't be either. I bring the kick to an audible volume that is loud enough to be felt but not overbearing in the track. I then bring the snare drums up so they sit above the kick because the snare drum is what keeps the beat of the entire song. Hence Eminem saying in the beginning of "Cleaning Out My Closet," "Where is my snare? I can't hear the snare in my headphones." Once these drums are in place, I bring in the bass as this sets the groove for the track and, in my opinion, is the most important non-drum instrument in music. I was told in the beginning of my career that the bass should be felt but not necessarily heard in the mix. While this is going to be dependent on the preference of the artist and producer, I keep this in mind during every mix that I do because this way I keep the driving groove in the track but don't create muddiness or excessive low end build up as I add more elements in the mixing process. Once I feel as though I have a good balance and separation on these three instruments (unless there is more than one kick, snare, or bass being used), I begin leveling out the rest of the track.

Of course, as I keep mentioning, this is all a personal preference and a process that I have developed for myself over the years that works for me but may not be viable for everyone. For example, the engineer I trained to take over as the main engineer in the studio I work at doesn't use this method and rather starts with all his faders at 0 dB and levels out from there. His balance process is based on the explanation below.

Start by setting the snare fader at 0 dB and bringing the rest of the drum mix in around it. The snare is the beat's foundation, and typically one of the loudest elements in the mix.

Next, bring the kick fader up until it sounds almost as loud as the snare. It should be loud enough so that the low frequencies are rich and powerful, but not so loud that it masks the bottom-end of the snare drum.

Then, bring in the toms. These can be almost as loud as the snare if they're used sparingly, but if they're heavily featured, they should sit a little further back in the mix.

Last, bring in the cymbals, overheads, and room mics as needed. The level of these tracks will vary from genre to genre, but they should definitely all be used to support the featured drums, not overpower them.

One key component of balancing the drum mix is planning. Use the pan knob to add separation between the toms, widen out the overhead mics, and add depth to the room mics. Make sure to frequently check your mix in mono, you never know where your track will get played, and you want to make sure it sounds good in every format. Most audio interfaces feature a mono button at the top for quickly referencing your mix in mono. If it sounds good in mono, it will sound great in stereo. Vice versa is not always the case.

Once the drums are balanced, bring in the bass. This can be tricky because of the low-end similarities of its frequencies with the kick drum. The bass should be loud enough that the low end is big and powerful, but not so loud that it overpowers the kick drum. I was taught that when mixing the bass, you want to feel the bass but not necessarily hear it. Using this rule will allow you to create a powerful bass that doesn't interfere with the low end of your kick drum. Always check your reference mixes to make sure you're staying on course.

A second bass aspect you will undoubtedly come across in today's music is the 808. The 808 is technically considered a bass drum, however in some genres the 808 is used more as the bass than a drum. Because of the different aspects of the 808, engineers take different approaches when mixing. Some will not touch the 808 other than volume level, because this is already a digitally created sound manufactured in a way that doesn't need much touch up. Others will mix the 808 as if it's a bass or a second kick drum. I have heard one engineer say the only thing he does to the 808 is fade or lower the volume of the initial hit, thus dampening the impact and creating more headroom for the drums overall. Sometimes you will have to go a step further as there will be a kick drum, bass, and 808 all playing at the same time. How you mix your 808 is going to depend on whether it's acting as a bass or secondary kick drum. Creating good low-end separation between these three instruments can be difficult. They all occupy the same frequency range and can cause a low end build up that muddles/overpowers the whole track. High-pass filters and compression are going to be your best friends here.

Once you have the bass level where you want it, don't be afraid to adjust some other drum faders. Mixing is fluid, and every move affects the rest of the mix. Changing the volume or sound of one instrument may mean you need to tweak the overall balance.

Last, bring in the remaining instruments in order of importance. If it's a rock song, start with guitar one, then guitar two, and so on. Then move on to the keys, and all the way down the list to the triangle used in the outro. Understand, only one instrument can be the focal point, the rest are the supporting cast. Think of them as the background vocals. They need to be present and heard but not overpowering to the focal instrument.

Learning how to balance all the elements in a mix can be difficult, especially since tastes change from genre to genre. In rock music, the guitars are the loudest instruments. In hip-hop, it's the kick or 808. In EDM, it's the bass. In pop music, the vocals are everything. Balancing all the elements in your session first (before any EQ, compression or efx), makes it easier to address frequency and dynamics issues later. Reference tracks will keep you on the right path from start to finish. Remember, it's the ear, not the gear. The best equipment in the world can't make up for a bad balance.

When the balance is all said and done, spatially the frequencies of the mix should follow some resemblance of the diagram below:

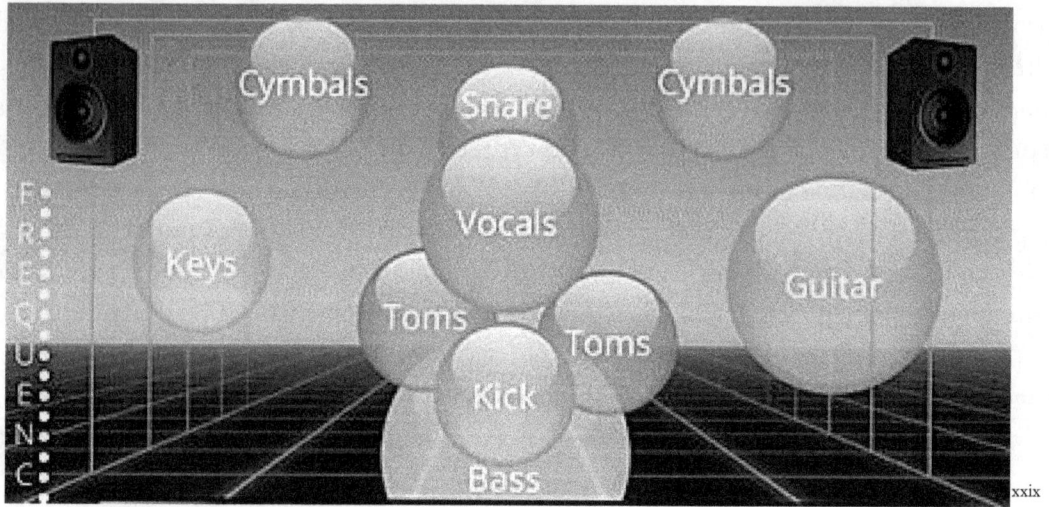

xxix

After all of this, you are probably saying to yourself, "This is way too much. I don't know if I can mix my song myself. Can I just release the song without mixing it first?" I will answer your question with this.

When listeners flip through radio stations or a playlist to find what they like, every song gets a few seconds before the dreaded 'skip.' We make snap judgments about the sound of a song within the first five seconds. In that short timeframe we learn what genre the song is, whether it's mellow or energetic, simple or sophisticated, if the mood is interesting, and does it sound professional or not. If the sound grabs us, we leave it on. And the thing that makes perhaps the most difference in a song's sound is the mix.

Every song you've ever heard on the radio was professionally mixed. All the great bands and artists handed their music to a professional mixing engineer. Even today when many musicians do the production and recording on their own, they work with mixing professionals. The mixing process is deep and requires an abundance of skill and practice. As you have spent the past decade singing or playing instruments, a professional mixing engineer has been mixing for that same time frame. Mixing makes a tremendous difference to the outcome of a song, more so than whether you recorded that guitar player or background vocal, more than which microphone you used, more than mastering.

A good mixing engineer can make a song pop out of the speakers and come to life. That's why today, top mixing engineers such as MixedbyAli or Dave Pensado have a rock star status. In the music industry mixing engineers have tricks in their bag to bring out the best in a recording. A good mixer will know how to make vocals sound powerful and, in your face, bring out the breathiness in a vocal performance, make a scream sound exceptional, make drums sound explosive, fix timing, and transform instruments or vocals into ear candy. A good mix can enhance your performance, while an awful mix can make a good vocal performance sound small and buried, a good drum track sound like nothing but hi-hat wash, and a song sound like an unflattering mess.

Most of us have heard countless songs, and because these songs were professionally produced, our ears are used to hearing a top level of production. Think of the last time you saw a bad sit-com pilot. Did you cringe? It's likely because the myriad of amazingly written sit-coms you've watched made you expect more. The same holds true with the music industry professionals who use 'sound quality' to judge an artist's level. A mediocre mix can make a great song sound like a demo.

Now that you have a beautiful sounding mix, the last step in postproduction is mastering. During mastering, additional audio treatments are applied to correct problem frequencies and enhance the musicality. Since magnetic tape replaced straight-to-lathe cutting in the late 1940s, audio mastering has become its own art form. An audio master is the final version of a song that's prepared for sale, download, streaming, radio play, or any other form of mass consumption. The audio master is used to make all future copies of the recording. It's what is pressed on vinyl, burned to CD, and what digital services use to encode the files of music they make available. When you listen to a song via streaming, download, or physical format, you're listening to a copy of the master audio.

Skipping the mastering process will gravely affect how your song sounds and compares to other commercial releases. Mastering puts a final sheen on the recording you worked so hard to create and the mix you went over with a fine-tooth comb. It brings the sound of your recording to the same level as the millions of songs available. When one of your tracks is placed on a playlist, you don't want your song to suddenly be softer than all the rest. Lil Jon has a stipulation for all of his songs. He wants all of his tracks to be louder than the competition because when his songs are played in the clubs or on the radio the audience automatically knows it's a Lil Jon song.

Not mastering your music before release is like working tireless hours designing and manufacturing a beautiful car and then putting it on the showroom floor without a paint job. Mastering will make your final mix sound better, but only if the mix is already good. Mastering won't save a terrible mix, but it can ruin a good one. One award-winning producer/engineer has been at the center of two high-profile cases of a poor mix being unsalvageable by the mastering engineer. His mixes for two high profile rock/pop bands were too compressed when sent for mastering. The mastering engineer stated the mixes were "already brick-walled before they arrived." "Brick-walled" is a term for a mix or master that is too loud. Similarly, a third band's 2002 album received backlash for being overly compressed and distorted. In this case, it's not clear if the over compression came from the mix or the master, but the band asked a second high profile engineer to remix the entire album in 2013.

Finding a mastering engineer can be as easy as asking the engineer who mixed your music, as they might have some favorite mastering engineers to recommend, or the mixing engineer might be a mastering engineer as well (though mixing engineers don't like to master their own mixes). There are many mastering studios available. Do your research, compare rates, and be sure to listen to what those engineers have worked on, ensuring you like their work. As with mixing, the price of a master will vary depending on what you need done, how many songs you're mastering, and the length of the songs. If it's just a quick touch up it could cost $50-$100 per song. For full services such as adjusting EQ, volume and additional post-production effects, the average cost is about $150 per song.

This might sound expensive, but you're not just paying for the engineer's expert ears. Mastering studios have state-of-the-art audio equipment and are built to be an optimal environment for listening to music. This environment enables the engineer to make accurate adjustments that you might not have heard if you were to master on your laptop.

Mixing and mastering your music are critical elements of creating the best listening experience. Gone are the days of releasing mixtapes where the tracks only have an adequate rough mix. If you release your music without any post-production work, it will be skipped over in every playlist by every listener. Put as much time (maybe more) into the mixing and mastering of your tracks as you did in the recording process. Releasing an unfinished product is the fastest way to get skipped.

Chapter 4   COPYRIGHTING YOUR MUSIC

You're now ready to release your music for public consumption. There are two final steps you must complete to ensure you get the most out of your music. Copywriting your songs and signing up with a performance rights organization (PRO).

A PRO is an agency that ensures songwriters and publishers are paid for the use of their music by collecting royalties on behalf of the rights owner. PROs collect public performance royalties, meaning when a song is played in public, on any kind of radio (AM/FM, streaming, or satellite), in a venue, or TV shows and commercials, it's required they pay for the use. Restaurants, music venues (bars, amphitheaters, performance halls), sports arenas, stores, shopping malls, bowling alleys, golf courses, amusement parks, airports, hospitals, and any other public site that plays music must purchase a license from the PROs to play that music. PROs will pay out the licensing fee as a performance royalty to songwriters and rights holders (publishing companies). The biggest PROs in the United States are ASCAP, BMI, and SESAC. They collect public performance royalties as defined by the US Copyright Act and ensure that payment is issued appropriately.

When songs are streamed digitally on a service like Pandora or SiriusXM, or on a cable music channel (Music Choice), due to their utilization of the music's statutory license, SoundExchange collects what is called "digital public performance royalties" and distributes these royalties to the artist and sound recording copyright owner. ASCAP, BMI and SESAC collect and distribute royalties for the songwriter, composer, and publisher. Both satellite radio providers and webcasters pay SoundExchange when they stream music due to their utilization of the statutory license. These are collected for works covered by the Digital Performance Right in Sound Recording Act of 1995 and Digital Millennium Copyright Act of 1998, though services like Spotify, Apple Music, and Radio have negotiated deals with many labels and publishers directly, bypassing SoundExchange when dealing with royalties.

While each of the three PRO companies works similarly, each has a slightly different way they represent their artists. Choosing which PRO company is right for you can be as simple as deciding if you would like to pay for your membership or not, or it could be far more intricate. Unless a SESAC affiliated artist gives you a referral, you won't be able to become a SESAC member. ASCAP and BMI are open for any artist to join. However, ASCAP has a registration fee to join, while BMI is free to join for artists (publishers have a registration fee).

Here are some key differences between each of the PROs:

ASCAP is the oldest working PRO, having launched in 1914. It's also the second largest in the US, boasting about 10 million works from approximately 660,000 members. For publishers and songwriters, there's a one-off $50 registration fee. Well-known members of ASCAP are Ariana Grande, Katy Perry, Kelly Clarkson, and Justin Timberlake. Some benefits of ASCAP:[xxx]

- Membership discounts to the songwriter's hall of fame.
- Membership in the USA Alliance Federal Credit Union.
- Discounts on dental, health, instruments, and life insurance through the MusicPro program.
- Discounts on the web tools of ASCAP (digital marketing, selling tools and more).
- Discounts on retail products and services related to music.
- Vehicle rental and hotel discounts.
- Access to the annual 'ASCAP I Create Music Expo.'

As the largest PRO in the US, BMI represents about 12 million musical works and over 750,000 musicians. Its membership is entirely free for songwriters. For individual publishers, the cost is $150 and for companies $250. Notable members of BMI are Lady Gaga, Kendrick Lamar, Taylor Swift, Carrie Underwood and Sam Smith. Some benefits of BMI:[xxxi]

- Discounted registration for the billboard Latin conference only offered to certain BMI affiliates.
- Discounted membership from LARAS.
- Exclusive discounts with NXNE.
- Access to Fan bridges.
- Exclusive discounts from Video Games Life for their particular LA show.
- Access to Musician's Atlas.
- Discounted registration The Billboard touring conference and awards.
- Access to Muzlink.
- Access to the production marketplace.
- Songwriters' hall of fame.

SESAC is the smallest and the only PRO that's a for-profit organization. It caters over 400,000 musical works from over 30,000 affiliated writers. SESAC pays out in the same way as BMI and ASCAP, in quarterly royalty checks. However, SESAC members also have the option to get monthly radio royalty payments. There are no fees required to join SESAC. Famous members of SESAC include Mariah Carey, Bob Dylan, Adele, Neil Diamond and Mumford and Sons. Some benefits of SESAC:[xxxii]

- The option to get monthly radio royalty payments (instead of the usual quarterly royalty payments).
- 10% discount at Sprint.
- 10% discount at Bertleemusic.com.
- 15% discount on the first year of SONGTRUST.
- Discounted Nero Multimedia Suite 10.
- Discounts for airport parking.
- Discounted rate on CMA's Sterling person's membership.
- Available 3-month free Musician Atlas online account.
- 20% discount on the legacy learning system.
- Special 33% discount to the American songwriter magazine.

Even though you are affiliated with a PRO that doesn't mean that your song is copyrighted. While the PRO may assist with the copywriting process, you still need to go through the process to have a proper legal copyright for your song. A copyright provides the owner with the exclusive right to a particular work for a defined duration of time. For a work to be copyrightable, it must be original and fixed in tangible form, such as a sound recording recorded on a CD or a literary work printed on paper. There are many copyrightable works. Some include: original literary works, dramatic works, choreography, musical works, audio-visual works, and other graphic artistic works (logos, album cover art, photo and music videos are all potentially protected).

Music copyrights are unique, as each track contains two copyrights. The first is a copyright of the song (i.e., the musical composition), which comprises the lyrics and underlying music (beat, instrumental). The other is a copyright of the sound recording or master recording itself. For example, Bob Dylan is the original writer and composer of "All Along the Watchtower." It has been subsequently performed and covered by several artists, including Jimi Hendrix. In this situation, the copyright of the underlying musical composition (the lyrics and musical arrangement) is owned by Bob Dylan (or his publishing company), while the copyright of the Jimi Hendrix version of this track, is owned by Jimi Hendrix (or his record label).

There are five exclusive rights that a copyright owner holds for their created work.

The owner, as well as authorized third parties, has the right to:[xxxiii]

- Reproduce the work, (i.e., mechanical reproduction of the music for CDs, downloads, and vinyl).
- Distribute the work (i.e., stream or otherwise make the music publicly available).
- Prepare derivative works.
- Publicly perform the work (i.e., in a concert or on the radio).
- Publicly display the work.

This means that the owner has the sole and exclusive right to publicly distribute copies of the work by sale, rental, or lease, and to publicly perform or display the work, such as selling copies of a novel or publicly playing a musical recording at a restaurant. A compulsory license is one the songwriter (or publisher) cannot refuse, i.e., it does not require the songwriter's permission for you to record their song. The Harry Fox Agency, the foremost mechanical rights agency In the United States, administers and issues compulsory licenses and collects and distributes the mechanical royalty license fees to the parties. Here is how you can register your song with The Harry Fox Agency:

- You can register your songs, and provide them with related recording data such as Artist Name, Album Title, and ISRC, using one of our standard formats:
  - **Common Works Registration (CWR):** An industry standard for the bulk submission of composition information.
  - **eSong®:** HFA's proprietary system for registering compositions.
  - **eSong® Bulk:** HFA's solution for high-volume registrations for publishers that are not CWR-enabled that utilizes an Excel-formatted template

To register your songs, you must set up an HFA Online Account. Note, having an HFA Online Account does not entitle you to the benefits of HFA affiliation.

Once your claim has been received, HFA researches the song ownership information in their song database. If a discrepancy arises between your claim and the song information in their database, a 'Notice of Claim' will be sent to the publisher of record to start a resolution of your claim. Otherwise, if your claim is concurrent with the results of the research, the song information will be updated in their song database.

Copyrighting your song used to be daunting. Finding the right lawyer and a law firm, then keeping them could be expensive. However, nowadays you can register your song for copyright through https://www.copyright.gov/registration/, thus making the six-step process relatively easy.

Step 1: **RECORD YOUR SONG IN A "TANGIBLE MEDIUM."** Before you can get copyright protection, you must record your song either in written form or on a taped or digital sound recording.[xxxiv]

Step 2: **REGISTER FOR AN ACCOUNT AT THE US COPYRIGHT OFFICE WEBSITE.** You can also register a copyright by mail, but electronic registrations are cheaper and can be processed much more quickly. You can register electronically, even if you plan to mail a copy of your work to the copyright office.[xxxv]

Step 3: **FILL OUT THE COPYRIGHT REGISTRATION APPLICATION.** Once you have signed up for an online account, you can fill out online copyright registration forms. Be sure to carefully follow the instructions. If you register your copyright by mail, you must complete a paper application.[xxxvi]

Step 4: **PAY THE REGISTRATION FEE.** You can pay the copyright registration fee online with a credit or debit card, an ACH transfer, or a copyright office deposit account. If you register by mail, you can send the fee by check or money order. Basic registration fees range from $35 for an online registration of one work with a single author to $85 for a paper registration.[xxxvii]

Step 5: **SUBMIT A COPY OF YOUR SONG.** You may mail copies of your song in paper form or as an audio recording. You may also be eligible to upload your song digitally. The copyright office website describes the number and type of copies you must submit for both published and unpublished songs.[xxxviii]

Step 6: **WAIT FOR YOUR REGISTRATION TO BE PROCESSED.** Processing times for copyright registrations can vary, but it takes three to five months to process an electronic registration and seven to 10 months to process an application by mail. When you register a song copyright, you take an important step toward protecting your intellectual property. Registration is easy, but you need to carefully follow the copyright office instructions for filling out the forms and submitting copies of your work.[xxxix]

As a new artist you may be thinking to yourself, "Why should I copyright my songs?" Truth of the matter is unless you have a documented copyright to your work, anyone can make a copyright claim on your songs forcing you to either take them down from all websites or face legal action. Copyrights are important to register for and understand. Here are eight basic facts about copyright law every musician should know:

- **COPYRIGHT PROTECTION IS PRESENT AT THE CREATION.**[xl] The moment you create your music is the moment copyright protection begins. Creation occurs when music and/or lyrics are recorded, set to paper, or otherwise "fixed in a tangible form," according to the US Copyright Office.

- **TO PROTECT A COPYRIGHT, THE OWNER SHOULD REGISTER:**[xli] While the copyright is formed when you create, you need more to go to court to enforce your rights. To sue and claim damages, creators must own a copyright registered with the US Copyright Office.

- **A COPYRIGHT ESTABLISHES VARIOUS RIGHTS FOR THE OWNER:**[xlii]
  - To reproduce the work.
  - To adapt or arrange the work.
  - To perform the work.
  - To display, distribute, and/or sell copies of the work.
  - To incorporate the work with visual images.
  - To license others to do any of the things listed above.

- **PROTECTION FOR MORE THAN A LIFETIME:**[xliii] For published works created after January 1, 1978, copyright extends for 70 years beyond the life of the author. If there is more than one author, the copyright usually extends to 70 years from the death of the last living author. A work created by two or more individuals, where they intend to merge or otherwise mesh their works together at time of creation of the work, is considered a joint work. This means that the joint creation must be prepared "with the intention" that the different creator's contributions will be merged "into inseparable or interdependent parts of a unitary whole" with each author contributing material that, "could have been independently copyrighted." However, each author's contribution to the final work doesn't need to be equal and the authors don't need to be in the same physical area or create the work at the same time. When musicians create work for corporations or limited liability companies, this is considered "work for hire," and the corporations or limited liability companies are the owners of the copyright for 95 years from its first publication or for 120 years from the year of its creation, whichever expires first.

- **FOR COPYRIGHT PURPOSES, A SOUND RECORDING IS SEPARATE FROM A COMPOSITION:**[xliv] Sound recordings are copyrighted separately from the copyright of a musical composition as they are not considered the same work under copyright law.

- **PUBLISHED AND UNPUBLISHED MUSICAL WORKS MAY BE COPYRIGHTED:**[xlv] Work does not have to be published anywhere in order to be copyrighted.

- **SPECIAL RULES APPLY TO THOSE WHO WANT TO PERFORM COVER VERSIONS OF COPYRIGHTED SONGS:**[xlvi] For those who want to perform a cover version of a copyrighted song, set rates must be paid to the copyright owner to acquire "mechanical rights" to use the music. The current rates are set by the US Copyright Office, but you may also go through a private, non-profit organization called The Harry Fox Agency.

- **"POOR MAN'S COPYRIGHT" ISN'T GOOD COPYRIGHT PROTECTION:**[xlvii] You may have heard that you can establish the date of creation for copyright law purposes by mailing yourself a copy of the work and keeping it in a sealed envelope. In reality, this evidence is not likely to prove useful in a future copyright case. The best advice is to go through the copyright registration process for complete protection.

Another related copyright concept is the "work for hire" doctrine. This means an individual is commissioned by a third party, an individual or corporation, to create a specific work for the third party. This third party is then the owner of the work. For a work to be considered a "work for hire," an employee must prepare the copyrighted work within his or her employment for their employer. While this may seem straightforward, an analysis of who is considered an "employee" and whether a work was created "within the scope" of the employee's employment are determined on a case-by-case basis. In addition, a work may also be considered a "work for hire" if a "work is specifically ordered or commission for use as a contribution to a collective work, as a part of a motion picture or other audiovisual work, as a translation, as a supplementary work, as a compilation, as an instructional text, as a test, as answer material for a test, or as an atlas" as long as "the parties agree in writing that the work is a work made for hire." For works made for hire and anonymous and pseudonymous works, the duration of copyright is 95 years from first publication of the work or 120 years from creation, whichever is shorter.[xlviii] Once the work is registered and the certification is issued, the benefits of the registration begin immediately and are retroactive to the initial filing date. A formal registration of the creative materials with the U.S. Copyright Office within three months of public release provides additional valuable benefits to the owner of the work. This now allows the work to become a matter of public record and available for search within the U.S. Copyright Office and the Library of Congress. A work must also be registered in order to bring a copyright infringement lawsuit.

Copyrighting your creative work is arguably the most important legal process you will go through as an artist. Without the correct legal documentation of your work, it cannot be held up in a court of law that you are the proper owner of this creation. Think of the lawsuits you hear regarding one artist "stealing" a part of another artist's work. Metallica and Dr.Dre refused to release music and sued Napster because they saw sharing their music over the internet without each person paying for the song as stealing, which eliminated Napster as a service, forever changing how music is listened too. Marvin Gay sued Pharrell, Robin Thicke and T.I. for recreating a part of his song in "Blurred Lines" and won the case in court because what they created was his intellectual property. Yellowcard sued Juice WRLD for using a sample of their guitar in his first single "Lucid Dream." Although this suit was dropped after his untimely and unfortunate passing, Yellowcard would have won the suit, and Juice WRLD would've had to pay millions of dollars for copyright infringement and a possible royalty settlement (meaning Yellowcard would now own a percentage if not all of the royalties to this song). Without the proper copyright documentation, any artist can take what you have created, sample or directly use your material, and claim it as their own. If this were to happen and the artist were to then copyright their material, you (even being the original creator) can be sued for wrongfully using their copyrighted material without their consent. Yes, the copyright process can be long, but is necessary before you release any music.

Chapter 5   MUSIC DISTRIBUTION

Music distribution is as old as the music industry itself. Even when sheet music publishing companies ran the business, they needed someone to print out the scores and deliver them to the stores. That is where the distributors came in. While the core role of music distributors stayed the same for over a century, their workflow and business models have been subject to constant change, and those changes had a massive effect on the music industry. From the pre-2000s "era of CD" to "the era of streaming" that is used today, we still use the dominant distribution medium to define the stages of the industry's development. In 2001, the recording industry was almost exclusively physical. Two decades later, physical sales make up less than 1/4 of all global recording revenues with the share going down to 10% for the more developed digital markets. Most of the music distributors turned from supply chain managers into providers of digital infrastructure and rights administrators.

Today, you're able to make your song available to listeners worldwide by simply uploading your song to the internet. So, why would there still be a need for distribution intermediaries? Can't the artist just "Do It Yourself?" Not really. The distributors are still an integral part of the recording chain, taking upon themselves a few core roles:

DISTRIBUTING RELEASES TO DSPS

There are "direct artist platforms" like Bandcamp or SoundCloud that don't require a distributor. You set up an artist page, upload your music, and that's it. However, they're just a fraction of the plethora of digital distribution resources. With streaming services like Spotify, Apple Music, Deezer, Google Play Music, Pandora and Tidal to social media platforms like Instagram, TikTok, and Facebook, in today's digital environment, a well-oiled tech pipeline is a must, because most DSPs don't allow direct music uploads, forcing the artist to go through distributors/aggregators. Spotify recently closed off its direct upload program after a year of beta-testing, stating "music distribution is best handled by partners." DSPs would rather work with distributors to save themselves from dealing with unstandardized metadata and payout distribution. Artists can (technically) upload their music on iTunes themselves, but Apple will suggest you go through a distributor to ensure the release metadata fits the platform's requirements. Some of the broadest digital distribution networks claim to source over 600 online stores, and all the different DSPs have different metadata standards that make it virtually impossible to handle digital music distribution manually.

ROYALTIES ALLOCATION

In the world of streaming, the rights owners now earn money the second the user presses play. The value of that stream depends on dozens of factors, and with the royalty calculation as complicated as it is now, imagine if Spotify, Tidal or Apple Music had to pay out those royalties directly to every artist. The administrative costs would go through the roof, even if they'd gotten the metadata and banking details correctly, and the rights owners themselves wouldn't be too enthusiastic about getting paid separately from each digital platform. The distributors fill that gap serving as a sorting plant for royalties from DSPs to rights owners, ensuring every "master" dollar goes back into the recording industry (while the composition/publishing royalties go through a separate pipeline of CMOs, PROs, and publishers).

MARKETING DISTRIBUTION STRATEGY AND TRADE MARKETING

A customer walks into the record store where they're presented with hundreds of options. The "Stuff Selections" offers an eclectic mix of new releases, the "Point of Sale stand" promotes the latest blockbuster release and there is a "Premium Shelf" at the entrance of the store.

Today we don't have many record stores anymore, but the same principle still applies. A person opens Spotify, clicks on "New Music Friday" and presses play. The track that plays is the #1 song of the week, the *"record that every customer will see,"* the DSP equivalent to the premium record store shelf. How do you get there? A handful of DSPs dominate the digital market and while some streaming giants are putting their algorithms forward as mediators of music discovery, the most popular playlists and the *"feature spots"* are curated by the service's editorial team. To get that desired distribution push, you need to go through them. However, the editorial team can't speak to thousands of managers and labels every week, just like streaming services can't distribute royalties directly to rights owners.

As an artist it may be time consuming to singularly upload each track to each streaming platform individually. If you're independent, it's hard to track the metrics for each platform and ensure your tracks were uploaded properly. What options do you have to make this process easier? First, you can hire a company, but this will cost varying amounts depending on the size of the company and the campaign you are looking for. Second, you can build your own team to monitor these platforms. Third (and most likely your best option), you can sign up for one of the many distribution channels available to independent artists. Last, you can get distribution through one of the major labels including Sony ATV, Kobalt, Universal, Warner, Columbia or Atlantic. However, as an up-and-coming independent artist, you probably don't have access to one of the major label distribution channels. That still leaves you with a variety of independent options. Each one has its own platform with different stipulations, partnerships, connections, splits, rights, and subscription fees, but each of the following independent distribution channels will upload your music to all streaming platforms. Here is a breakdown of a few of the independent distribution channel options you can sign up for as an artist:

DISTROKID[xlix]

A music distribution service that distributes tracks to all the major music stores and streaming platforms. Users pay a yearly fee of $19.99 to upload unlimited albums and songs and artists always keep 100% of their rights and royalties.

CD BABY[l]

Distributes your music to 150+ streaming and download services around the world for a fee of $9.95 per single, $49 per album, and 15% of your royalties. CD Baby also gives you access to key demographic and geographic data when you distribute your music using their service.

TUNECORE[li]

For a flat fee of $9.99 per single or $29.99 per album, Tunecore distributes your music to over 150 digital stores and streaming platforms. TuneCore artists keep 100% of the profits they earn from sales, downloads, and streaming revenue.

AWAL[lii]

A distribution service that delivers your music to all the key stores and streaming platforms in over 200 territories worldwide. AWAL is free to join, but they take a minimum 15% share of all your streaming and download profits once your track is released. One of the major differences of AWAL is that they don't automatically accept every artist who wants to join the platform. They believe that having a curated artist roster allows them to support their artists with a higher quality of service.

UNITED MASTERS[liii]

While it's free to distribute your music and deliver your tracks to 30+ stores and streaming platforms, including all the majors like Spotify and YouTube, they do take 10% of the profit from your streams and downloads. Every artist has access to an analytics dashboard which tracks your real-time data.

DITTO[liv]

With unlimited releases starting from $25 USD per year, Ditto distributes your music to over 200 stores, including all the major streaming platforms like Spotify, Apple Music, YouTube and more. Ditto has three distribution packages available for music makers at every stage of their career: Artist, Professional and Label. Ditto lets you keep 100% of your rights and royalties, has 24/7 artist support, and lets you track sales and trending data with daily analytics reports.

RECORD UNION[lv]

A distribution platform that lets you register a free account and then charges you for every release. There are three distribution packages available depending on the amount of stores you want your track delivered to, with single releases priced from $7. Record Union artists are charged per year for every music store or streaming platform they want their track added to and take 15% of all artist royalties.

SPINNUP[lvi]

An independent record label and music distribution service owned by Universal Music Group. You can sign up for free to use their social data dashboard and special artist features, but then you pay to release every track. Single releases start at $9.99. SpinnUp delivers to 44 music stores and streaming platforms, artists keep 100% of their rights and royalties, and the top tracks uploaded from their platform are sent to the Universal Music Group A&R team, giving you a chance to be discovered and signed by their record label.

LEVEL[lvii]

Allows you to release your music on Spotify, Apple Music, iTunes, Amazon Music, Google Play, TIDAL, Pandora, Deezer and Napster. While still in Beta, you can distribute your music free of charge, but when the full platform is launched, Level will take 8% from each of your release royalties.

If you choose to sign-up with a "Distributor," understand this isn't a specific company, rather it's a role other parts of the recording chain can internalize. Because of this, there are a wide variety of distribution channels you can go through.

MAJOR DISTRIBUTORS

The majors are perhaps the only players in the recording market that own a catalog big enough to negotiate with prominent DSPs and get direct access to their editorial teams. They don't need distribution partners, rather the label's distribution department works 99% of the catalog. It's not only about distributing their own catalog; major labels also distribute a sizable portion of independent labels. Beggars Group is distributed in the US by Warner Music's ADA, Fool's Gold and Mass Appeal by Universal's Caroline International. On the US market, 85% of digital revenues go through Universal, Sony, or Warner (or distribution companies under their umbrella). To counteract that, digital platforms and independent labels are trying to level the playing field, and digital rights network Merlin has success mediating relationships between independent labels, non-major distributors, and DSPs. That said, the current system is far from perfect. Independent labels don't have the same 1:1 editorial team access as the major labels, and it's still easier for artists to be visible on streaming platforms if you're signed or distributed by a major label.

INDEPENDENT DISTRIBUTION PARTNERS

Major deals aren't for everybody, and for the top-tier independent artists, there's another option. There's been a trend of major labels buying up independent distribution companies. Recently for example, The Orchard became a part of Sony in 2015, and Universal bought INgrooves in early 2019. Today, the primary players left are Believe Digital, Idol, Redeye

Worldwide and recently launched Ditto Plus (not to be confused with Ditto's open platform solution). The important thing is, for distribution partners aggregation is a side-service whose actual value is in the hands-on approach to promotion, trade marketing, and digital release strategies. From the moment you sign a distribution deal, you have a dedicated consultancy and pitching team with direct contact to editorial across the major DSPs. The deals with dedicated distribution partners will always be percentage-based, meaning distribution partners will take a portion of the recording royalties, which can be as high as 50%. The distributor will often offer an advance to the artist, recouped by the future cash flows. The independent distribution partners are more accessible than their major-affiliated counterparts, but in both cases, the up-and-coming artist has to show their worth as an investment.

WHITE-LABEL DISTRIBUTION SOLUTIONS

Not all the independent labels are looking for distribution partners. Some top-level indie labels have an in-house distribution department that only lacks the technical infrastructure. To bridge that gap, record labels can use white-label distribution services like Consolidated Independent, Sonosuite and FUGA. White-label solutions provide a technical pipeline, focusing on delivering audio and metadata to DSPs, and distributing royalties back to right holders at scale while their customers keep complete control over distribution and retail marketing strategies. Their business model targets top-end independent labels with a sizable catalog and output or distributors looking for a tech pipeline, rather than someone who wants to distribute a handful of songs.

OPEN DISTRIBUTION PLATFORMS/AGGREGATORS

Every music professional/artist has probably heard of CDBaby, TuneCore, and DistroKid. The business model of open platforms revolves around two types of services. First is the aggregator package: go on the platform, upload your music, and they make your release available across hundreds of DSPs. This is the basic service that all of the online distribution platforms offer, and depending on the service, the distributor either charges a flat per-song/album fee, an annual recurring subscription fee, or a percentage-based commission up to 15%. The second package is "premium artist services." That could mean playlist, pitching bundles, publishing administration services, airplay plugs, physical distribution, or anything in between. The quality of those artist services will be nowhere near what a Believe Digital partnership can offer. However, those services are available to anyone who is willing to pay.

The ability of open platforms to properly represent their customers on the trade marketing field is limited. With 40 thousand songs uploaded on Spotify every day, it doesn't matter how big the team is, they won't be able to provide personalized promotion services at this scale. Most of the time, the deal is a value proposition: "Distribute your album to every DSP for $50 and keep 100% of the royalties," However, if you go with a flat-fee distribution deal, you're on your own if you want to stand out across the DSPs.

SEMI-LABEL DISTRIBUTION SERVICES

This last type of distribution company is relatively new. As of now, only two companies fall into that category: AWAL and Amuse. The idea of semi-label distribution is you don't need a record deal to release your music, but you still need a distributor. The thinking of these companies is, let's release your music and if it gains traction, upstream to a record label-type deal. Similar to open platforms, AWAL and Amuse offer a basic service of distribution administration of getting the music out there. When the artist gets a distribution deal, the consumption data gathered across the DSPs ends up with the company's A&R. Meaning if these companies see the artist is doing well, the initial deal can be upscaled to a distribution partnership or a full-blown record licensing deal. This allows them to offer their basic distribution service pro bono for the sake of powering its A&Rs with data. Labels are now focusing solely on release marketing, and it's hard for independents to expand down the chain and take on distribution unless they have special relationships with the streaming editorial community.

It comes down to which distribution channel and situation fits your needs best as an artist. Some have major partnerships with different companies and organizations (United Masters having partnerships with the NBA), while others give you better splits and royalties on your music. They all offer relatively even splits, all of which are beneficial to the artists compared to what you would receive at a major label. The best part about going this route is that you can keep close to 100% ownership in your songs and catalogs. This means you own your masters; you own your copyrights; you own your songs in their entirety. If you were to sign with a label, especially as a new unproven artist, you would give up a majority of the percentage of not only your songs but also your masters (which you may not own at all).

Chapter 6   RELEASING YOUR MUSIC

As an independent artist, it's enticing to release your music on every digital streaming platform possible to garner the largest listenership possible. Realistically, unless you align yourself with one of the distributors, I mentioned in Chapter 5, this is an unobtainable feat. The vast majority of popular digital streaming platforms don't allow for individual artists to directly upload their music to the platforms. This means as an independent artist you have to find the digital streaming platforms that allow direct uploads to their platforms. Your best and most popular options in this category are going to be YouTube and SoundCloud.

To release on YouTube and SoundCloud is free. Create an account on each and you're able to upload music and videos with ease. YouTube allows you to upload as much as you want as long as it's a video. If there is no accompanying video, that's ok, you can use iMovie (free with all Mac computers) to create a still image with your song playing and upload it to your account.

It may not strictly be a music streaming service, but YouTube has an undeniable presence in user base size, interaction and consumption. In May 2019, YouTube CEO Susan Wojcicki revealed that YouTube counts 2 billion monthly active users, accounting for 45% of the world's entire online population (the total number of internet users in the world is around at 4.4 billion). YouTube is the number one site for web traffic worldwide (8.6 billion monthly visits) and in the US (1.6 billion monthly visits).[lviii] What are some other reasons that you should use YouTube as a platform for your music?

- 1 billion hours of YouTube watched per day.
- YouTube accounts for 25% of global mobile traffic.
- 44,000 YouTube channels had at least 250,000 subscribers in early 2019.
- 80% of YouTube views from outside the US.
- 500 hours of content uploaded to YouTube every minute.
- YouTube localized to 100 countries, and accessible in 80 different languages.
- Video accounts for 47% of global music streaming, with 77% of music listeners using YouTube monthly.
- 20 million YouTube Premium/Music subscribers.

- 2 million subscribers to YouTube TV.

SoundCloud is a similar concept. Create a free account, and you can upload music for public consumption. However, SoundCloud only allows you to upload four hours of content with a free account. Once you reach this mark you must subscribe to SoundCloud Premium ($10/month) to upload more content, or you will have to pick which songs you would like to stay up and which one to take down to stay under the four-hour limit. If you upgrade, you can upload content unlimitedly with no restriction.

SoundCloud is one of the most well-known and popular platforms for independent and unsigned artists to upload their music. Like all streaming services, you must market yourself and provide listeners with an idea of who you are as an artist, by having a solid visual presence and offering links to your social media channels. The easier it is for listeners to share your work, the more likely you are to be noticed. Artists like Lil Uzi Vert, the late XXXTENTACION, and the late Juice WRLD all made their name from SoundCloud. By focusing on this single platform, they could captivate a large audience that propelled each of them to star status. While SoundCloud doesn't offer overall listener statics, each artist can see their own personal statics through their SoundCloud artist profile account. You will see your monthly listeners, number of subscribers, number of listens on each song (daily and overall) and where those listeners are coming from. SoundCloud is still one of the biggest platforms for up-and-coming artists to grow their fanbase and get noticed.

What about the primary streaming platforms? How do you upload your songs to Spotify, Apple Music, and Tidal (among others)? For this there are a few options. Using your Apple ID (which most likely you have because you had to create one when you bought your iPhone or Mac), you can sign up for Apple Music for Artists, allowing you to upload your music onto the iTunes store. Once your songs are uploaded, be sure to claim your artist profile so you will receive royalties from the purchase of your songs. If you would like to upload your songs to Tidal or Spotify, you will have to go through a third-party distributor, as you cannot upload directly to their platforms. To publish music through Tidal, you must use either Indigoboom, Record Union, Distrokid or Tunecore (these are the four major distributors listed on the Tidal website). However, as we spoke about in the previous chapter, each independent distributor has its own set of stipulations in regard to sign up and distribution.

With the wide variety of digital streaming platforms and uploading options, how do you know that you're choosing the right one for your music? What does each platform offer you as an artist? What are the benefits and drawbacks for each platform? Before answering those questions, you as an artist need to understand that each stream is counted differently.

This means that a stream from a free account counts differently than one from a paying account, which counts differently from a playlist stream, which counts differently from a song download, which counts differently from an album stream, which counts differently from a downloaded album, and so on. Each different stream type for individual songs and albums is calculated differently when your total amount of streams is counted in their totality.

Spotify is arguably the leader in all the streaming platforms. In Q1 of 2020 alone there were 286 million monthly active users. Of these, 130 million were Spotify Premium subscribers (meaning they are paying to use the service). This is up from 271 million monthly active Spotify users and 124 million Spotify Premium subscribers in Q4 2019. Year-on-year, it's a 69 million increase in users (32%), and 30 million increases in subscribers. (30%) A few other statistics to note for the Spotify streaming platform:[lix]

- Spotify claims 36% of the global streaming market.
- Spotify listeners average 25 hours of streaming per month.
- 44% of users listen to Spotify daily.
- Over 50 million tracks available on Spotify.
- Around a third of Spotify listening time is spent on Spotify-generated playlists, with another third going on user-generated playlists.
- Average users listen to 41 unique artists per week.

Apple Music boasts 30 million subscribers and is one of the most significant platforms in terms of musical exposure. Features such as internet radio, genre-based stations and user satisfaction feedback promote and strengthen this platforms music discovery. It's vital that you get your music onto this platform to generate plays and streams. More so than other streaming platforms, Apple Music actively asks for feedback on songs to provide more tailored auto-generated recommendations. If you want your music to be suggested to users, you must familiarize yourself with the artists surrounding your genre and know which acts are recommended to audiences consuming your genre. Get comfortable with your fanbase and design your Apple profile with them in mind. It's important to brand your work appropriately, and Apple Music will reward artists that do so. Apple has also branched out to video content and visually focused work, meaning it's more important to provide imagery alongside your sound.[lx]

Tidal differentiates itself from the competition with a focus on high-quality playback and a wide selection of music videos. While not as large a contender as Spotify or Apple Music, Tidal is a service that prides itself on higher artist royalties and emphasis on minor acts. The Tidal streaming platform boasts 4.2 million subscribers in 53 different countries and has a catalogue of over 60 million songs. Tidal has also established a pedestal for smaller, unknown acts to get recognized with the 'TIDAL RISING' playlists. You'll want to make the most of this if you're going to get recognized.[lxi]

Google Play offers a more minimal and stripped-back aesthetic while still keeping much of the expected features of a streaming platform. Users can create new playlists, add albums and artists to their library, stream radio, and explore freshly recommended acts. Google Play Music is a branch of the Google Play service, which has 1 billion active users. Getting on this platform will open your music up to a number of new listeners. To get your music on this platform you must upload your music to TuneCore, which will then upload your music to the Google Play music store.[lxii]

An extension of the Amazon Prime service, Amazon Music has a catalogue of two million songs. The number of Amazon Music listeners in the United States amounted to 30.4 million in 2018. Much like other platforms, playlists can be curated and shared with options to download and save certain albums or artists. If you would like to upload your music to the Amazon Prime store, you can do so by signing into your RouteNote account (or create one if you don't already have one), create a "new release," upload your audio file and fill in the metadata, and from there go to "manage stores" and you can select which stores/services you would like your music uploaded and distributed to.[lxiii]

Another well-known music streaming and sharing platform, much like SoundCloud, is BandCamp. This platform allows users to share and distribute musical content and merchandise with specific catering to independent artists. The site is primarily driven by new music listening and browsing, so it's an ideal place to gain potential audiences. Similar to SoundCloud, BandCamp doesn't offer overall listener statics. However, each artist can see their personal statics through their BandCamp artist profile account. You will see your monthly listeners, number of subscribers, number of listens on each song (daily and overall) and where those listeners are coming from. Getting your music uploaded to BandCamp is simple. Create an account (if you don't already have one), select "add," click "add tracks," choose the audio file you want to upload and save the draft.[lxiv]

BlueJay, an app tailored toward music socializing, enables artists to host their own public radio shows, playlist share, follow artists and engage with group chats during live sessions. It's free for Android and iOS, and the ideal platform to broadcast your sound and similar sounding artists, having already been implemented by the likes of Equate London, DJ David Mortal, Challenge, and The Isle of CC. With a strong focus on community, BlueJay is a useful place to share and spread the word about your music and brand.[lxv]

Deezer boasts 40 million tracks available, 30,000 radio channels, and 16 million monthly active users. With a 'hear this' tab inside the app, smaller artists can get their work spread to more listeners. You can share and discuss songs with friends through integrated social media accounts, making Deezer an essential platform for up-and-coming independent artists. Adding your songs to the Deezer platform is simple. Click on "favorites," go to "my MP3," select MP3s and choose which files you would like to upload.[lxvi]

A free broadcast and internet radio platform, iHeartRadio supplies a variety of services, including song recommendations, podcasts and on-demand music selection. Available across over 90 devices, the potential audience for your work is massive. In 2019, 8% of Americans reported using iHeartRadio each week. iHeartRadio has 128 million global users as of April 2019, with 250 million monthly active listeners, and 858 radio stations in 150 markets. Getting your music to play on an iHeart radio station can be a little difficult. Unlike some of the other platforms mentioned here, to be a part of the iHeart rotation you have to submit your music through a third-party aggregator that has distribution rights and agreements with iHeart (try TuneCore or CD Baby).[lxvii]

With an exclusive focus on the listening and distribution of radio shows, DJ mixes and podcasts, Mixcloud is a great way for independent, musically minded people to share their compilations, remixes, and playlists, and it's easy for registered users to upload content. You'll want to use Mixcloud's social networking widget to broadcast your work to as far of a reach as possible. To add your songs to this platform you must have an account. Through your account page click "upload," choose the file you would like to upload, add a title, click "upload," and you're good to go.[lxviii]

Founded back in 2000, Pandora Internet Radio is America's leading online radio company and sees around two million average active sessions per month. Designed to be a more streamlined experience, Pandora offers millions of songs with personalized playlists and handfuls of radio stations. Unlike the iHeart radio stations Pandora is a bit easier, but you still have to go through a process that includes their curators who decide which songs to play. You can (through your account) submit your songs to their music page and a representative will listen and decide if your song is a good fit for one of their stations.[lxix]

Jango is a free platform with an emphasis on custom radio stations and was first introduced in 2007. The service allows independent artists to promote their music alongside larger artists for a fee. With a well-designed album cover, music video and song, Jango is a solid platform to gain exposure and attention from audiences.[lxx]

Available in the US and Canada, Slacker Radio enables the creation and sharing of customized music stations, with over 300 radio stations curated by music experts. Using social media platforms, music creators and users can use the Slacker name to promote songs, bands, and artists, making it a great place to promote and establish a fanbase. Just like the other radio stations mentioned above, you must submit your tracks to their curators and/or producers who will listen to your tracks and make the final decision if your music is the right fit for one of their stations.[lxxi]

There are a tremendous number of DSPs and websites that you can upload your music to for public consumption. The tough part is deciding which one(s) are going to be the most beneficial to you. When you're starting out, it's best to focus on one platform rather than spread yourself too thin. Finding a core audience on one platform and building from there will benefit you more than attempting to grow a large following on every platform, only to have an insignificant fan base on each.

Chapter 7   MARKETING

In today's climate of all digital, social media marketing has moved to the forefront of marketing interactions. While a social media marketing campaign is tantamount to a successful release and career, guerrilla (or street team) marketing still has its place because a social media marketing campaign (unless done with a huge budget) can get lost on the timeline of the people you're trying to reach. Posting flyers across the city has the possibility to reach exponentially more people because they can't help but notice all the flyers when they walk by. And there are other guerilla tactics you can use. For example, hiring people to walk high traffic shopping neighborhoods wearing sandwich boards touting your tunes or setting up counters about your music at street fairs and meet and greets. Because we now live in a digital-age, artists don't think about the physical side of marketing and only focus on the digital side. While this is a sensible strategy, face-to-face interactions aren't dead yet.

Personal interaction is the number one way to make a lasting impression. Speaking with a follower on social media will create a fan for a moment, having an interpersonal conversation with a fan at a meet and greet creates a fan for a lifetime. Each generation has a shrinking attention span and thus forgets about videos and photos as fast as they appear. Having a physical item that they see daily during a normal routine creates a lasting impression. Guerrilla marketing can be time-consuming as you will need to physically be out in the world for meet and greets, posting flyers, handing out merchandise and making connections, but in the long run this marketing technique could prove to be rampantly beneficial in growing your fan base. A loyal local fan base is more impactful than a large social media following in the eyes of most music industry executives. Social media numbers can be inflated, can be faked, and not all followers are actual fans. A local fan base that will buy your merchandise, attend your shows, and stream your music will allow you to reach heights your social media following won't.

There are a variety of social media platforms, and each platform consists of a different audience that requires a different marketing strategy. As an artist you should have an account on every platform (Instagram, Twitter, Facebook, LinkedIn, Snapchat, and TikTok), although it's hard to provide and maintain great content and activity on each platform by yourself. If you're doing this on your own, I suggest choosing one or two platforms to focus on at first.

Eventually, you will need to be present on each platform, but keeping the focus on one or two in the beginning will be beneficial. Creating a large following on one platform can translate to those followers following you on a different platform.

Take DJ Khaled for example, he utilized Snapchat when it first came out to propel himself to superstar status. While it's true as a DJ and producer he was already popular, by utilizing his personality through SnapChat he became a larger-than-life public figure. Reaching millions of people with each video post, he was able to take his brand to an astronomical level on this singular platform which then translated to his other social media accounts. Videos of him dancing, walking around his house, being with his wife and son, working out and more, gave him mainstream appeal that increased his public recognition, music sales, and brand partnerships. Did you know who he was or what he looked like before the Drake vocals came in?

Almost the entire world uses social media. Without a digital footprint or social media presence, for all intents and purposes you don't exist. However, social media is not intended as a straight person to person, or company to person, marketing platform. Rather, it is a catalyst for word-of-mouth marketing. Your posts should have around an 80%/20% split of personal posts to advertising posts. This doesn't mean that your personal posts can't be promotional. You just need to frame the promotional content within the post in subliminal ways. For example, if you're in the studio, you could share a video of you working in the studio, post a photo of you recording or a snippet of the song. When you're on tour, take photos at the venues and videos of the performance. These posts are subliminal promotional posts because they don't directly promote products, but they do represent you and your music. Understand that social media management takes a huge time commitment that takes time away from your creative process. As an artist you need to focus on your music, social media isn't the end-all-be-all for promotion.

Your social media accounts are ways for fans to connect with you outside of listening to your music. When fans or industry people see you in photos, that is what they expect to see in person and on stage. Make sure you are being your most authentic self. Are you expressing yourself to the fullest? Are you stepping outside your comfort zone? Remember to give your fans opportunities to relate to you and your personality.

"But what do I post about?" This is a common concern with a simple remedy. Your posts should be focused around your hobbies, talents, passions, hometown, and everyday life. Think about what makes you, you. Your first theme should be music, but what about the other four? Is your location a huge part of who you are? Do you work out every day? Are you an animal lover with three dogs and two cats that sometimes don't get along? Once you narrow down your social media themes an entire world of content ideas will open up.

Each social media account today applies some marketing strategy to reach as many users and create as much engagement as possible. What are some of these strategies and how can you make them work best for you?

- Defining your brand
- Engaging with fans, venues, other brands, and more
- Channel differentiation
- Social media analytics
- Boosted posts and advertising

While engaging in the above methods, it's important to think about the image you're attempting to portray. If the audience can connect with you as a person, the connection with you as an artist will be that much stronger. The stronger the connection, the more willing your fans will be to support and share your content. I'd suggest starting with the five themes below:

MUSIC

This is the most important kind of content you should post, and you should be posting this frequently. Posting song snippets, previews of upcoming songs, videos of you in the studio, anything that shows your fans and followers you're working on new music will create anticipation.

HOBBIES

Let your fans know what it's like to hang out with you for a day when you're doing something you love other than music.

SUPPORTING THE LIVE MUSIC SCENE

Connect with them over your love for live performances and invite them to meet you at someone else's show. Creating these meet-and-greets will allow your fans to interact with you on a personal level, rather than an artist level.

EXPLORING NEW CITIES

Share photos of the restaurants you try while on the road, or during your daily life.

CHASING YOUR DREAMS

Nothing is more "you" then sharing your experience as a young musician pursuing your dream.

Most of the time, it doesn't occur to artists that they can't just post a picture and expect to get the maximum number of likes. There is analytical research about the best and worst times to post on each social channel. Analytics are your friend. Being on top of the trends can boost your social media presence. There is a reason each social media platform now allows users with certain types of accounts to see all of their analytics. As an artist you have to use these analytics tools so you know when and where to post your content.

- Facebook users are usually on during work hours. Having a video that captures the viewer in the first 20 seconds is key.
- Twitter is the fastest moving social channel, the average lifespan of a tweet is about 15 minutes, meaning you can post more often on this platform.
- Instagram users have been described as nocturnal so schedule your IG posts any time after 9 PM.

If you're blindly posting on your accounts without using analytics, your posts will not reach the maximum number of followers. Take Instagram, for example: this platform allows you to see what day and time your followers are active and the most engaged with your content. It makes little sense to post at 6 AM on Wednesday if your followers are typically on Instagram at 10 PM on Thursday. By then your post has been lost in the Instagram sphere and is unlikely to be seen on a followers' feed due to the millions of other posts appearing on their feed.

A social media feature you need to take advantage of is story posts, as these differ from feed posts. A feed post is a post you put on your page that will stay there in perpetuity unless you take it down. You can instead create a post that is only shown for 24 hours called a story post. These story posts don't have to be on brand rather they can showcase different daily activities because they will disappear the next day. Your story posts can also be converted into "memories," allowing you to take an entire day's worth of story posts and keep them on your page in perpetuity. This allows your fans to see entire events they may have missed from your story posts any time they want.

Each of these platforms have algorithms that account for how each post is shown. Hashtags, tags and follower engagement, are all parts of these algorithms. The hashtags you use determine where your posts are seen the most. Who you tag in the post determines which audience sees the post? The engagement of your posts determines what place on the feed and discovery page your posts are shown. The more engagement you get, the higher your post will rank on different pages and the better your next post will do. Research trending topics and hashtags to see which ones you should be using. Be careful though, because if you use the same hashtags all the time, or if your content doesn't align with the hashtags you are using, these platforms can ban your account (meaning that you will be less or non-visible to the public or you cannot post at all). In order to make the most out of your social media posts and take advantage of the algorithms you should:

INTERACT WITH YOUR AUDIENCE

Algorithms on social media platforms treat engagement like a snowball effect. The more engagement your post gets, the more likely it is to be rewarded by the algorithm. One of the easiest ways to encourage engagement is by asking questions of your followers. Serving as a call-to-action, question-based posts are a simple way to encourage interactions and connect with your audience at the same time.

TAG OTHER ACCOUNTS IN YOUR POSTS

By tagging other accounts in your posts, you're sending notifications to them to view your posts. When you post if you're using a product, wearing a specific brand, or eating at a restaurant, tagging that company not only notifies the company of your post but draws the eyes of their followers to your page.

HASHTAGS

Hashtags are how people search and find topics and people on social media. Using the correct hashtags makes your posts and account more searchable to the general public.

OPTIMIZE YOUR POST TIMING FOR WHEN YOUR FOLLOWERS ARE MOST ACTIVE

Timing is everything. By correctly timing your posts for when your follower base is most active on a platform you are greatly increasing your chances for their engagement on that post. Use your analytics to see what days and times your follower base is most active and schedule your posts around those times.

CREATE A POSTING SCHEDULE

Social media algorithms reward activity on their platforms. The more you post, the more traffic you will see. These platforms want you to spend as much time using them as possible, so they try to encourage you to post more by boosting the accounts that post on a more frequent basis.

POST VIDEOS ACROSS ALL NETWORKS

All platforms are vying for your attention, this means they want you to post with them and not use them as a third-party posting site. They designed their algorithms to look favorably on posts that are directly posted to their app. For example, if you post a video on Twitter, the platform will make this video post more searchable than if you posted a link to the same video to be viewed on an outside site.

LINKS AND CAPTIONS

Social media algorithms are like grandparents, they don't want you to dump and run. They react unfavorably to accounts that post links and walk away. Spend time with the posts and comments, be engaging, be creative, then you can drop your link.

TRY DIFFERENT CONTENT TYPES

Posting repetitive content is the easiest way to bore your followers. If you're posting the same type of unengaging content every day, much like a sitcom that has been on for too long, the viewers will know what to expect and stop viewing the content. Experiment with different content types to see what your followers engage with the most. For example:

- Images versus text posts.
- Long versus short videos.
- Links versus no links.
- No hashtag versus multiple hashtags.

Experimenting can give you the most insight in regard to what performs well and what doesn't.

STUDY YOUR ACCOUNT ANALYTICS

If you don't look at the numbers, you won't know how your content is performing. The numbers don't lie. They will show you the type of content that resonates with your fanbase and which content you should stop creating.

To have effective music promotion you need to control your message on any platform where fans can see you and listen to your music. There are hundreds of thousands of artists vying for the same fans. You can't post your music and run. You have to create your place, own that space, and make the platform work for your message. What are some aspects to consider when promoting on social media?

WHO AND WHERE ARE YOUR FANS

To get the most out of your promotion efforts, find out who your fans are. Knowing details like the location and age of your audience helps you build a marketing strategy to accurately reach them. Some platforms give detailed information like when fans came across your music, and through what channels or search terms they used.

DON'T ALIENATE EXISTING FANS TO ATTRACT NEW ONES

Without fans you have no career. They are essential to your success. The size of your fanbase doesn't matter. Whether it's five or five million, you have to create a meaningful connection. Posting music, photos or videos, and hoping for the best is not good enough. You have to cultivate an image and brand that resonates with a specific group of people. Being true to yourself is the easiest way to do this, as it will come off as genuine rather than fake and needy.

CREATE COMPELLING NON-MUSICAL CONTENT

It takes more than just music to capture a fan in today's microwave music climate. Fans will be drawn to you because of your story, image, and brand before they will be drawn to your music. If they see you as someone they can connect with, they will be more than happy to listen to your music. You create these relationships by providing fans with non-musical content. Through interviews, videos and photos, you can show the non-artist side of you that the general public can relate to. People are captivated by people before they are captivated by music.

WRITE A PRESS RELEASE FOR PLAYLISTS AND BLOGS

These platforms and media outlets are a powerful force for the promotion of your music. Even coverage from smaller press outlets can be effective in broadening your listener base. Playlists are no different. The biggest curated playlists have millions of daily listeners. However, getting media coverage as an up-and-coming artist is difficult and getting playlist curators to notice your music can be a daunting task. Blogs such as "Pigeons and Planes," and "Ones to Watch," have become a steppingstone for rising artist to gain mainstream appeal. In the same token, the smaller music blogs can help newer artists garner a ton of attention as well. Research music blogs that feature songs and artists with a similar music style to yours. While playlists aren't technically media outlets, they are still considered vital in promoting your music. Without knowing the curator personally or having a big budget (usually a few thousand dollars), you won't be able to directly submit your music to the upper echelon playlists. However, streaming platforms have thousands of user-generated playlists that do allow for up-and-coming artist submissions, which is a good place to start when trying to attract the attention of the larger playlists. Identify which playlists accommodate your music genre and contact the curators. There's a ton of nuance when reaching out for coverage and adding an electronic press kit (EPK) to your website and outgoing messages will be a great benefit. Your EPK provides a singular place for your digital assets (pictures links, artist bio, etc.) for media members (bloggers, radio directors, DJs, event promoters, etc.) to easily access. Your EPK should include:

- **BIO:** A concise overview of who you are, your influences, the music you make, and any acknowledgements you have received so far.

- **PHOTOS:** Provide downloadable Google Drive or Dropbox links to high quality photos and include photo credit info if necessary.

- **MEDIA FEATURES:** Include positive quotes from media outlets that you have been featured in.

- **MUSIC LINKS:** Provide a central link with your songs.

- **PERSONAL LINKS:** Media members like to see your digital links (social media, profiles, websites) so they can keep up to date with your activities.

- **ANY PERTINENT INFORMATION**: New EP or album releases and any information around the releases.

CREATE A WEBSITE

Personal websites are critical in building an identity and reaching fans. Social media still does this to a degree but is becoming less effective due to algorithm updates limiting accounts reach. Creating your own website allows you a clear path in reaching different audiences and allows you to shape your message and identity with no limitations. Websites allow the creation of e-commerce stores that social media platform don't.

PROMOTE AND SELL ON YOUR WEBSITE

Your website should never be out of date. It should always reflect new events, appearances, and milestones. You want fans visiting your website as often as possible. The more they visit your site, the more exposure to your albums, merchandise, and tickets they have. As a rising artist, you probably don't have many updates other than the occasional release or local show. In this case, starting a blog is a simple solution that's easy to set up within your website. Post on your blog once or twice a week, sharing anything that's relatable to your fans. This could include song inspirations, new lyrical concepts, artist stories, or a look inside your studio. Landing pages are crucial for your website as they can collect email addresses, house your links, provide fans with information, or sell your merchandise.

EMAIL PROMOTION

Your email database is possibly the most valuable asset in your music promotion, because unlike traditional media outlets, this database provides a continuous marketing avenue. When someone signs up for your email list, it means they are invested in you and are interested in your career updates. Use this to your advantage and premiere new content and update new music, merchandise, tickets and show dates.

PR AND RADIO CAMPAIGNS

Unfortunately, the success of these campaigns revolves around the budget you put into them, and the results you're probably looking for won't come unless you have a few thousand dollars in your budget, and even then, there are no guarantees. These types of campaigns are great because they can garner massive attention and exponentially grow your fan/follower base, but these campaigns largely rely on personal relationships unless you are at a certain artist level.

Now that you know how to create your social media pages, it's time to understand the differences in each platform. While every platform is utilized by a massive amount of people, each platform has a different demographic. Understanding the demographics using each platform is tantamount to getting the most out of each platform.

Instagram is the leading marketing platform in the world and is driven by graphics and videos. This is where most of the world spends most of their time for social media consumption. Instagram is great, as it connects directly to Facebook (it is owned by Facebook) so you can cross-promote without having to post on both platforms separately. Instagram now has 1 billion monthly active users. The top three countries that use Instagram are the United States (116 million), India (73 million), and Brazil (72 million). Over 60% of users log in daily, making it the second most engaged network after Facebook. Males between 18–24 years old are the biggest demographic group, while 75% of all users are between 18 and 24. 37% of US internet users are now on Instagram, and 90% of Instagram users are younger than 35. A few other Instagram usage statistics to be aware of:[lxxii]

- Over 500 million Stories are posted every day.
- 3.5 billion likes every day.
- 95 million posts are made every day.
- 63% of users use the app every day.

In August of 2020 Instagram introduced a new feature called, "Reels." The feature was made as a response to the growing popularity of TikTok and a way to create similar content within the Instagram platform. Here are some quick highlights about reels:

- They're short-form video content in full 9:16 portrait mode.
- They can be from 3–15 seconds in length.
- They can be filmed directly within the Reels and/or uploaded from your camera roll.
- They can be filmed as one full take or a series of takes edited together.
- They can only be uploaded on mobile devices.

You'll recognize an Instagram Reels video by the icon in the lower-left corner of the video when scrolling through your feed, or in the upper-right corner when looking at someone's profile. If someone you follow uploaded a Reel, you'll see that video in your home feed as you scroll through. You can also see the Reels for an account by going to their profile. If they've uploaded a Reels video to their feed, it will appear on their profile like any other post. In addition, the Reels tab will display any reels they've uploaded but didn't share to their feed. You can also discover reels from other accounts on the Explore page. The top of the Explore page will show a big Reels video selected for you, and as you scroll through the Explore feed, you'll see more Reels videos interspersed as vertical videos and labeled as Reels.

There are a number of limitations when using Instagram Reels. If you're familiar with TikTok, you'll notice some of those features aren't available in Reels, and if you're accustomed to using Instagram Stories, you're going to feel like Reels are missing some key functionality. Here are some other limitations to be aware of:

- There's no progress bar when viewing a Reel so you don't know how long it is.
- You can pause a Reel when watching it but you can't rewind or fast-forward it. You have to let the video play and then it will loop back when finished.
- For a Reel you've created, you can't edit the caption after uploading it, you would need to delete the video and re-upload it to make changes.
- The caption for any Reel is there on the video but the preview shows only one line of text.
- Other than a view count, there aren't any Insights available for Reels.

Instagram Reels give you another avenue to interact and share content with your followers and fan base. Because we know that not all of your accounts will have the same followers (even though most people that follow you on one platform most likely follow you on multiple platforms) creating Reels or converting your TikTok videos into Instagram Reels is a way to reuse content to captivate a different audience. Be mindful it's not always best to recycle content on multiple platforms as it can become redundant to your followers, but also because it may not translate the way you intended. Not all content is meant for every platform. Just because the video worked on TikTok doesn't mean it will attract the same reaction from Instagram Reels. Creating new content geared towards each platform-specific audience is always the best way to go. Even though it may be easier to reuse the same content, your fan base will appreciate the effort. Being lackadaisical is the fastest way to lose your followers and fan base.

1.62 billion users visit Facebook daily, and a fan page on this platform is beneficial in keeping your fans up to date on your career. Coupling these two platforms together is essential in building your online presence. These platforms are a great way to create promotions for fans to win prizes and increase fan participation. You can also use countdown timers on Instagram for your next release to increase anticipation. While Instagram Stories are slightly more popular, Facebook Stories are where Facebook users spend a lot of time. Creating Facebook Stories requires a different marketing strategy than creating other types of Facebook posts.

In 2019, the most significant change in Facebook user demographics was among users born in 1945 or earlier, aka the "Silent" generation. This age group had grown on the platform from 26% in 2018 to nearly 40% in 2019. Interestingly, Millennials and Boomers only increased by a maximum of 2% and Generation Xers even reduced their Facebook use. In 2015, 71% of teens were active on Facebook. Now only 51% of American teenagers between 13 and 17 use Facebook. Facebook use is prominent among high-earners, surpassing LinkedIn, which reaches 49% of users making more than $75,000. YouTube is the only social media platform with more reach at 83% of high-income earners. Facebook's overall active users continue to increase every year across the platform. Among active US Facebook users, 74% of people use the site every day, and 88% of Facebook users are on the platform to stay in contact with friends and family.[lxxiii]

There are 500 million tweets sent each day, 6,000 tweets every second. Twitter is the platform where everyone talks about every topic in the world. The Twitter community has the ability to make 240 characters go viral in an instant. This same community has the ability to make a person go into complete obscurity overnight. There are 330 million monthly active users and 145 million daily users, 22% of which are Americans. This is the number one social media platform for news updates and information. Fewer people are watching the news, instead receiving all information through Twitter. Use this platform to engage in more personal conversations with your fans, giving them a glimpse at a different side of you as an artist. We have all seen the "Twitter rants" people go on. For good or bad, these rants show the ranters' personal side. Because of the inter-personality of this platform, Twitter is the perfect platform to communicate with people you wish to collaborate with, as users are more apt to answer when you tweet them or send a direct message on this platform than most others (expect maybe LinkedIn).

In November of 2020 Twitter introduced a new feature called, "Fleets." Because they disappear after a day, Fleets allow people to feel more comfortable sharing casual thoughts, opinions, and feelings. You can Fleet text, reactions to Tweets, photos or videos and customize your Fleets with various background and text options. To share a Tweet in a Fleet, tap the "Share" icon at the bottom of the Tweet and then tap, "Share in Fleet." Your followers can see your Fleets at the top of their home timeline. Anyone who can see your full profile can see your Fleets there too. Also, anyone who can send you a Direct Message can reply to your Fleets. If you want to reply to a Fleet, tap on it to send a Direct Message or emoji reaction to the author. Replying or reacting to a Fleet starts a conversation in your Direct Messages. Fleet authors can see who views their Fleets, including accounts with protected Tweets, by clicking into their Fleets and tapping on the 'Seen by' text at the bottom.[lxxiv] This new Fleet feature is similar to the stories feature on other social media platforms like Instagram, Facebook and LinkedIn. Allowing you to momentarily share thoughts that disappear is a great way to interact with your fans and user base on trending topics and current events. While the feature allows for the Fleet to disappear after 24 hours, remember once you put something on the internet it never really goes away, so be careful what you post because even though it has been removed from your timeline doesn't mean it has been removed from history.

Snapchat and TikTok are best used for short videos (usually comical) that show a different side of you as an artist. These platforms are generally used for personal videos that don't always pertain to you as an artist. If you look at some of the most famous people on these platforms, they are posting the same videos as the everyday Joe. Most of the videos consist of them in their house, with their families doing everyday things, or the next challenge or dance craze. Snapchat has fallen off the radar from most social media consumption (unless you're a Snapchat girl behind a paywall meaning that the content you are paying for is not safe for work and rated R), but TikTok has emerged as a thriving platform for the younger generation to create short videos that usually pertain to different challenges, dances, and what seem like "impossible" tasks. These platforms are a great way to use influencers to create a challenge or dance revolving around your song to gain more attention. Drake created the song, "Toosie Slide" for a TikTok dance. Let that sink in for a moment. The biggest artist in the world created a song strictly so it could be a worldwide dance craze on a social media platform. Not because he wanted the song as a single, not because it was his best work, but because it had a simple dance to it, and the lyrics literally told you how to do the dance. Cardi B used the same technique with her song, "WAP," featuring Megan Thee Stallion. While this song wasn't directly made for a TikTok dance craze, one has ensued. Besides being two of the top Hip-Hop artists in the world and being a catchy song, (at least as it pertains to females), the internet has created multiple dances for each part of this song, which has propelled the song to number one on most music charts across the world.

TikTok is a platform you as an artist not only need to be aware of but must take full advantage of. TikTok has helped push undiscovered artists to further growth, including Lil Nas X, Ambjaay, StaySolidRocky, Powfu, BENEE, Y2K, bbno$ and others. Meanwhile, artists like Curtis Roach, Curtis Waters, Breland, Tai Verdes, BMW Kenny and others have used TikTok to promote their music. Some, like ppcocaine and Avenue Beat, preview original music directly on the platform. Several emerging artists, like Shuba, Blu DeTiger and Kid Sistr, have even used TikTok as a platform for creative performances.

Recently, the social media video platform completed two deals with some of the music industry's most notable labels and distributers. TikTok created its first music distribution partnership with indie music distributor UnitedMasters. The deal will allow artists on TikTok to tap into the platform's ability to make their music go viral, then distribute their songs directly to other music streaming services like Spotify, Apple Music/iTunes, SoundCloud and YouTube. TikTok says its new agreement with UnitedMasters will also involve promoting their artists on its video platform. That means artists will have more opportunities to reach new fans who could then, in turn, use the artists' music in their videos. TikTok will also add the music from UnitedMasters' artists, with their permission, to its Commercial Music Library. This catalog gives verified businesses access to royalty-free music for use with their promotional content. "TikTok artists who are creating music in their bedrooms today will be featured in the Billboard charts tomorrow," said Ole Obermann, global head of Music at TikTok in a statement. "Our mission is to help those artists achieve their creative potential and success. This partnership with UnitedMasters gives us a turn-key solution to help artists who are born on TikTok to reach their fans on every music service." The deal allows indie artists to effectively circumvent traditional record labels by reaching young music fans on the social video app, then translate that to charting success.[lxxv]

They compiled a second deal with Sony Music Entertainment that will allow the short-form video app to continue to offer songs from Sony Music artists for use by creators on its platform. The agreement will also see the companies partnering on efforts to promote Sony artists. TikTok also noted it would work with Sony to support "greater levels of TikTok user personalization and creativity" and "drive new and forward-looking opportunities for fan engagement with SME's artists and music." TikTok had already struck short-term licensing deals with Universal, Sony, and Warner earlier this year reports indicated. This had allowed the labels more time to hammer out the particulars of their agreements with TikTok without having to yank their music from the platform in the interim.[lxxvi]

Last, LinkedIn, though underutilized, is your best friend. This platform is Facebook for businesspeople, and every single businessperson in every industry has a LinkedIn profile. You can connect with people you could never get a meeting with in person through this platform. Label heads, managers, A&Rs, TV/Film sync personnel, and agents all have LinkedIn profiles (along with every one of their assistants and interns). With a simple click of the connection button, you can send your music and speak with these people through messenger (just like Facebook) and create relationships otherwise unobtainable for an up-and-coming artist. A few reasons as an artist you should use this business platform:[lxxvii]

LINKEDIN HAS 675 MILLION MONTHLY USERS

That's a 14% increase since the end of 2018, when LinkedIn reported 590 million users.

57% OF LINKEDIN USERS ARE MEN, 43% ARE WOMEN

29% of American men are on LinkedIn, while only 24% of American women are.

27% OF AMERICANS USE LINKEDIN

That makes LinkedIn the 5th most popular social media platform for Americans (more popular than Snapchat, Twitter, or Whatsapp).

51% OF AMERICANS WITH A COLLEGE EDUCATION USE LINKEDIN

Among college-educated Americans, LinkedIn overtakes Instagram and Pinterest to be the #3 platform. Same for Americans who make over $75,000 per year.

70% OF LINKEDIN'S USERS ARE OUTSIDE OF THE US

While the US is LinkedIn's biggest market at 167 million users, it has gained traction around the world. This includes 211 million users in Europe, and 179 million in Asia Pacific.

61% OF LINKEDIN'S USERS ARE BETWEEN 25- AND 34-YEARS OLD

Nearly half (44%) of Americans aged 25-29 are on LinkedIn.

ENGAGEMENT HAS INCREASED 50% YEAR OVER YEAR

LinkedIn's algorithm has been updated to rank personal connections over "superstar echo chamber" effects, to make sure the feed stays relevant to users.

30% OF A COMPANY'S ENGAGEMENT OF LINKEDIN COMES FROM EMPLOYEES

Boosting brand reputation via employee advocacy is a winning strategy for companies that install a comprehensive program.

EMPLOYEES ARE 14X MORE LIKELY TO SHARE CONTENT FROM THEIR EMPLOYERS THAN OTHER TYPES OF CONTENT ON LINKEDIN

Statistically, a company's employees average 10x more reach across all social media platforms, compared to your company's official profiles.

Each platform has a different strategy associated with how to post and connect with followers. At the same time, each platform has a different marketing strategy in regard to paid advertisements as well. Paid ads on these platforms allow you to select a specific demographic with specific parameters to show your advertisement to. You can create your own graphic or video, choose your advertising demographic, strategy, budget, and length, and the platform will run your ad for you reaching your specified desired audience.

If you want to advertise on Facebook, it's a good idea to use Facebook Targeted Ads. This feature is run on a bidding system where advertisers bid on several ads based on their target audience, then that bid will be put into a lottery for a chance to be picked to run. Other than the lottery, Facebook Ads lets you show ads to your customers based on their behavior. This is helpful because you can keep advertising to your existing Facebook customers based on what Facebook tells you about their use of the app. Using Facebook Ads helps you build new leads and generate brand awareness, and the analytics Facebook gives you opens the door for experimentation, trying different ad formats and seeing what your audience engages with most.[lxxviii]

Twitter reports that 41% of users purchase a product after seeing an ad within a month, and when using their ad software, you can target a specific demographic. Twitter provides ad settings based on your budget, such as how frequently your ad will be seen, and the ad type to run. As a consumer, I barely know I'm looking at a sponsored tweet because they look similar to regular tweets. As a marketer, this means more eyes are on your ads because they're not as blatant as other social channels.[lxxix]

60% of people discover new products on Instagram, and 200 million accounts visit at least one Instagram Business profile each day. Business profiles on Instagram mean you can set up e-commerce and run ads from your Instagram account. Since Facebook owns Instagram, you can run ads on both platforms and they will be managed in one place (on Facebook), so campaigns can be run and analyzed concurrently. While the platform is ripe with exposure possibilities, Instagram Ads are against the changes of the app's algorithm. Instagram wants users to stay on the platform as long as possible and they do this by using algorithms to target each user with content they would be interested in and showing them content the user will be more likely to click on. Ads being against the algorithm means when Instagram changes their platform's algorithms some posts might not show up on user's feeds based on that user's search history. However, paid ads will continue to appear on all user feeds regards of the changes in the platform's algorithms. Using Instagram Ads, you can choose your budget, which is tied to the length of the ad run and your ad runs for as long as you pay for it.[lxxx]

On LinkedIn, millions of professionals have found a wealth of professional connections. The platform allows you to reach thousands of industry professionals. Fortunately, ads let you do the same. There are 630 million professionals on LinkedIn, with 63 million in decision-making positions. With the potential to reach 60 million decision-makers on the most popular social platform for lead generation, it's good to consider LinkedIn as an optimal platform for advertising. LinkedIn's targeted ads let you type in keywords and select audiences by category for a more focused advertising campaign.[lxxxi]

Marketing is an essential aspect in creating a successful music career. Without a proper marketing strategy, your music will be lost in the abyss that is social media. Using a combination of social media marketing, paid advertising, and guerrilla marketing will ensure you reach your target audience. Social media channels are making advertising functional for businesses of small size. It's about learning how to use them to benefit your brand and get the highest ROI.

Chapter 8   ASSEMBLING YOUR TEAM

Perhaps you should have your team in place before you completed any of the previous steps, and to a certain degree I can concede that point, but I am putting this step here because the former can be done by yourself, while the latter will be difficult to complete alone.

Your team will essentially be broken down into 3 categories:

1. The core team, who work 24/7 in a partnership deal on revenue sharing.
2. The service provides available for hire on flat fees or a percentage.
3. The creatives, who help bring the art to life, on fees per project or a percentage of royalties.

Before you break down your team into these three categories, there are a few traits to be aware of when picking your team members. First, bring on team members when the need arises. Early on, your team may consist of only friends and family. It's important to recognize that as you build a team, members come on board when there's a financial incentive to do so. This is for two reasons: one because as with any job the employee has to make a living; second, because people will see the potential you may have and they want to be part of the financial gain, even if they offer no benefit to your team.

Next, assign roles and responsibilities. Each member has different skills they bring to the table, and you'll get more done if you divide up tasks. Take a look at the jobs that need to get done. You may need to consistently be posting on social media and engaging with your fans. **You may need to construct weekly newsletters**. Maybe you need to be contacting venues and booking gigs (and promoting those gigs). Or perhaps you need to design t-shirts to sell at your gigs. Once you have a list, brainstorm who might be well-suited to take each task. Do any of you know photographers, artists, or website designers you could work with? Is one person more comfortable talking to people and pitching your music to venues? Do you know a social media guru who spends hours online? Once you delineate tasks, you're able to get things done faster and move on to new ideas and complete goals. Once the responsibilities are assigned and you have delineated a team member to each task, it's important to fill in the gaps.

While you will use the talents of many designers for various duties throughout your career, it's smart to use one person who can work in different graphic mediums. Websites, advertisements, stickers, merchandise and album art, all need graphic work. Outsourcing for each individual project can get expensive, so developing a relationship with a talented artist or learning to do it yourself is necessary.

You're going to need someone to handle the more complex web coding duties. These duties can mean developing marketing tools for contests or coding you a great website. A personalized website is a crucial aspect of your online presence. Your website creates a centralized place where your fan can access music, merchandise, tickets, and updates. Having a dedicated web designer and developer will ensure your website is constantly updated and maintained.

Getting your videos promoted can be a tremendous step in gaining more exposure. While promoting to traditional TV outlets is nearly impossible on your own, using online video promotion is by far the strongest method for promoting videos. If you're using YouTube updates, acoustic videos, music videos or vlog (video blogs) content, you're going to need help filming and editing them. A dedicated videographer will assist in developing and creating your videos, while also shooting behind-the-scenes videos for promotional purposes. Your photographer will be responsible for background photos for social media postings, and professional photo shoots for branding.

Once you have these promotional aspects in place, a social media manager is key to creating your online presence. Your social media manager will maintain all of your social media accounts, ensuring you're always on brand and creating engaging content to increase your follower base. In the midst of the thousands of things you as an artist will be doing, posting on social media isn't always at the forefront in your mind. A social media manager will ensure the correct pictures and videos get posted at the appropriate time. They will monitor your accounts, engage with your followers, and keep your fan base abreast of the latest updates from your career.

A merchandise manager is key in manufacturing and selling through your website, and when you begin performing live shows. Thankfully, this can now be an automated process, but if you choose you can have a team member do this job as well. Most websites will allow you to set up an e-commerce store where fans can purchase your merchandise. This website will track orders, optimize the shipping process, and in some cases manufacture the merchandise once ordered so you don't have to worry about storing excess or selling out.

If you are touring, you will need a crew that consists of many roles such as tour manager, merchandise, instrument tech, sound, lighting and countless other roles depending on the size of the tour. Each of these roles will ensure the shows run smoothly and without technical difficulties. These crew roles are responsible for setting up and breaking down the equipment before and after shows, scheduling travel, working out tour logistics and much more.

Beginning with the core partners, there will be five principal business partners who work on your behalf for a percentage of revenues. These four business partners invest time and money up front, rather than getting flat fees. The main five include:

1. The Manager
2. The Agent
3. The Publisher
4. The Record Label (and/or Distributor)
5. The Attorney

Your manager should be your right hand, negotiator, and music industry "parent" set to guide you through the musical career waters that are now your life. Managers know the ins and outs of the music business and should be the first building block in your team, mainly because they assist in building the rest of the team. They should have pre-existing relationships with agencies, publicists, publications, writers, lawyers, distributors, and should be able to understand your vision so they can build your brand on your behalf. Your manager will be by your side in everything from helping you build your aesthetic to pitching you for large brand partnerships. Though you will always make the final call, you should take their opinion and guidance seriously. It's your manager's job to maximize your potential. They're the team leader, they coordinate strategies and ensure the rest of the team is on the same page. Your manager is responsible for the daily behind the scenes management, which includes checking the accounting, coordinating schedules with and for the rest of the team, and keeping the infrastructure intact. You should be focused creatively/musically rather than business oriented, so leave that aspect to your manager. Outside of your production and creative team, your manager is going to be your most valuable asset.

A good booking agent is possibly the most difficult team member to find. Because of this, in the beginning of their careers many artists are their own booking agents. A booking agent's job is to pitch and negotiate live show deals on your behalf. They are pros at helping curate shows and festivals lineups and should have relationships with local promoters and venues allowing them to book your tours, take care of guarantees, and get you on tours with compatible acts. While this member of the team is usually scarce, taking this job seriously is do-or-die for you if your fanbase is built through live shows. Having an agent is particularly essential in the US, where personal managers are forbidden from procuring employment for their artists. It's left to the agent who is required to have a license. Outside the US managers do often work to secure bookings. Agents help with the logistics of routing a tour, advancing gigs, booking flights, and creating itineraries for the team. It may seem easy to do on your own, but having an expert negotiate the best deal(s) is more appealing than having to break your artistic "character" to ask a promoter what the venue capacity is, ticket cost, and your gig fee.

It's impossible for the layman to collect royalties every time your song is performed or synced which is why there are music publishers. A publisher's necessity is twofold: one to spread the word about your music, and two to collect royalties from wherever your music is heard on your behalf and pass them through performance rights organizations like ASCAP, BMI, and SESAC. Your publisher can do a lot for you to get placements, licensing deals, and make you money through these avenues. A publisher such as Kobalt even works to offer creative support and find places to sync your music in TV, movies and ads, while providing comprehensive reports of all music sales, downloads, and those sync placements.

In today's music climate, artist managers are not as versatile as they used to be. This is because in most cases labels will provide the artist with a publicist, distribution team, marketing budget, and radio/video promotion, and most deals will take care of the recording budget and network too. Some labels go above and beyond in these areas, while others take a more hands off approach. Each label has their own process. However, there are few universal standards in recording contracts, which can make it difficult to know if you're getting a fair deal or a boiler plate agreement. Most artists think of getting a record deal as the ultimate goal and the solution to all of their problems, but in today's music industry it's more of an ingredient than the whole cake. If you utilize the deal to its greatest potential, it will positively affect your career, but if you rest on your laurels and don't take full advantage of the opportunity, you will be yet another cautionary tale. We'll get more into this in later chapters.

Once you're in the position to sign contracts, you'll need a lawyer to take care of those contracts, and you're going to want to deal with a single lawyer for all of your matters. The lawyer will either receive a fee on all earnings you make through the lawyer's help or work on a flat hourly rate. It's safe to say no matter what stage your career is at, it pays to befriend a talented lawyer. An entertainment lawyer specializes in creating and reviewing contracts for you in all aspects of the music and entertainment industries and will help protect your intellectual property and ensure you've earned and collected all the revenues and royalties you deserve. Your lawyer can also shop your music for record deals and licensing if you begin working with them before signing to a label. If you notice anything suspicious regarding your relationships with others or the money you're making, having a lawyer around is the best way to settle your nerves or take action to right any wrongs.

If you don't have these principal partners, or have holes in these areas of your team, you have the ability to hire people for these roles and create an independent team resembling that of a major label. These roles include:

- Publicist
- Radio promoter
- Playlist curator or plugger
- Marketing/digital marketing specialist

How are fans going to hear your music if your name doesn't appear in their searches? This is where your publicist comes in. They are content strategists and brand builders. They take your story/music and pitch it to writers and publications that have an audience your message will resonate with. Publicists often work with photographers and videographers to create promotional content on your behalf, which is necessary for social media, press, and promotional items for upcoming shows or releases. Publicists know exactly when and how to create buzz about your music and career, which can be difficult when talking about yourself. Doing publicity is time-consuming and takes an intricate understanding of marketing and relationship building. Writing countless emails and searching publications that will talk about you is a never-ending job. Having someone that's good at building relationships is a key asset.

Radio isn't dead yet, and you can always find a new fan in someone who hears your song by chance. Having someone around who specifically works with music directors at local radio stations is a significant benefit to get your music heard by a wide audience. A radio plugger may work not only with local stations to get one of your tracks on a steady rotation, but also with podcast hosts, YouTube channel stars, and other key influencers who have a demographic following complimentary to your own. Many PR companies have in-house or third-party radio pluggers they like to use, but know that this role is important to have on your team to reach a greater audience altogether.

A digital marketing manager develops, implements, and manages marketing campaigns that promote you as the artist. They play a major role in enhancing brand awareness within the digital space and drive website traffic. Your digital marketing manager can be your social media manager, but sometimes the social media manager doesn't have an in-depth knowledge of SEO (search engine optimization), email marketing campaigns, and websites. In this case, the digital marketing manager will assist in these areas to increase your digital presence outside of the social media sphere.

Look into signing with a music distributor or aggregator. This final and essential team member (or company) can deliver your release to hundreds of digital stores and services around the world, helping to connect your music with tons of new fans. AWAL, for example, delivers music to over 198 countries around the world, and tracks all delivery dates and royalty income. Many streaming services only accept music submissions from a select number of distributors, so do your research and select a distributor that can distribute to your top choice platforms. If you need a refresher on how this works refer back to Chapter 6.

Besides creating your own faux record label, you also must develop your creative team. Your creative team often varies from session to session, project to project, show to show, or in some cases artists work with the same creative team for their entire careers. A major part of your creative team will be your A&R. In the beginning stages of your career, you can either be your own A&R, or your manager can act in this role. The purpose of an A&R is to coordinate all aspects of the music creation process for you. Your A&R will schedule studio sessions, coordinate sessions with other artists, producers and writers, keep track of budgets and schedules for song and album creation. This team member will be your lifeline in the backend of the creation process so you as the artist can strictly focus on the actual song creation. Knowing the background business as an artist is crucial to your success and you should be involved every step of the way, but with that said, a great A&R and manager are infinitely important so you can concentrate more on the creative aspect of your career and not constantly have to split focus.

On the recording side of the creative team, the A&R would usually coordinate:

- Producers
- Writers
- Engineers
- Musicians
- Mixers
- Masters
- Music Studios
- Graphic Designers

Today's record producers aid in the directing and creation of the musical sound, the song structure, and arranging the vocal/instrumental contributions. The producer also offers coaching assistance in regard to notes, pitch, and phrasing during the recording sessions. The executive producer enables the project by arranging its financing and business partnerships. Neither is to be confused with a beat-maker who only programs the beat, sends it to the artist and has nothing more to do with the creation process.

The audio engineer is the principal person during the recording process. They are the ones responsible for recording all the instruments and vocals. They ensure all audio is recorded clearly and proficiently at the direction of the producer. In some cases, the audio engineer will act as the producer when there is no formal producer present. As I spoke about in chapter 2, a professional audio engineer is crucial to creating a great song and achieving great sound quality.

Musicians are going to be the session instrument players. If your production needs actual instruments to be played and recorded in the studio, hire studio musicians during your session time to play these instruments. These session musicians will either be paid a flat fee for their performance or per hour. They are Work for Hire, meaning they will be paid once for their work in the studio that day and will not receive any percentage or points on the royalties of the song.

A mixing engineer is the person you hand all of your recordings to. They are going to take all aspects of your recording session, put them together and have them sounding radio ready. The mixing engineer could be your recording engineer, but in most cases, these will be two different people.

A mastering engineer is a person who does the final touch ups on your mix to prepare it for distribution, which can be by physical media (CD), vinyl record, or streaming.

A recording studio is a specialized facility for sound recording, mixing, and audio production of instrumental or vocal musical performances. This can be your small in-home project studio or a professional music studio large enough to record for a full orchestra of 100 or more musicians.

Graphic designers are going to be the driving force behind your digital brand. Working hand in hand with your social media and digital marketing managers, the graphic designer will create all of your graphics and logos, ensuring they are all on brand and in the style that fits you best as an artist.

The second part of your creative team will be your touring crew. In the future, you should hire a music director for your live shows, but as an up-and-coming talent on a budget, it's better to be your own live music director. This touring team may include:

- Musicians
- Sound Technician
- Lighting & Digital Effects
- Wardrobe & Beauty
- Back-up singers

- Back-up dancers
- Photographers
- Videographers

Live musicians will be your accompanying instrument players while on stage. Not every artist has or needs these, but they add a layer to your live show that is beneficial. For the audience, listening to live instruments creates a unique feeling rather than listening to a prerecorded backing track played by a DJ. These live musicians can include a drummer, bass player, guitar player, keyboard player, and any other necessary live instruments. Playing with live instruments allows you to create specialized versions of your songs that will only be played during a live performance.

Your live sound technician is an audio engineer who helps produce a live performance, balancing and adjusting sound sources using equalization and audio effects, mixing, reproduction, and reinforcement of sound. The live sound technician is responsible for the sound quality you hear in the stage monitors, your earpiece, and the speakers playing to the audience.

Lighting and effects are a crucial part to your live performance. Any time you see a live show by an established artist they have cues where lighting and other special effects are used to create an ambiance to their show, creating a memorable experience for the audience. These effects are run by a team of people responsible for setting up and implementing these effects at specific moments throughout the show.

Your stylist is the person who picks out your outfits for public appearances and live shows. They will keep you in image and on brand every time you go out of the house. If you are a female artist, this person can also be responsible for your make-up and hair or these can be two-three different people. Either way, they do the thinking for you, so you always look good to the audience.

Back-up singers and dancers are another layer and aspect that can be, but don't need to be, added for your live show. Most rappers don't use either during their live shows. Most singers use both. Deciding to use back-up people during your performance comes down to a few simple questions:

- Do you have choreography?
- Do you have background and/or harmony vocals in your songs?
- Do they add anything to your show?

If the answer to any of these questions is yes, it may be beneficial to implement back-up singers and/or dancers to your live performance.

Last but not least are your photographer and videographer. As I spoke about earlier in this chapter, these two team members are going to be shooting content for promotional purposes. Pictures and videos of your live shows are important to post and promote on social media for the fans that couldn't make it to a specific show, and to get the fans excited for your upcoming shows. If you're using a single person for both roles make sure they have crisp, clear and quality work when it comes to both video and photos

If you have a complete team in place willing to work as hard as you, together you will reach great heights. But if only one link in the chain is out of place, the entire operation will break. There is a reason most artists have their team in place when they are on the rise because they have a close relationship with these people and know they won't go behind their back (Dame Dash to Jay-Z). The cohesive team with the same mindset will always win. One rotten apple will always spoil the bunch.

Chapter 9   REHEARSALS

The next step is preparing for live shows and performances. However, before you consider doing a live performance, it's crucial to rehearse your live performance. I can't express enough how critical it is to be prepared to go on stage in front of an audience. Just because you can record in a studio and perform in front of a camera (keeping in mind these are edited for the best takes) doesn't mean it will translate to a live show. A good live show that showcases your energy and gets the crowd involved can be that deciding factor in winning over an A&R even if they have never heard your music before. If you can captivate a crowd at a show, you have just created a fan base that will now stream your music purely because they loved your live show. The opposite holds true, if your live show is boring, you lack energy, you're missing cues, and not performing all of your lyrics, the crowd will become uninterested and most likely forget your name before you leave the stage.

What are some ways you can rehearse? You may think this is a simple question to answer, but I have seen a laundry list of artists who not only rehearse wrong, but don't know where to start with rehearsing. Rehearsal is different for an artist performing a one man show (maybe including the hype man and/or a DJ) than it would be for a full band. For a one man show, you will most likely have a DJ accompany you, playing your songs with cues when to play the next record and distinct drops to keep the audience engaged. Most artists also have a hype man to keep the energy up during the performance. It's also possible that for your first few appearances you're performing alone. In this case it is best to practice stage presence so you're not standing in one place, but rather working the entire stage, and engaging with the entire crowd.

First, let's begin with the DJ. You as the artist are dictating when you want the next song to play, when you want (if at all) there to be drops in the records, if you want the DJ to be part of the performance (acting as your hype man) or just in the background playing the records. These are all different roles the DJ must understand, as a missed cue or fumble in record change can hinder the entire performance. Rehearsing with your DJ to make these transitions flawless is tantamount in creating a brilliant performance. Even if you as the artist are on point during your performance, if your DJ is not on the same page as you, how well you performed won't matter. The audience won't see the DJ as the problem, they will only see a bad performance and attribute that to you as the artist.

Adding in the hype man creates another layer of synergy to your performance. The job of the hype man is to keep the energy up throughout the performance and emphasize what you're doing and saying as an artist. You and your hype man should perform in tandem, having a routine in place for every song you perform that night. They should know every word, line and ad-lib to every song, and be prepared to emphasize what you're saying when you would like them to. The hype man is essentially a live stack track, but also serves the purpose of keeping the crowd engaged throughout the performance. A great hype man can take over a performance for an artist who may struggle on any night. Flavor Flav for Public Enemy and Spliff Star for Busta Rhymes are recognized as some of the best hype men in hip-hop for how they could accompany their leading acts.

For live bands the rehearsal is exponentially more important, because now there are anywhere between three to sometimes ten or more people playing instruments and each person has different cues for each song. The drummer is keeping the beat and usually the one giving cues to the rest of the band. The bass player is keeping the grove. The piano and guitar players are coming in and out at different points and sometimes playing multiple instruments depending on the song (sometimes also acting as background singers). If one person in the band does so much as play a single wrong note, is a beat ahead or behind, loses their place in the song or plays the wrong song at the wrong time, it will hinder the entire performance. It's important that the band knows what the set list is for each performance, as depending on the show, the setting, and the city, the songs in the set can change nightly. The lead singer usually creates the set list prior to the show, but I have seen singers take until the last minute (literally five minutes before the show starts) to hand out the set list. This is stressful for the band because if they don't know what songs and in what order they will play that night this could greatly affect the performance. As a band, you should be rehearsing weeks and sometimes months leading up to the show (especially if you are doing multiple shows during your tour). Performing each song should be second nature for you and the band. As cliche as it is, practice makes perfect. Even the greatest artists and performers in the world prioritize their show rehearsal. Beyonce and her band rehearsed for an entire year for two 90 minutes performances at a single festival.

A few ideas to keep in mind while rehearsing:

PRACTICE MAKES PERFECT

Practice your set until it becomes second nature. Sounding natural is crucial when performing live. The audience can tell if you're unsure about certain aspects of your performance. You need to know your set like the back of your hand because you're trying to create a performance that truly is astonishing.

PRACTICE TRANSITIONS

Artists that are new to live performance don't take into account the transitional on-stage time. There will be "down time" in between song for instrument changes and the band preparing for the next song. If you're working with a live band or playing instruments yourself, this will inevitably be part of your show and you have to prepare for this. By rehearsing these transitional periods, it will ensure them to go smoothly on stage and not take the audience out of the show experience.

TAPE YOUR REHEARSALS

The tape doesn't lie. Watching yourself on tape can be terrifying for some artists. But if you can get over the awkward feeling of watching and critiquing yourself, you will be on the path to creating a better live performance. These recordings will show you and your team what does and doesn't work in your live performance, allowing you to tighten up those little details. Everyone in the show needs to understand how they look and sound during the performance. Reviewing the tape is not meant to humiliate anyone. It's intended to help them get better by showing them what they can improve on to get the best performance possible. Here are a few of the things to work on after you have the songs down:

- Transitioning in your set from one song to another.
- Any audio effects or volume rides.
- Lighting cues for mood and maximum dramatic effect.
- Guitar or costume changes.
- Staging cues for performers and scenery/gear changes.
- Where you'll be speaking with the audience and the general gist of what to say.

With touring, you have to be on your A-game every time you hit the stage. One poor performance can be the ultimate detriment for future dates in that city. Every person in the crowd will have a phone and/or camera that will film your every move, while simultaneously posting on every social media channel. Ask any artist what happens after they had a bad show. Rehearsing tirelessly is a sure-fire way to make every performance the best it can possibly be.

Take the advice of Barry Stemley, aka Barry Bee:

"The experience of Recorded vs Live always reminds me of something Dizzy Gillespie once told me sitting next to him at the piano as I was trying to address the best way to approach the improv of a difficult song as well as how to organize melodies for composing. He said, 'You play sax, I play trumpet. We only play one note at a time. But if you look at all the great artists, they either play guitar or piano in addition to their horns. When you do that, you get to hear all the colors of the sounds you might want to play.' I've had this same experience with guitarist Dave Smith, one of the best recorded and live performers I've known who also plays sax and flute, as well as with pianist Kenny Kirkland. Recording is our repetition of how we put our sound out there. It's always laced with what we want to say and how we connect with our audience.

Once in conversation with Prince he said, 'I can't do what you do, and you can't do what I do. All I ask is that you respect the music. Push it as far to the left as you can and as far to the right as you can. You don't have to make it a hit song. Just address it with the seriousness of what it is trying to say.'

The recorded and live experience is the reason why we play. Music is human emotion put into sound, so it is important to address it with the seriousness of that conversation. Recording and live are equally important entities. One gets our audience, the other keeps our audience. Every bar should be written with the idea of reaching the audience coupled with the genuine nature of the things we want to say. A hit record is not the attempt to write so much as it is the attempt to communicate with the fans. Music is the universal language everywhere we go in the world, so it's important to find the common grounds of the sounds we want to put out there.

In the realm of recording or live I find it's very important to decide what is the emphasis you are trying to give to your audience. In composing, sounds can be stronger if you double the notes that you find are important to the lyrics or to the other parts of the music. They tend to emphasize a point you are trying to make in a song. However, you can bring out more emotion by splitting up the harmonies or subtlety using harmonic inversions, I think of them as small waves on a beach that move in and out of each other in harmony with the whole body. Also, doubling tracks can add to the effectiveness and strength of the sound. Think of it as the crash of a wave on the shore.

This is also true for live performance.

Another thing that I've found is that if you go through a number system backwards you will find that minor scales are also intervals derived out of major scales. Never be afraid of putting the ninths, thirteenths, or the seconds in the bass or chord structure to add a softer rounder melody. The best type of music for me has always been cerebral and emotional, giving me something to think about as well as something to feel.

One of the things people often ask is where do you start? Do you start composing from a melody or instrumental, or do you start with lyrics and write the music around the lyrics? The truth is that all three are good. Often the melody will give you the lyrics, or the lyrics will give you the mood of how you would like to compose the music around them. Regardless of which approach you use, the goal is to reach into the hearts and minds of your audience."......*Barry*

Having a great live performance starts with rehearsal. We have all been told, "Practice makes perfect," and this couldn't be truer for live performing. If you don't take your rehearsal seriously, your live show will reflect this. There is nothing worse as a fan than going to a live show and walking away upset you spent possibly hundreds of dollars to see your favorite artist bomb on stage. The same holds true for new acts. If you're unprepared and crash and burn as a show opener, it's extremely unlikely you will have many future opening performances. I can't tell you how many times I have seen artists lose possible deals based on their live performance. At the same time, I know artists that have been signed strictly off of their live show. There have been times an A&R has gone to live shows because of personal connections with managers or promoters only to sign an act they have never heard of based on their live performance. Don't lose out on opportunities because you think you can go on stage with no practice. Live shows are a different animal that chews you up and spits you out if you're not prepared.

Chapter 10   MERCHANDISE

A major part of transitioning from local up and coming to regionally and nationally known is your merchandise. Now that you are prepared for live shows, it's time to manufacture some merchandise to sell at these live shows, as this will enhance your brand two-fold. First, you will sell this merchandise, thus creating a revenue stream for your career, and second, to have your fans indirectly spread the word of who you are by wearing your logo. This coupled with the online marketing strategies I spoke about in earlier chapters will take you from being known by a hundred people, to being known by a hundred thousand people.

What is the best type of merchandise? Where can you get it? How much will it cost? What is the best way to sell the merchandise? How much should you sell it for? These are all questions you need to have answers to if you are thinking about creating your own merchandise. There is a vast amount of merchandise options you as an artist can sell, but it's all going to boil down to your brand, image, target audience, and budget.

Start with smaller, inexpensive items such as, stickers, buttons, posters, and guitar picks. These are great merchandise options for fans on smaller budgets. Due to their inexpensive cost, you can also use these items in free promotional giveaways or to bolster your merchandise bundles. I once went to a new franchise company location a few weeks after they opened. To promote their business, they were giving away free stickers to each party before they left as a thank you for coming in. While they could have probably sold these stickers for a few dollars (and I would have bought them because of the hospitality we were shown), they gave these small items away for free because it was an advertisement for their business and the customers that come in from seeing these small stickers provide a greater profit to the company then selling the stickers.

Pricing will depend on how you're using your small merchandise items and could range from free to $2 or $3. Smaller posters could be $10 or less, and higher quality larger posters can be as much as $20. A few places you can order these are: Sticker Guy, Vistaprint, and Zazzle.

Next is the larger merchandise options such as shirts, hats, pants, hoodies and other clothing articles. These are your bread and butter for merchandise and are something most fans expect to see at a merchandise table. The key factor in your clothing is the artwork. The simplest form is printing shirts with your project cover art on the front. If you're financially able to, hire a graphic designer to create personalized graphics. Good clothing with clever designs can bring in an untapped fan base because they like your merchandise. A poor design on a cheap shirt could deter people from listening to your music and taking you seriously as an artist.

You should think about your fan demographic when ordering shirts and clothes. If your fanbase is male-centric, female clothing items could be a waste of money. Your geographic location plays a major role too. If you are performing in the Southwest, long-sleeve tees and jackets probably aren't a popular clothing item. You're better off selling tank tops and hats. Don't feel as though you have to go crazy with designs. Too many choices can sometimes overwhelm fans who are quickly making purchases before and after the show. A few places you could order these are Merch.ly, Curly & Spike, Cravedog, My Custom Band Merch, and Bands on a Budget. However, if you live in a metropolitan area, there will be a variety of local stores that can do these jobs for you as well.

Rule number one in merchandise is know your fans (KYF) so you can create a product line to suit them. What is the gender ratio of your fan base? What is their age range? Are they casual or more sophisticated? It's important to understand that kids can't wear profanity, sexually explicit designs, alcohol, tobacco or firearm images to school, so they and their parents will be reluctant to buy items containing these. Men generally don't buy clothing with photos of other men on them. Ladies go for more trendy and fashionable designs. An older crowd is likely to buy larger sizes than a younger crowd and will shy away from edgier items like cropped shirts, distressed tops, and neon or loud colors. So where can you find this info? Here are a few ways:

- Use analytics from streaming and distribution services to see who is consuming your music.
- Pay attention at shows, and if you can't, ask someone on your team to take notes for you.
- Use analytics from social media to see who is engaging with your page.

How much should you pay for merchandise, and how much should you sell it for? At an independent level, $20 is the average price fans are willing to pay for a t-shirt. Larger clothing items (hoodies or sweatpants) average between $30-$40 because they cost more to produce. Most fans will want to buy more than one item at a time, but this can become pricey. In this case, it's a good idea to offer a discount bundle for multiple items, or to create merchandise packages that contain multiple items from your collection at a lower price than purchasing them individually. For a low-cost shirt, you shouldn't pay more than $5 to produce it and shouldn't sell it for more than $15. If you are working within a strict budget, the key is finding the best quality product for your money, while keeping in mind the price point that you think you can sell it for. As a general rule, make sure that the price you can sell an item for is at least twice what you're spending on it.

Not every fan has the same budget so you will want to have items at different price points so every fan has something accessible to buy. By diversifying your merchandise, you're lowering your risk of leaving money on the table. While they may not want to buy that $20 shirt, maybe they'll be okay spending $10 or $15 on another item. With the right product mix, you can offset lower cost items against higher cost items and maximize your profitability.

Now that you have your merchandise plan in place, it's time to begin your sales strategy and this should begin with promoting your merchandise from the stage. Let the crowd know you have a merchandise table, tell them where it is, and tell them you'll meet them there after the show. Offer Special deals at the merchandise table such as buy-one-get-one-half-off, bundles. Offer exclusives/limited edition items only available at the show. A 2013 Nielsen study showed that fans would spend $2.6 billion more a year if they had access to exclusives, and I can only guess that the dollar amount has grown since. If you're touring or have a web store, start a new season with items that will only be available for a couple of months or during the tour. If you want to get more personal, design merchandise items that indicate something specific about what you're doing. Run contests with a call to action and empower your fans to be your brand ambassadors. For example, if they post a picture with your merchandise using a specific hashtag, they could win a meet and greet at your next show. Ask fans to share their latest merchandise purchase on social media and in their network with a special code or link for others to buy it. If a purchase results because of that share, reward them with more merchandise, a special item, or a ticket to your next show.

Take advantage of "Fear Of Missing Out" (FOMO) and Second Hand Reach (reaching people who couldn't make it to the show but are likely to engage on social media during it). You can do this by promoting your merchandise on social media the day of the show to let fans know about the merchandise they might miss at the show and give them a way to buy it. You can also have someone post about your merchandise during the show to reach those who couldn't make it and direct them to where they can buy it, whether it be your web store, your social media pages, or via an app like Merch Cat Fan, which lets fans buy merchandise in app at shows or from home.

Get fans involved in your merchandise process by inviting feedback. Since your fans are the number one consumer of your merchandise, ask them what they'd like to see on your next merchandise run. You may think they'd want a beanie, but maybe only a few fans wear beanies, and the majority would rather a trucker hat. Inviting your fans to contribute to merchandise ideas will keep them engaged and increase your chances of selling the merchandise they suggest. There are some powerful benefits that come with your own brand of merchandise:

IT EXTENDS YOUR INFLUENCE

When you've got people wearing your clothes, they're basically a walking advertisement for your music.

IT BUILDS A CONNECTION

People buy merchandise at gigs because it's a shared experience they want to remember. By creating custom merchandise designed specifically for a tour, you're offering your fanbase the opportunity to deepen their relationship with you and each other.

IT DOESN'T REQUIRE MUCH INVESTMENT

This comes down to the quality and creativity of your merchandise. People won't wear it if it doesn't look good. You want your fans to wear your merchandise, not throw it in the back of their closet.

IT'S A GREAT ADDITIONAL REVENUE STREAM

Making and selling merchandise can seem like a big step for an up-and-coming artist. Realistically, you can't rely on this as your primary source of income.

SETTLE ON AN IMAGE

Use your merchandise to solidify your image. What type of gear do you want to be associated with? Pay attention to the styles and fashion tastes of your audience.

IT'S A PLATFORM FOR YOUR CREATIVITY

Merchandise is a great platform for you to experiment. The more effort and creativity that goes into your merchandise, the more money you can charge.

ANALYZE YOUR AUDIENCE

There's a major distinction between creating music people like to listen to and music people will share. Analyze your audience and determine if they are true fans and willing to purchase your merchandise.

WHAT ARE YOUR FANS MERCHANDISE PREFERENCES

Interact with your fanbase to see what their merchandise preferences are. It doesn't make sense to invest in clothing items if your fans would prefer posters.

PROMOTE

You have to do everything in your power to properly promote your merchandise collection. Digital marketing has made this easier. You can post pictures and links on social media platforms, include store links in your profile bios, or you can do old-fashioned street marketing and wear your merchandise in public.

As a new artist, the idea of designing and purchasing merchandise can seem like a daunting task. Not knowing what your fanbase will gravitate towards, not knowing what a good price point for purchase and sale is, and the relentless fear of purchasing bulk orders and not selling the inventory are all reasonable fears for you to have. There are a few Dos and Don'ts to follow in regard to artist merchandise:

DO'S

- **STAY TRUE TO YOUR IDENTITY, BUT GIVE YOUR FANS WHAT THEY WANT:** You want your merchandise line to be authentic to who you are as a musician. A lot of artists try to make merchandise with clever sayings, but that's only going to hit home with their biggest fans. You need to design for a wider fan base.

- **CREATE TOUR DATE SHIRTS:** Tour shirts are always popular. People like to show they were at their favorite artist or band's show, and they do this by purchasing shirts with the dates of that specific tour. Generally, the tour dates are printed on the back. However, if you want to switch it up, you can print the tour dates on one of the sleeves of the shirt instead.

- **CREATE A CONCISE COLLECTION:** In the beginning there is no need to have an extensive merchandise collection of 30 items. This can be overwhelming to the buyer and deter them from purchasing anything at all. Having a collection of around five items is a good starting point. You want to provide a cohesive collection while at the same time having enough of a diversity to entice your fans to purchase each item. If all of your merchandise has the same logo, there is no incentive for the fan to buy multiple items.

- **BE PRESENT AT YOUR MERCHANDISE TABLE:** This is unrealistic once you have reached the star or superstar status. However, for up-and-coming artists this is a great way to interact with your fans who came to the show. Showing your appreciation for them attending the show creates an interpersonal relationship that deepens their connection with you and your music.

DON'TS

- **FOLLOW TRENDS:** Younger artists try to make their merchandise look like everybody else's. When you're following the trend, how will your line stand out from the rest? And when the trend ends so do your merchandise sales.

- **GET AHEAD OF YOURSELF:** Everyone wants to offer their fans a ton of cool items but 'having a huge merchandise line never makes sense when you're starting out. A lot of new acts try to move too fast, looking at pop-up shops and what the major acts are doing. You can go into debt quickly if you get too creative too soon.

- **CLING TO IDEAS THAT AREN'T WORKING:** You should be open-minded beyond your perceived vision. The customer is brutally honest, and things that you think are going to sell might not. If you have a great idea, your fans will let you know.

- **BE SHY ABOUT WEARING AND PROMOTING YOUR MERCHANDISE:** Bigger artists always wear their merchandise onstage, even if it's just for one or two songs. Machine Gun Kelly always posts about his merchandise and he's happy to because the pieces look amazing. If you won't wear your merchandise, why would your fans?

Where do you get this merchandise? For starters, shirts are the easiest, as you can do a quick google search and find a cheap production center that will bulk sell you shirts with logos (or possibly you already know somebody). Or you can go to a department store (Walmart, Target, Kohl's) where you can buy blank shirts for cheap and send them to someone to print the logos (which could be cheaper because you don't have to buy the shirts from the manufacturer). The other merchandise will have to be bought and produced by a company, and these companies can be found all across the country (or internationally) for cheap depending on the product, how many items you purchase, and what type of logo you are looking for (warning, colored logos will cost more to print and produce than black and white). Most manufacturers will want a deposit or the entire payment up front before they start the work, and will give you varying turnaround times normally somewhere between a few days to a few weeks, not including shipping which can take a few weeks, and we all know the faster you want something the more it will cost to ship it. Earlier in the chapter I briefly mentioned a few companies you can get different merchandise items from. Here is a more in-depth explanation of a few companies with more being available in this chapter's section of the appendix:

- **MY CUSTOM BAND MERCH:** Makes t-shirts, hoodies, zip-ups, hats, stickers and all other artist merchandise items.[lxxxii]

- **BANDS ON A BUDGET:** BandsonaBudget.com is an online company that custom prints all types of merchandise, varying from shirts to stickers, banners to tour posters.[lxxxiii]

Once you have decided what designs to use for your merchandise and what types of merchandise you will start with, here are some places to sell your merchandise:

- **EBAY/AMAZON:** Creating your own store on Ebay and Amazon is a seriously easy way to sell your products. It's simple, easy, doesn't cost much and will give you complete control.[lxxxiv]

- **POP-UP STALLS:** Having a physical presence at a gig or festival is a great way to get your name out there. It also lets you communicate directly with your fanbase. Nothing says dedication more than hitting the stage than heading to the merchandise table after to sell products yourself.[lxxxv]

- **BANDCAMP:** The platform offers the opportunity to sell physical merchandise and digital music.[lxxxvi]

- **E-COMMERCE PLATFORMS:** There are plenty of sites out there which will help you create and manage an online e-commerce store. Companies like Music Glue allows your fanbase to buy music, merchandise, tickets and experiences with ease.[lxxxvii]

Merchandise when done correctly becomes free advertising. Anyone wearing, posting or promoting the merchandise item they bought from your store is a personal endorsement to everyone that sees it. A great design, an interesting logo, or tour dates will make people ask questions about what it is or where they can find it. Creating a great looking merchandise line opens your artistry up to an entirely untapped market your music may not have reached. I know people who wear artist merchandise strictly because they like the design, having never heard the music or even knowing who the artist is. Great merchandise becomes a live billboard you didn't have to pay for. Bad merchandise gets tossed in a drawer, never to be seen again.

Chapter 11   MUSIC PUBLISHING

Music publishing is the business of promotion and monetization of musical compositions. Music publishers ensure that songwriters receive royalties for their compositions and work to generate opportunities for those compositions to be performed and reproduced. Through an agreement called a Publishing Contract, a songwriter or composer "assigns" the composition copyright to the publishing company. In return, the company licenses and monitors where the composition is used, while collecting and distributing royalties to the composers. Music copyright is split into two distinct parts: the master recording and the underlying composition:

1. The composition is a musical work (harmony, melody, etc.) that may or may not include accompanying lyrics.
2. The sound recording (aka Master) is the underlying composition, produced and recorded by the recording artist(s).

In the most basic scenario, these two sets belong to the same person, if you've both written and recorded a song from scratch. However, that's not always the case. If you record a Beatles cover, you will only get the master recording copyright. The composition rights will still belong to whoever owns the Beatles catalog. The structure of music rights can get extremely complex. Imagine a song featuring twelve songwriters, two lyricists, a handful of samples, and a re-sung line. With all of these cooks in the kitchen, there are a lot of hands in the pot. Each of these different people that contributed to the song are going to want a percentage, and each person is going to feel as though what they contributed was the most important. This means each of these people, along with their managers and legal team, have to enter negotiations to determine the exact percentage each of them will receive.

Making (and monetizing) a successful composition requires a unique skill set compared to the one on the master. The way publishing royalties are calculated is a subject of copyright legislation, which means the mechanisms regulating the publishing business can vary from country to country. That means the industry has to rely on disconnected sets of local legislations, which creates thousands of marginal cases and grey areas. Under the US law, in order for a work to qualify for copyright protection it must be "original to the author," "independently created by the author," and possess "at least some minimal degree of creativity." Once the copyright is obtained, the author of the musical work is granted the exclusive right to:

1. Reproduce and distribute the musical work.
2. Perform or display the musical work publicly.
3. Create derivative works based on the musical work.

The copyright owner has the power to allow or prevent third parties from using the composition. If anyone wants to exercise those rights, they must get a license from the copyright owner and compensate them in royalties and/or an upfront payment.

There are four main types of publishing royalties: mechanical, performance, sync and print, to pair with the three subsets of composition copyright. The first type is mechanical royalties. These royalties compensate the songwriters for the reproduction of the composition, paid by third-parties that want to record, manufacture, and distribute the musical work. In today's streaming environment mechanicals are primarily generated whenever the user plays a song on a streaming service. The "play" part means that non-interactive streaming, like Pandora's ad-supported radio, doesn't generate mechanical royalties. There are a few ways in which mechanical royalties are paid out, depending on the medium. For interactive streams (Spotify, Apple Music) the mechanicals are paid out to publishers directly by DSPs. For on-demand downloads and physical sales, the mechanicals are paid out to the owner of the sound recording first, the labels who distribute the royalties due to the publisher. In both cases, the DSP/record label will pay fees to the mechanical rights organization (HFA in the US, MCPS in the UK), that distribute them to the composition owners and their publishers. In most of continental Europe, PROs claim both public performance and mechanical royalties. In the US, the mechanical royalty rates are set by CRB (Copyright Royalty Board, a panel of three federal judges appointed by the Library of Congress) depending on the medium used to host the composition. For digital downloads and physical mediums, mechanical royalties have a flat rate of 9.1 cents per copy (for songs that are less than 5 minutes long). For the longer tracks, a mechanical rate of 1.75 cents per minute applies.[lxxxviii]

The resulting figure is an All-In Royalty Pool of everything that streaming services need to pay the songwriters. Then, the streaming service will deduct the public performance royalties (set through negotiation with PROs) from the All-In Pool (both mechanical and public performance royalties). What's left is the mechanical royalties due, distributed between the songwriters on a per-rata basis, same as payouts to the master owners.

Second is the public performance royalties, compensating composition owners for the "perform or display of the musical work in public." Every time a composition is publicly performed (radio broadcast, a background playlist at a restaurant, or a digital stream) the rights owners get paid through their PROs (ASCAP, BMI, and SESAC in the US, PRS in the UK). Public performance can be separated into two parts: royalties paid by streaming services, and royalties paid by conventional public "broadcasters." In the first case, the DSPs will pay out a share of their revenue to the PROs, split between all right owners on the platform. As mentioned above, that share is a subject of negotiation between streaming services and PROs. Based on the quotes available, this should fall somewhere between 6-7% of the service's total revenue, deducted from the All-In Royalty Pool.

Then there are all the public performance users: venues, clubs, restaurants, TV channels, radio stations and so on. To get a right to publicly perform music, broadcasters gain a blanket license from PROs. This blanket license allows broadcasters to play any song, with the overall cost depending on the platform's potential audience. Users regularly report their playlists to the PROs through cue sheets, broadcast logs, etc. If you hear music playing in a public space, there's a blanket license behind it. The PROs then use that data to calculate royalties due to rights owners, factoring in a wide range of variables, unique to the public performance medium. Every calculation system aims to link the royalties due to the performance. A song played in prime time on national TV will earn much more than a song played in the middle of the night on a non-commercial college radio station.

Third is sync royalties. Sync royalties are generated from your copyrighted music, when it is "synced" with visual media (television shows, commercials, movies, video games). Music publishers usually have the sync license to a song, which means they have the sole right to use the copyrighted music in visual media. As such, music publishers usually sell this sync license to people who want to use the song and sync it with visual media.

The fourth and last type of music royalty is the print music royalty. Print music royalties are less common because they are generated when copyrighted music is transcribed to a print piece, such as sheet music, and then distributed through a music publisher; or print music royalties are generated when sheet music that is copyrighted is sold on-line.

There are two main conceptual differences between sync licensing and mechanicals/public performance royalties. First, sync agreements target a specific piece of music. Unlike performance royalties, syncs are always directly negotiated by music users and copyright owners (or their representatives). It costs the same to play Drake as it would an unknown artist on the radio. However, if you want to sync those songs to an ad, Drake will cost you about a million times more. Second, syncs have to be negotiated with both composition and sound recording owners, so licensors have to go through representatives from both the songwriters and the recording artists. Synchronization cash flow is shared between the recording and publishing sides of the music business.

Then, there are international royalties which are generated from plays outside of your domestic market. On paper, CMOs across the globe work together and exchange royalties, but in reality (because of the same publishing chaos), this isn't always the case. That means songwriters have to register with all the CMOs across the globe to get 100% of their royalties. Songwriters need a dedicated publishing administration representative who will register, audit, claim, and dispute other's claims on their behalf to get anywhere close to 100% of the royalties due.

Because of the intricacies of international royalty collection, the publisher needs to cover all the markets across the globe to claim effectively. Often, smaller publishers will delegate their catalog to international companies for worldwide representation (known as sub-publishing). Usually, these independent publishing company will claim and audit royalties in their domestic market, while outsourcing international collection to major publishing companies, like Sony ATV, Warner Chappell, BMG, UMG, Peermusic, Downtown Music Publishing (Songtrust) or Kobalt in exchange for a small share of the royalties.

The degree of the publisher's involvement in the artist's career depends on the artist. For some acts, publishing is just a side revenue stream. Think of an artist that both writes and records their own music, most of their revenue will be made on records, merchandise, ticket sales, and everything in between. For these artists the publishing royalties are an additional revenue source, but it won't be their priority. A lot of the artists have two musical lives, recording their own music and writing music for other recording artists (or TV shows, movies, and video games). Take Ed Sheeran, for example, everyone knows him for his songs "Shape of You" and "Perfect." However, some don't know that he writes songs for the biggest names in the business, including Justin Bieber and Major Lazor. There are songwriters who focus entirely on writing for other artists and publishing. These are the writers and composers at the back of the music industry and, while they are less visible, they have a tremendous impact on the music industry. For instance, Max Martin, he's written and produced, from Katy Perry "I Kissed a Girl" to Backstreet Boys' "Everybody." Top songwriters can generate millions in royalties every month, but how do you go from writing for yourself to writing for the Drakes of the world? Here's where publishing A&R comes in, and for songwriters and producers who focus on writing for other artists, publishers become an instrumental partner.

The role of an A&R is to find and sign music talent and develop the artist's career. However, there's one crucial distinction between a publishing A&R and a label A&R. The goal of the publishing A&R is to maximize the long-term revenue generated by talents. When Ed

Sheeran wrote, "Love Yourself" for Justin Bieber, his label didn't make a single penny. However, his publisher made millions in royalties and sync fees. While the label A&R is focused on the monetary success of the sound recording featuring the artist, publishing and recording A&Rs have similar roles, but their priorities (and their day-to-day work) are very different.

Picture this. There are two A&Rs: one is working with a beat-maker/producer, the other with an artist. These two artists create a song together and now they have to split the royalties. Here's how the splits could be structured:

Beat-maker/producer's share

- The musical part of the composition, 50% of the publishing copyright.
- The producer's share of sound recording, usually about 2-3% of the master rights.

Artist's share

- The lyrics, making up another 50% of the publishing copyright.
- The lion's share of the master (split between the artist and their label).

For these two, the scales are tipped in different directions. The beat-maker/producer will make money mainly on publishing royalties, while the artist will rely on recording revenues. Because of this, the goal of the performing artist and by extension their A&R is to make the most successful sound recording possible. While the role of the beat-maker/producer's A&R is to make the most successful composition, which means getting the most popular artist on the beat. The bigger the performing artist, the better, and if you get Drake consider your work done. It's now the label's job to promote the song. That makes the publishing A&R perhaps the most connection-dependent job across the music industry. Songwriters have to collaborate, and the only way to grow the songwriter's career is to build their name across the music industry and write for the most prominent recording artists.

Another key function of the music publisher is to defend the interest of the songwriters and maximize their share of the rights. For instance, when multiple songwriters are working on the same song whether it's a couple of "guest songwriters" or a four-piece band each person owns a percentage of the song. So, who owns which portion of the copyright of the songs? The commonly accepted practice is for all songwriters to split the copyright in equal parts, regardless of their respective contributions. However, this is generally not the case, and publishers will enter negotiations on behalf of their songwriters to establish the final splits.

This process can get very complicated, because songwriters are sometimes contracted to work on a specific part of the song, like chorus melody or verse, and a producer might be dedicated to just programming the drums. But what happens if they also come up with a line that makes it to the song's hook? Who owns what? Publishing representatives will often have to enter fierce negotiation over those percentages, especially if the song is an unexpected success.

Something to be mindful of as a new artist in regard to writing and production, a general split for music collaborations is 50% to the producer and 50% to the writer. If there is more than one producer or writer, they each will break down the respective 50% equally or based on how much each person contributed to the song. Meaning that if one person wrote the hook and one person wrote the verse, the writer on the hook could get more because of the importance of the hook compared to the verses. However, when working with more established artists, they are going to take a bigger portion of the percentage because based on the fact they are on the song the song is going to be more popular. While you may not think this is fair, there is very little you can do other than being taken off the song completely or not receiving credit. As harsh as it may sound, it's better to take 1% of a pie than 100% of a raisin. There are a litany of examples of up-and-coming artists getting no credit or recognition for their contribution to certain songs because the major artists on the songs took everything, and unless you had signed paperwork you have no recourse. There is another concept called "ghost writing" which means you contribute to the writing or production of the song but are not credited. In this case, you will either act as a "work for hire" or be grateful for the opportunity to work with established artists.

We live in an age where music is continuously repurposed and re-recorded. Sampling is a widespread technique nowadays, spreading far beyond electronic and hip-hop music. From the copyright standpoint, if the composition features a sample, the author of the original song becomes a songwriter for the new composition. It doesn't have to be an actual sample of the recording. Just adopting a famous line from another song will fall into this category.

The "let's split everything equally" rule doesn't apply here. Instead, sample users will negotiate the license with the publisher of the original catalog defining the share of copyright. Sometimes, the author will allow use of the sample pro-bono. However, if you're sampling Notorious BIG, you will relinquish a majority of the copyright. Depending on the samples use in the new composition, the publisher can claim anywhere from 5-100% of the copyright. These sampling negotiations can get messy, but if you want to monetize the music that uses a sample, you must go through the corresponding publisher or risk losing 100% of your copyright plus monetary ramifications.

Two of the most recent and prevalent examples are, "Blurred Lines," by Robin Thicke,

Pharrell and T.I. and "Lucid Dreams," by Juice WRLD. With "Blurred Lines," a judge entered a nearly $5 million judgment against Robin Thicke and Pharrell Williams in favor of Marvin Gaye's family in the lawsuit involving copyright infringement surrounding Thicke and Williams' song "Blurred Lines" and Gaye's 1977 hit "Got to Give It Up." In 2016, Williams and Thicke appealed a verdict that awarded $5.3 million in damages (the initial March 2015 jury verdict resulted in a $7.3 million award, but the judge agreed to cut that to $5.3 million), seeking to overturn the ruling, but a federal appeals court upheld the verdict in March 2018. According to California federal judge John A. Kronstadt's judgment, Thicke, Williams and Williams' More Water From Nazareth Publishing Inc. are jointly required to pay Gaye's family. They jointly owe damages of $2,848,846.50. Meanwhile, Thicke has been ordered to pay an additional $1,768,191.88 and Williams and his publishing company will pay another $357,630.97 to the Gaye family. All because the bass line used in the "Blurred Lines" beat was close enough to the one used in "Got to Give it Up" that it was considered copyright infringement.[lxxxix]

As for Juice WRLD, he was served with a copyright infringement lawsuit over his breakout hit "Lucid Dreams" by the now-disbanded punk rock band, Yellowcard. Band members Ryan Key, Peter Mosley, Longineu Parson and Sean Wellman-Mackin filed a complaint in California, claiming that Juice WRLD stole "melodic elements" from their 2006 song "Holly Wood Died." The band was suing Juice WRLD for $15 million in damages and wanted shared ownership of the song, along with damages collected from Juice WRLD's tours. The band's suit claims that "The Infringing Work and Infringing Sound Recording peaked at No. 2 on US Billboard Hot 100. The song was on the chart for 46 weeks. The Infringing Work and Infringing Sound Recording peaked at No. 1 on Billboard Hot R&B/Hip-Hop Songs. The song was on the chart for 34 weeks. The Infringing Work and Infringing Sound Recording peaked at No. 1 on Billboard Rhythmic Songs. The song was on the chart for 28 weeks." However, Yellowcard dropped the lawsuit upon the untimely passing of Juice WRLD.[xc]

In music publishing the contracts and agreements can be difficult to understand, and terrifying if you don't fully know where your money is coming from or who it's going to. It's a must that you have someone that understands entertainment contracts review your publishing deals before you sign on the dotted line. This is one area artists get taken advantage of the most and why you hear new artists complain on social media that their "label is robbing them." This is because they didn't fully understand the language and terms of the contract they were signing and were only looking at the payout numbers up front. Think of when you hear Russ speak about owning his catalog so he can make money from home because most of his music royalties aren't going to different representatives and companies. Russ is one of the few artists that owns all of his masters and his whole musical catalog, so every cent he makes goes directly to him. Most of the artists who sign to major labels aren't so lucky. They now have to split their earnings between the labels, the publishers, and the managers before getting anything their music financially generated.

There are a variety of different music publishing contracts that a label can offer to you as an artist, writer, or producer. Some of the more common ones include the single song agreement, exclusive songwriter agreement (ESWA), co-publishing agreement (co-pub), administration agreement (admin), collective agreement, sub-publishing agreement, and purchase agreement. All of these are contracts and agreements between the artist and the publishing company that cover a variety of publishing rights associated with song creation and ownership. Each agreement provides the artist and publisher with different rights and ownership percentages for the songs. For a complete explanation of each of these agreements and how they are structured, please refer to the Chapter 11 section of the appendix in the back of this book.

Music publishing is a godsend, especially for new artists, as it provides a lane to get your music placed and heard through different mediums that can garner huge results both financially and career wise. Be mindful of the contract you're signing, as the wrong deal could drastically set you back in your career. Placements and syncs in most cases will garner a bigger financial gain than record sales and streams. Think of Pusha T owning 40% of the Arby's theme song that gets played on every commercial or being the musical mind behind the McDonald's commercial theme song (granted for the McDonald theme song, he got paid a onetime payment, but think of the continuous royalty payments if he owned a percentage). Where your music will eventually either drop in sales and streams, or sometimes completely stop altogether, a placement like this is a perpetual revenue stream that never goes away.

See Appendix for additional information on music publishing.

Chapter 12   SUBMITTING YOUR MUSIC TO LABELS AND A&RS

Sending music to A&Rs and label representatives can be intimidating, because you never know what to expect. There are a litany of questions that are undoubtedly going through your mind as you prepare to send your music to different labels with the hopes of something great happening. How do you introduce yourself? Are you sending it to the right person? What do you put in your initial message? How will they react? Will they react at all? What is the correct way to send your song submissions? How many songs should you send? And you should know that sending out a bunch of unsolicited emails will not net you an answer or even be opened. There are a few different ways to submit your music to labels, A&Rs, and managers, to get on their radar.

Music blogs are still the leading places for rising artists to become discovered. Blogs like Dancing Astronaut, YourEDM, Nest HQ, EARMILK, and Run The Trap can provide artists with greater notoriety among industry professionals and listeners, as these blogs average around 1 million unique viewers per month. But how do you get in contact with these blogs and their writers? The best way is to go for personal interaction as this can greatly increase the chances of your music begin heard and featured. First, it's important to identify which writer covers your music genre and where similar music to yours gets covered, which you can do by googling reference artists.

Say your track is sonically comparable to Lil Uzi Vert, by searching "Lil Uzi review," a list of blogs that have covered his music through the years will appear. Once you have identified the bloggers, on most sites the author of an article is listed either at the top or bottom of each article, with a link associated with the writer's biography which has links to their social media accounts and a personal email.

Another avenue is Hype Machine. Hype Machine is a website that ranks tracks by up-and-coming artists based on the number of blogs that feature your track, the number of likes your track has, and the number of followers on the blog. Labels, A&Rs, and industry personnel use these metrics to keep abreast of the newest music trends and to find the next big star. Hype Machine is considered the "cream of the crop" when it comes to music blogs, because each track that is featured on this site comes with a list of other blogs where the track is mentioned. What makes this site even more credible is each of the blogs mentioned with the track are handpicked by the Hype Machine staff, and they don't show any blogs that have commercial interests. All the blogs on this site are legitimate, meaning you only have to worry about figuring out which blogs would be the best to reach out to.

Most playlist curators and blogs that curate their own playlist on streaming platforms have submission forms in their profiles or on their sites where artists can submit music. Tracking down the individual curators can be difficult but most likely increase the chances of your track being heard. Starting a conversation with these curators can be tricky. First, you need to identify which playlists are popular and include artists similar to your style. For example, if you're in the electronic music space, you may have come across Spotify's dance music curator, Austin Kramer (SiriusXM's BPM, Electric Area, Tiesto's Club life). He created a meritocracy to how tracks move to the top of the playlists called "mint." (multi-directional incubation tool). How it works is your track will be placed on one of the smaller playlists at first. Then if you follow your first release with other quality releases that resonate with the playlist's audience, your track will begin to appear on the larger playlists with larger followings.

Playlist curators are looking to keep their playlists up to date with the most popular songs. Getting your music on a curated playlist is a sign that your music is being heard. In most cases (unless you have paid for specific playlist placement), they will place your songs on the playlists based on the initial popularity of the song. This means when your song is first placed on the playlist (no matter the size or popularity of the playlist) you will be towards the bottom. As your song receives more plays in the playlist, your song will rise in the rankings. As your song rises on the playlist, it will be picked up by more popular playlists.

YouTube Channels are still extremely effective for rising artists and producers, as you can reach millions of potential fans. YouTube personalities hold the same power as Spotify's curator or labels when it comes to breaking an artist. Here are some of the follower bases for the more popular YouTube music channels:

- NCS (13M subscribers)
- Trap City (8.6M subscribers)
- Mr. Suicide Sheep (7.6M subscribers)
- UKF Dubstep (6.1M subscribers)
- Proximity (5.3M subscribers)
- The Sound You Need (4.2M subscribers)
- Majestic Casual (3.6M subscribers)
- CloudKid (1.6M subscribers)

Submitting your music to these channels is relatively simple. Most of their contact information is posted clearly on their pages on the about tab or under "Details," "For business inquiries." There's sometimes a hidden email address of the page's owner (just prove you're not a robot). This is the most underrated method to submit music, but it's one of the most effective.

If you're calling is composing music for movies, ads, radio, video games, and websites, then Music Libraries are where you need to go. Music Libraries are catalogs of music available for professionals in need of legally cleared music to license. When you hear background music being used, most likely the music director got the track from a music library. These tracks are not commercially released or distributed by labels or publishers, rather they are made specifically for the music library based on the criteria given by the artist. In order to sell your music through these libraries, you first need to have an extensive back catalogue of quality music, and then you need to apply through the library. You need to provide the library with a private folder of custom music, and it's a plus if you can show releases through a major label. Even as an artist who may not be a composer, you may want to consider this option since licensing tracks can generate large royalty payments, and music libraries are the best avenue for this. Here are a few of the most reputable music libraries:

- Pond5
- Musicbed
- Artlist
- PremiumBeat
- Music Vine
- Marmoset
- AudioJungle

There are three options if you wish to submit your tracks to these labels: find their general submission email, a submission form, or contact their A&R. A&Rs are the ones who sift through demo submissions and deal with artists directly. Fortunately, with the amount of information available at our fingertips on the web and social media, it's easy to discover who these people are. The most straightforward way to get started is looking on Google, and type "label name + A&R," or subscribe to the A&R Directory which garners you a complete list of every A&R at every music label (updated quarterly). You have to set yourself apart from the thousands of other artists also submitting tracks to these labels, and you can do this by interacting with their representatives constantly. When they post on social media, interact with their posts, leave thoughtful comments that show genuine interest in what they are doing. Sometimes they post, "casting calls," where they ask their follower base for new and interesting artist, they may be unaware of. In these cases, avoid sending them your own music. After you have garnered this relationship and they see you're not just spamming them with links (like so many artists do), they will be more open to speak with you and accept your music links.

Nowadays, most artists and label personnel host their own radio show/podcast. This is a platform for creatives to help creatives by supporting and showcasing other artist's music. Some podcasts have created segments where they ask for and play listener submitted songs. Possibly the most notable podcast to do this is "The Joe Budden Podcast," which ends each episode with the "Sleeper Segment," where each person on the podcast plays a song from an artist they like that the listeners may not have heard before. Artists have used this opportunity to expand their listener base, and possibly secure a song release with a label that is affiliated with the podcast. Try to meet other artists, producers, DJ's, publicists, booking agents, label staff, fans, and anyone else in the music industry, as these connections could lead to opportunities.

With the variety of ways of getting your music noticed by the public, it comes down to separating yourself from the crowd. Tens of thousands of songs are released daily, by both new and established artists, so having something that sounds like everything else may garner some attention, but it won't gain you the overall attention you are looking for.

What happens after you have a few placements on these blogs and playlists? What is the next step in getting your music heard by the labels and A&Rs? Signing with an established record label is the most streamlined way to reach a global audience. But how do you get a label to listen to and/or release your demo?

The first step is preparing your demos. Before you send a demo to a record label, ensure your music is sounding the best it can. Don't waste an A&R's time with poor quality tracks. Make sure your tracks are finished, mixed, and either mastered or ready for mastering. Ensure you're exporting your tracks in the correct format and tagging them properly. Most labels prefer links to stream demos over downloading them. Find out what file format a label prefers and use a service like Dropbox, Box.com, or SoundCloud. Labels often prefer MP3 files over other formats because of the smaller file size, and be sure to give your tracks clear file names and ID3 tags. For example, Artist Name, Track Title, and Contact Information. Think iTunes metadata. Last, don't send demos with copyrighted material unless it's cleared for use. Labels will reject tracks that could land them in legal trouble. Avoid sending remixes and mashups as labels want original work so as not to worry about copyright issues.

Many record labels specialize in a specific genre and style, so it's essential that you research a label before sending them your demo, making sure your music aligns with the music they release. Check out the other artists signed to the label you're researching. Does your style of music fit into a similar sound category? Research artists that produce the same style of music as you and find what labels they are on. Compile a list of the labels your music will connect with the most. Find names and contact information such as the A&R's email address and locate their demo policy. The more you know about the label, the better. The information you collect will help you personalize your message during the submission process and will help you reach the right people. It makes zero sense, sending a future house track to a techno label.

Once you have your list of labels, locate and carefully read their demo policies. Most labels have a demo policy displayed on their website. A demo policy outlines a set of guidelines they require for demo submissions. Demo policies often include:

- **UNSOLICITED DEMO SUBMISSIONS:** Most A&Rs and labels will not accept unsolicited demo submissions.

- **COPYRIGHTED MUSIC:** Send only your copyrighted music. Labels do not want to deal with copyright claims on any songs, especially those that they don't own.

- **ACCEPTABLE DEMO FORMATS:** For example, private SoundCloud or Dropbox links, MP3 or WAV attachments.

- **MASTERING AND MIX PREFERENCES:** Some labels ask for specifics like a mixed down track with -6db of headroom.

- **EMAIL FORMAT AND ARTIST DETAILS:** A label may request artist name, track names, and contact info. Other labels may prefer an EPK (Electronic Press Kit), a bio, music career achievements, photos, or other artist details.

- **CONTACT INSTRUCTIONS:** These could include email or submission form guidelines and other contact information.

- **FOLLOW UP EXPLANATIONS:** Some labels offer follow up instructions for your demo submission. The hard truth is that if they don't respond, it means they aren't interested.

- **ADDITIONAL INFORMATION:** Some labels explain how many demos they receive and the hardships of listening to everyone. They may also offer insight into how they handle demos.

The easier you make it for someone to access and listen to your music, the better. Record labels can receive hundreds of demo submissions a day, so personalizing your message is vital to stand out from the crowd. A few guidelines to adhere to when submitting your music to labels are:

DO'S

- Craft a subject line that will entice them to open the email.
- Mention what city or country you're from or currently living in.
- List some well-known artists you've collaborated with.
- List a few gigs you performed at.
- Mention other tracks or artists you like from the label.
- Ask for feedback.
- Give a brief explanation of your work.
- Keep your emails small. The more space they take up the more likely they will get deleted.
- Videos make your work seem polished and "finished."
- Great artist and track names matter.

DON'TS

- List artists you think you sound like.
- Give your music a specific genre.
- Link to demos with lots of plays.
- Oversell yourself, adding spammy details or being unrealistic.
- Add too many links.
- Include a long bio.
- Use inappropriate language.
- Send CDs, WAVs, or even MP3 downloads unless specifically asked for.
- Send CCs, BCCs, or mass emails to multiple labels at once.
- Presume you're a perfect fit for the label.
- Talk about your age.
- Send more than three tracks at once unless specifically asked for.

With an understanding of where to look for A&R, label and managers information, and a grasp on how to submit your music, what are they looking for in an artist submission?

PRESENTATION

When you submit your music to an A&R, label or publisher, they are going to check your digital presence. You need to ensure this all has a professional esthetic. The best way to do this is to cross link all of your pages together, this means that on each of your social media pages you have links to your other social media pages as well as your music.

GRAPHIC DESIGN

A unique personalized logo and individualized creative artwork is what sets you apart from the crowd. Work with a talented graphic designer to create the best logos and graphical representation of yourself as an artist as possible.

IMPECCABLE WEBSITE

You have to own your own domain. This means finding a dedicated hosting website such as GoDaddy or Wix and purchasing a personalized domain name from them. Nothing says, "I don't support my own career," like a website titled artistname.wix.xom/artistname.

MAKE THEM LISTEN AND BUILD THE RELATIONSHIP

When submitting your demos to labels, they will generally provide you with both their submission and follow-up policies. Patience is key here. It can sometimes take weeks or months to hear back on your initial submission. This doesn't necessarily mean they aren't interested. It could mean they just haven't had a chance to listen to the song yet. Following up with them is a good idea, but do it respectfully. Nothing will kill your chances faster than being impolite and pushy.

Once you get a point of contact with someone at the label, you need to nurture that relationship, as this will go a long way in expanding your contacts within the company. Networking is everything in the music industry. You want to stay on their radar. This can easily be done by interacting with them on their social media pages. Congratulate them on new accomplishments, comment on their press releases, and share their artists new releases. This all shows that you are staying up to date and are interested in the success of their company and not just spamming them for an opportunity. It's ok to send them updates on your music and career happenings but be sure to do this respectfully and sparingly. "Thoughtful consistency" is a concept you want to implement into your contacting strategy.

It's important to personalize each message. This shows effort on your part. The fastest way to receive a rejection is to mass send a blanket message that shows no personalization. It takes time to go through demos, especially for labels that receive hundreds a day. It could take several weeks before getting a reply. If the label provides a follow-up policy, it's best to stick to that. The hard truth is, you will get a reply if they find your demo is a good fit for the label. Otherwise, you should not expect a response. Don't despair if a label rejects your demo, perhaps the rejection has nothing to do with your track's quality, but rather it doesn't fit with the label's sound. Take it as a learning experience. Accepting rejection and learning what doesn't work will help you grow as an artist. Send a polite email thanking them for taking the time to check out your music, and don't scratch a label off your list if they reject your demo. In the future you can always resubmit your demo to labels that have rejected you.

Be ready to accept everything that comes your way. You will spend hours, days, weeks, and months sending your music around the internet to people before getting a single song picked up by one publication. Scouring the internet for the correct contact information for the right person at the correct label will take an extraordinary amount of time. I have spent entire days searching the internet for contact information, just to find out the email I submitted tracks to is no longer served. I have also spoken directly (through LinkedIn) to A&Rs and managers who told me where to submit tracks, only to never hear from the representative again, even after sending a follow-up message.

Discount Kevin McCall's lyrics for Chris Brown collaboration, "It only took a year and a half to get on." It could take years to gain the traction and recognition you desire. Continue pushing forward through all the rejection, continue working even if no-one is noticing at the moment, because it will come to a tipping point. Think of all Kanye West stories about him literally jumping on tables in meetings and studios rapping, being told to sit down, because he was seen as just a producer. Everyone in the industry has stories of being turned down and overlooked. If you keep working, eventually it will all work out.

Chapter 13   PREPARING FOR LABEL MEETINGS

After all the years of legwork, you have got the ear of a few managers and A&Rs that are now interested in learning more about you as an artist and have reached out to set up an initial meeting. What do you do to prepare for these meetings? What should you expect from these meetings? How should you conduct yourself in these meetings?

First, understand what type of meeting you are walking into. Is this a meet and greet to learn the basics of you as an artist? Are they just looking to get you in the door to hear more of your music to gage whether they would like to move forward? Have you reached a tipping point in your music and popularity, so the labels are interested in signing you? These are all important aspects to know before walking in the door, as each of these meetings will be different and with different personnel from the label.

I can't stress enough how essential these basics are. To increase your chance of getting signed, you need to understand what labels are looking for from their artists. First and foremost, a record label is a business. They have operating costs (distribution, marketing, design, etc.) and like any other business they need to generate revenue to cover those costs. This revenue is generated by selling music and merchandise, collecting mechanical royalties, and hosting events. The type of artists they work with can vary, but at the end of the day they have to make ends meet. The labels do this by working with artists that have fantastic music, a loyal fanbase, good marketing, and dedication. The higher you score on these points, the more intriguing you are to the label. A few things to keep in mind when preparing and walking into these meetings:

- Be who you are.
- Dress on brand.
- Respect everyone in the room.
- Be prepared.

Don't overthink these meetings, it's easy to psych yourself out. Remember the K.I.S.S. concept (keep it simple stupid).

Come prepared with a USB containing your EPK, high-res photos, and blog features. On the same USB or possibly a different one (because they sometimes like to keep the USB for future reference), have a few of your best songs prepared. In most cases they will have already heard some of your music, but it is always best to come prepared. You might also want to bring a wireless speaker to play your music from to provide a better listening experience when showcasing your music. If you have merchandise, take a couple of pieces, although this is not imperative.

Come to the meeting on brand, represent yourself as the artist you are. This is your first opportunity to introduce yourself, and you only have one chance at a first impression. Be respectful and polite, and graciously answer any questions they may have. Undoubtably, you have heard the stories of artists acting crazy in meetings and then being signed, but these are few and far between. Don't do crazy antics if they are not on brand with who you as an artist or the image you are trying to portray. If your image is not the crazy out of control artist then these actions will be to your detriment. Also much like a WWE wrestler, the crazy antics are just for show. If you were to meet those artists off stage or in private, you would see a completely different person.

If they ask you to sing or play an instrument, be confident, this is a pretty common request. Label meetings don't always happen in the office. In fact, I have had several label meetings that occurred in lobbies, studios, and people's houses. It's not uncommon for other people to be present during these meetings as they walk around the office or building, so don't become scared by this request. Rather, take it as a compliment because they are genuinely interested in hearing you perform live (this means they think you can sing). I have seen multiple occasions when a label head has come to the studio and an artist was singing live in the studio to the amazement of the label head, and this led to a label deal for the artist.

The days of being handed a contract immediately are over. However, if you're offered a contract on the day of the meeting, don't sign it then and there. No matter how big or small the label, always take it to a music lawyer to make sure the terms are agreeable.

The first meeting you will have is just an introduction to meet you and your team in person. These types of meetings may not include you as the artist, as they are generally set up by your manager who already has some relationship with someone at the label, which is most likely why you got this meeting. These meetings are short and consist only of a brief catch up between the parties that know each other, an overview of who you as the artist, what you're about, the music you make, and what you have going on. The managers have to be prepared for these meetings, just like you will have to be prepared for the upcoming meetings. The manager has to represent you the best way possible. Don't come in like a hotshot, thinking you're the greatest thing since sliced bread when you're starting out and this is your first meeting. Be realistic.

Don't get discouraged if you don't receive the reaction, you feel the music deserves. Not all music is for everyone, and sometimes the music you play doesn't resonate with the person sitting across the table. This doesn't mean the music isn't good. Sometimes this means the music isn't the right fit for the person you're meeting with or the label. A group like Griselda has outstanding music, but if they were to take a meeting with Ultra (a mostly dance music record label) the meeting might not go well. Not because the music isn't great. Because they are not the right fit for that label. The manager has to understand what position you as the artist are in, and not be overzealous with the expectations of this initial meeting.

Which leads to the second meeting, where you have reached a tipping point. If your social media following is in the hundreds of thousands or millions, major labels will look to meet with you because of the number of records you can sell. If you have an incredible local following (Pop Smoke or Fivio Foreign in Brooklyn), labels will look at you because your star power locally can generate "X" number of sales that can then be turned into a national campaign. However, for a second let's assume you have got this meeting based on the quality of your music. This meeting (first for the artist, second for the manager) will be to meet you, the artist, in person and learn about your story, hear more music (released or unreleased) and learn what you have upcoming.

Come to the meeting in image, be on time (meaning at least 10 but more like 30 minutes early). Never show up late as this could either cut your meeting short or cancel the meeting altogether. Have your best five songs ready and in a specific order you want to play the songs so you can easily go from one song to the next without wasting time. If the representatives in the meeting like what they hear, they will either set up a following meeting to cement their interest in you or they'll wait and see how the next few steps you outlined in the meeting pan out. Not all meetings will conclude with a deal on the table, but that doesn't mean the meeting didn't go well. Sometimes having the representative react in any way, shape, or form to your music can indicate a great meeting.

One meeting I was a part of, we played music from a few different artists. The label representative only said, "I like the sound of this song." Nothing further was was said on the part of the label representative. Once we left the office, my partners were ecstatic, because the representative saying he liked a song indicated a great meeting.

There is nothing worse than walking into this meeting having little to no idea what you want or being unrealistic in what you're looking for. Not naming names, but I was in a meeting with a label division head where he told a story about an artist's team walking into a meeting so high on drugs, they didn't know which label they were at. On top of this, the dollar amount they were asking for was substantially more than what they were worth. All of this made the label second guess whether they wanted to proceed further with this artist, and the label ended up not doing the deal. Don't overplay your hand, just because the label is trying to court you to sign with them doesn't mean they will break the bank on an unproven artist.

Don't get greedy. If the girl likes you, take her to the prom. Don't wait for the more popular girl to say yes because you could end up alone on prom night. It's better to negotiate your worth rather than try to get the most money possible. I'm not saying to undervalue yourself or saying that you shouldn't get as much money as possible (who doesn't want a million dollars), but sometimes starting with a smaller deal will be more beneficial in the long run. Think of it this way, if you sign a massive deal and don't live up to expectations, when it comes time for your second contract you will give the label every right to negotiate your price down based on performance. Conversely, if you start with a smaller first contract and over produce, you have all the leverage for your second contract negotiation.

Think of some of the biggest artists of all time such as U2 who, after their massive success with "The Joshua Tree" and "Achtung Baby," were able to sign with London label Polydor for $200 million in 1993. Lil Wayne resigned with Cash Money Records (bringing along his own imprint Young Money which included Drake and Nicki Minaj) after his incredible success with his mixtape series and album series "The Carter" for $150 million in 2012. Bruce Springsteen signed with Columbia in 2005 for $150 million. Adele signed the largest record deal for a British woman in 2016 for $130 million. Whitney Houston signed the biggest deal in the history of Arista records in 2001 for $100 million. The list goes on. If you have success your negotiating ability and leverage in those negotiations is astronomical.

However, you have to be realistic about your worth because not all negotiations are equal. One hit single doesn't give you all the leverage in the world. I worked with an artist in Atlanta named DLow who became famous for his single, "DLow Shuffle." This song was a massive success on the internet and the label awarded him hundreds of thousands of dollars to sign based on this song's success. Once this song's flame faded out, and he wasn't able to match that success, he was released from the label and was no longer able to garner what he perceived his worth to be in future negotiations.

This unfortunately is the story for more artists than the former above-mentioned giant contracts. Artists have their whole lives to create their first single and first album which usually garners them the most praise, fame, and monetary gain. Their second project doesn't alway live up to the hype of their debut, and this leads their star to fade and their worth to the label to decrease. All of which puts them behind the 8-ball in the second contract negotiations.

Remember, listen twice as much as you speak. You have two ears and one mouth. The advantage to this is that you can play off of what the A&R says, listen for their needs, business ideas, and plans. You want to illustrate why they should add you to their artist roster. Understand, if they really knew why they needed you there, they probably would have signed you already. It's up to you to convince them you're their artist. What do you offer them? Why should they take a risk on you? How can you make them money? Why would their current fans listen to your music? They have all the information you need to know. It's your job to listen for the clues. You may think you're unique and one of a kind, but the truth is record labels talk to dozens of "one of a kind" artists every week. It should be your goal to stand out from the crowd and be especially creative when you talk to them. What can you do to be unforgettable?

Many business owners looking for investors develop what is called an "elevator pitch." This is the 30-second summary of your product and goals that you could pitch to the company president who is in the elevator with you for a brief time. It works just as well for musicians as it does for other businesses. Can you summarize yourself and your sound in just under two minutes? You may have set up an A&R meeting, but that doesn't mean they're going to give you an hour of their time. Your elevator pitch is important, just like your live show. Practice this pitch until it becomes second nature.

Engage in the conversation, but separate the person you're talking to from the company building you're sitting in. If you choose to sign to a label, in reality you're not signing with the label, you're actually signing to work with the people in the label. It's important to understand the difference between a personal agenda and a company agenda. The agenda of the person you may be working with doesn't always coincide with the company's overall agenda. Every A&R is different and therefor they have different reasons for signing certain acts. An A&R who signs an act from a gut feeling or genuine liking of the music is working and negotiating from a different place than an A&R who signed an artist strictly based off numbers and a financial perspective. It will be to your benefit to speak with the A&R to see what their personal agenda is and why they want to work with you.

Don't get blinded by the A&R or labels pitch when trying to sign you. It is their job to create a personalized and glamorous pitch to capture your attention and make you want to sign with them. Getting promising artists to sign with them is just like any other job and has proven strategies to entice artists to want to sign and work with them. Don't get me wrong, this doesn't necessarily mean what they are pitching and presenting you is less sincere, it means that they are trying to put their best foot forward and show you why they are the right fit for you because they are thinking you are most likely in talks with other labels at the same time.

Your team can only be in cohesion and moving toward a common goal if everyone knows what that goal is. The music industry is constantly moving and changing so you have to be adaptive to all situations. Having an agreed upon plan with your team makes adapting that much easier. The better your relationship with your A&R, the more diligent and proactive your A&R will be in your career. Be cognizant of abilities and limitations. The music industry is extremely connected, everyone knows everyone, and A&Rs within the labels and from different labels talk to each other on a regular basis. They talk about artists they are keeping an eye on, artists they have met with, and they exchange war stories. When meeting with multiple A&Rs, it's important to be upfront about it because most likely the A&Rs you're meeting with know each other and know the details of your other meetings. Information moves quickly through the industry and being labeled as two-faced and not above board is one of the most detrimental reputations you can have.

After your meeting you should congratulate yourself on a job well done. If you were disappointed with a particular aspect, note that for the next opportunity, but don't dwell on the results of the meeting. You may get lucky, and the A&R liked you, but it's more than likely that you receive a polite rejection. Everyone fails, and successful people probably fail more than anyone. It's how you deal with failure that sets you apart from the rest of the crowd.

Conducting yourself in the right manner during these meetings can be the difference between getting signed and getting passed on. Know your worth, but don't overextend yourself. Be prepared to answer all questions with concise answers. Have your best music ready and in a format that can be played on all media platforms. Most importantly, always be on time (this means early). Big Pun got his deal without ever playing any music in his label meeting because he showed up early to the meeting at a time where it was universally known that rap artists were always late.

Chapter 14   UNDERSTANDING AND SIGNING YOUR CONTRACT

To quote the first paragraph of the introduction to Jeffrey Brabeas' book, *Music, Money and Success: The Insider's Guide To Making Money In The Music Business*: "In today's world of constant technological changes and innovations, shifting income streams, global concentration of the record and music publishing businesses, the importance of social networking sites and the changing distribution of music models, it's more important than ever that the songwriter, composer, music publisher, recording artist and record company have the practical business and legal knowledge necessary to succeed and exist in the music business." Simply put, knowledge of how this business works is essential to making a living and achieving success. In the entertainment and music industries, there are a variety of different contract and agreement types that contain an incredible number of intricacies. Below are highlights of some of the key provisions and language common to a contract you as a performer or songwriter will have to sign. Understanding what you are signing is as important as your talent to the success of your career.

RECORD DEAL[xci]

An artist assigns and transfers ownership in their sound recording copyright(s) to a record label, (usually) in return for an advance and subsequent royalty payments. The record label often agrees to market, promote, and license the recordings to music users such as streaming services and consumers.

PUBLISHING DEAL[xcii]

A songwriter assigns and transfers ownership, or partial ownership, in their compositions to a music publisher, (usually) in return for an advance and subsequent royalty payments. The writer sells in whole or in part, their composition(s).

DISTRIBUTION DEAL[xciii]

An artist gives a company the right to distribute their copyrighted sound recordings for a set amount of time. The company usually collects a fee or takes a percentage of the royalties that the song(s) earns. The artist retains ownership in their recordings.

360 DEAL[xciv]

Refers to the label's efforts to obtain a share in all rights and revenue streams related to the artist, in addition to the exclusive recording rights, name and likeness rights, touring rights, music publishing rights, and more.

If you would like a full in-depth explanation including a legal breakdown of language, clauses and everything encompassed in a 360 deal, I suggest picking up a copy of, *"Understanding and Negotiating 360 Ancillary Rights Deals: An Artist's Guide to Negotiating 360 Record Deals"* by renowned entertainment lawyer and attorney Kendall Minter.

50/50 RECORD DEAL[xcv]

A 50/50 record deal can be viewed as a joint venture or partnership deal between an artist and a label (or between two labels). 50/50 deals are typically offered to the artists and labels that are at a superstar level, and it's far more common to see 50/50 deals with artists and independent labels as independent labels may not be able to offer an enormous advance or any advance at all.

PRODUCER DEAL[xcvi]

The producer agreement usually occurs between a producer and artist, though sometimes it can form between a label and a producer. The producer can often negotiate up to 50% of the label's net receipts for a given sound recording. This negotiation is always based around the producer's placements and syncs with artists.

CO-WRITER AGREEMENT[xcvii]

Often, songwriters compose songs in collaboration with other writers. In the absence of a formal written agreement, the law assumes 50/50 ownership in any song known to be co-written. Splits that aren't 50/50 (or evenly split between all writers) must be memorialized in writing in order to be recognized by the law as such. This is where split sheets come in handy.

WORK FOR HIRE[xcviii]

A work made for hire occurs when Party A employs Party B to create something, where Party A is the legal author of the work, and Party B is paid either an hourly wage or an agreed upon flat fee for their provided work. In the eyes of the law, Party B will no longer have any rights to the work whatsoever.

MANAGEMENT AGREEMENT[xcix]

Manager agrees to devote itself to artist's career and to do all the things necessary and desirable to promote artist's career and earnings therefrom (anywhere between 5%-20%). These duties shall consist of such activities as working to secure deals with record companies, booking agents, song publishers, and music instrument manufacturers, and advising artists on the recording process, song selection, producers, packaging design for records, etc. Artist hereby authorizes and empowers Manager, and Manager agrees subject to the limitations set forth in this Agreement.

Always read this section thoroughly so you can catch any harmful language, such as a power of attorney in favor of the manager which would allow the manager to execute contracts and other legal documents on your behalf without your approval. This section stipulates what the manager will be responsible for in regard to your career. The language laid out in this section will determine how the manager will act on your behalf, and what recourse you have based on the manager's actions.

It's important to understand the manager contract more so than the label contract because your manager is responsible for handling the daily aspects of your career where the label contract may only include dealings with your released music and promotional opportunities. Be mindful of how your manager contract reads, as the manager could be receiving commissions from your deals well after the contract has ended.

Other deals that you can be offered include but are not limited to: master use license, mechanical license (explained in chapter 11), sync license (explained in chapter 11), performance license, PRO affiliation, booking/performance deal, and merchandise agreement. These deals are tailored specifically to individualized aspects of song creation and licensing. These details can be dense due to their centralized nature. For further explanations of the inner workings of these deals please refer to the chapter 14 section of the appendix in the back of the book.

It's important to bear in mind that all of these agreements bind the parties to whatever has been negotiated. Experienced legal advice is essential when dealing in the world of contracts. Always retain your own personal legal counsel, it's never a good idea to use legal representation provided by who you're signing with. If you do this, more often than not the lawyer is going to create contractual language that favors the label. *They are the label's lawyer not yours.*

There are several conditions that need to be met for a valid contract to exist. You should always check with your own attorney regarding the validity of a specific agreement, because there are varying industry specific laws in place at state or federal levels which affect the validity of a contract.

There are five major conditions that encompass a valid contract: the offer, (the promise to do something in exchange for something else); the acceptance (agreeing to the offer); the consideration (each party brings something of value to the table); the legality (terms must be within the scope of the law); and the capacity (involved parties must have full legal capability to enter into the agreement). Full details of each of these conditions can be found in the chapter 14 section of the appendix.

The next phase of understanding your contract is the language in it. In most cases, you won't have a full grasp on the language used. How things are worded in a contract is how the label can withhold certain things from you. It's the responsibility of the legal counsel you retain to read through all of this, and ensure you get the best, most fair deal possible. A favorite quote of mine that relates to this perfectly comes from Joe Budden: "You will always get fucked as an artist in the music industry, you just hope they use Vaseline."

A few standard music contract terms to familiarize yourself with to have a better understanding of what you're signing are: Bilateral contracts (agreements that require some type of performance on the part of both); Unilateral contracts (require a promise from one party and performance from the other); Breach (when a party fails to fulfill all promises made in an agreement); Power of Attorney (gives a party the right to sign documents in place of another); Writer's Obligation (the number of songs a writer should deliver to the publisher); Assignment Rights (assignment of copyright of music from the writer or singer to the music publisher); Publisher's Commitment (the commitment of the publisher towards the writer or the singer); rights to Return the Copyright (abides by the publisher to give back the copyright in case of commercial failure after a certain period of time); Advance/Royalties/Recoup (sets the royalty rate, the quantum of any advances, and the definition of royalty base); Audit Provisions (allows the artist to ensure accurate accounting from the publisher); and

Jurisdiction (recites the law that governs the contract).

With the intricate legalese used when constructing contracts, unless you have a law degree it's almost impossible to fully understand the entirety of your contact. Besides getting legal representation, how do you protect yourself in these contract negotiations? A few legal tips for your contract negotiations are as follows:

GET IT IN WRITING[c]

There will be points that you might consider too insignificant to be on paper. Let me warn you, the label is always looking for that loophole. A handshake deal is tempting, but to prevent ugly disputes in the future avoid verbal promises. Make sure you have every detail of the contract mentioned on the legal front.

OBTAIN YOUR OWN LEGAL ADVICE[ci]

Musicians are found to be naïve about legal matters, which leads to exploitation of their talent. Even if you trust the person, do not depend on their legal advice. Take your time to understand the terms and conditions.

USE INDUSTRY SPECIFIC ACCOUNTATNS AND LAWYERS[cii]

Music law is an exclusive arena which needs specialization on its own. Don't settle for accountants and standard lawyers as music laws can be difficult to understand. Choose an advisor who understands the laws well and looks into every little detail for loopholes.

RELEASE COMMITMENT (RELEASE COMMITMENT)

A contract should bind both parties with a fair exchange of benefits. If the one party doesn't live to its obligation, you should have a clear way out of your deal. To make the deal safer and beneficial it's imperative to add a release commitment in the contract.

Music contracts include a ton of different clauses put in place to ensure the artist is exclusively obligated to the record label. You hear a lot of artists say, "Hold them hostage" in releasing music because these clauses are mostly in favor of the labels. As an artist, be sure you know the different clauses in your contract, as these different clauses and the language used in these clauses make a vital difference in your obligations to the label.

As an artist, if you don't reach certain sales goals, then you may not get the same budget or resources for your second release. The label may not count an album you turn in against your contract obligations if the album doesn't meet the agreed upon number of songs to be considered an album. If you're tied to a label for a five-album deal and each album must have at least 12 songs, and you release a mix tape with only six songs, this may not count as an album, even if the label receives a profit from the mix tape release. Labels will use these clauses and loopholes in language to keep you under contract for as long as they can to obtain as much financial profit from you as an artist as possible.

A few major clauses to understand in you contract is:

TERM AND DURATION[ciii]

The term of a contract is the time over which the agreement lasts. In music contracts, the term can vary by the agreement. For example, an exclusive songwriting deal with a music publisher could be for one year with the option to extend through several more, while a record deal could be phrased in terms of album cycles. It is important to note that the term is binding and if the clause says that the agreement lasts until December 31st at 11:59 pm, then that timing must be adhered to strictly. Legal disputes arise when parties seek to grant the rights to their works to other entities before the term of the current agreement ends.

EXCLUSIVITY[civ]

An exclusivity clause prevents you from obtaining an agreement with a similar promise from an outside entity. Record, publishing, distribution, and PRO deals are all exclusive because they involve the licensing of exclusive rights. The companies stipulate that for the duration of the agreement they are the sole entities allowed to exploit whatever rights granted to them by the musician in the contract.

ADVANCE[cv]

Both record labels and publishers often give musicians a sum of money before creating exploitable works. These advances are recoupable, meaning that the company earns back the money through the royalties garnered by the licensing of future works.

ROYALTY RATE[cvi]

In a recording contract, an artist's royalty rate is negotiable, albeit relatively standardized in the industry. The rate is usually somewhere between 7%-25%. Mechanical royalty rates are set by the government, and performance royalties are calculated by the PROs and are based on complicated methodology.

KEY MAN CLAUSE[cvii]

This section of a contract gives a party the ability to end a contract if a particular person or "Key Man" no longer works for the other party.

RELEASE COMMITMENT[cviii]

The artist should aim to secure a positive release commitment from the label, coupled with a minimum marketing spend to support the release. Should the label fail to release your record, you should be able to terminate the deal, and/or buy back your recordings, so they can be licensed to another label, or perhaps self-released.

PRODUCER ROYALTY[cix]

The artist is further expected to pay the producer royalty from their own royalty share. For example, a producer is paid a three percent royalty and the artist 15 percent, the artist will end up with an actual rate before deductions of 12 percent. Don't forget that the artist still has to pay their manager a percentage of earnings, recoup advances, and possibly split royalty income five ways with a band. It's important not to allow the record company to recoup from the artist's royalty income advances paid to the producer.

TERMINATION[cx]

The contract should expect scenarios that could give the parties the right to end the agreement. There should be safeguards where if the label goes into liquidation or fails to release the record or is in breach of contract, the artist should be able to end the agreement and get the rights to their recordings back. Otherwise, your copyrights could become the property of third-party creditors fighting over the remains of the now defunct label. A similar provision, but much harder to obtain, is to allow the artist the right of termination where the label is sold, merged, or taken over. Don't forget: the label is still obliged to continue paying the artist on all recordings sold, even after termination.

ARTIST OBLIGATION[cxi]

- Artist shall be solely responsible for payment of all fees and expenses incurred by Artist. i.e., advance/budget.
- Label/manager shall be entitled to recover the sum or sums advanced, and reimburse itself for such Expenses, after deduction of Commission from Artist's Gross Earnings.
- Artist shall not form or enter into any group, association or other entity for purposes of recording records, tapes or audio/visual devices, or for the purpose of performing live engagements, or for the purpose of performing in television, theater or motion pictures, without first obtaining approval.
- Artist warrants that Artist will actively pursue Artist's career in the entertainment industry and will follow all advice and counsel proffered hereunder.

NAME & LIKENESS[cxii]

You will want to retain full control of your name and likeness, because if you relinquish these rights, you allow them to be used without compensating you. This is the fight college athletes have been having with the NCAA for years. Because college athletes don't own the rights to their name and likeness, the NCAA is allowed to sell merchandise with their names and use their images on promotional material without having to compensate the athletes in any way.

CARVE OUTS[cxiii]

Carve Outs are designed to exclude income that may be unfair for a label/manager to commission. For instance, if you're an aspiring singer/songwriter who has been making a living as a freelance make-up artist, you're not hiring/signing with a label/manager to make you more money from being a make-up artist. It's reasonable to "carve out" that income from gross earnings.

SUNSET[cxiv]

This rewards label/managers for their work during the term of the agreement while at the same time affording you the ability to sign with another label/manager and avoid paying two commissions.

Secondary clauses to be aware of are: territory (places the contract permissions apply); grant of rights (enables licensee to use copyrighted work); controlled composition (limit on the amount the label is required to pay for songs); secondary income (artist split of monies earned by label for secondary use of songs); artists warranties (artists must perform duties to the best of their abilities); and re-recording restrictions (restriction on re-releasing records for a period of time after end of contract). For full details on these and other clauses, please go to the chapter 14 section of the appendix.

A major aspect of your label contract will be the royalties' section which states the amount of "backend money" you receive from your music. "Backend money" refers to the quarterly payout you receive from your songs streaming on DSPs, being played on radio stations, being played on TV shows/commercials, being placed on video game soundtracks, being placed in movies and so on. The Copyright Office sets the statutory rate for mechanical royalties, increasing every two years according to changes in cost of living as determined by the Consumer Price Index. The rate increases are by authority of the 1976 amendment to the Copyright Act. The controlled composition clause limits the amount of mechanical royalties the company is required to pay for releases and holds the artist responsible for the excess.

Today's royalty rate is set at $0.0755 and the artist only receives 75% of this which equates to around $0.056 per song. This is a fixed rate based on the delivery date of the master recordings and doesn't change based on the length of the song. If you think that is unfair, the labels further exploit the artists and this system by not paying for what they call, "free goods," (defined as 15% of the records they sell), meaning that the labels calculate the royalty payout on only 85% of the records sold. Furthermore, the last way they stick it to artists is by holding them responsible for any excess mechanical royalties. This means that if the total amount paid by the company exceeds the specified amount above, the difference is deducted from the artist's personal royalties.

Traditional contract royalties begin at 11%–13% and allow for the royalty amount to be further diminished through a process of standardized deductions within the industry. For example, if you sell your CD for $10, under the "net sales" definition, you're going to receive 85 of every 100 units shipped. This means that $2.50 is deducted from the original $10 before applying the royalty percentage. Then an additional 20% is deducted from your royalty percentage. To understand this royalty reduction better, multiply an 11% royalty rate by 85% for a "free goods" deduction. Then multiply that by 75% for a "packaging" deduction. Then multiply that again by 75% for a "new media" deduction. After this process of deduction, an 11% royalty is reduced to less than 6%.[cxv]

So, when a track is sold to iTunes for $0.99, iTunes takes off 30% (about $0.30), leaving $0.69, of which a label's distributor might take 15% (about $0.10), making the Net PPD $0.59. This is the money that is split between the label and artists based on the royalty rate. One of the most important aspects of your deal is negotiating a fair royalty rate.[cxvi]

Labels often enter these negotiations with a low royalty rate, serving as an anchor for future discussions. The larger entities often have a company culture that encourages this, rooted in the old business model of the industry. Your expected outcome should be varied based on the type of label you're dealing with. With majors, royalty rates of 20-25% on physical and 25-35% on digital are common. With indies, digital rates of 40-50% and physical rates of 20-30% are fair. Welcome to the business of music.[cxvii]

Understand that what I have presented you with in this chapter is only the tip of the iceberg. It's critical to fully understand everything in the contract you are signing. There is nothing worse than signing a contract only to realize after your first big release you're not fully getting what you're owed by the label because of terms, language, and clauses in your contract that you didn't know were there. Take it from Meg Thee Stallion, her initial production deal with 1501 favored the label, and when her first single made her an international star she was losing a certain amount of money to her label based on the fact she didn't know everything in her contract. Not only was she contractually obligated to 1501, but she entered a management deal with Roc Nation, meaning that not only was she giving part of her money to 1501 but also giving a percentage to the management team at Roc Nation, all before she is getting anything she earned from her music. Lil Yachty during an appearance on "Everyday Struggle" stated that he didn't read or know what was in the first contract he signed.

As an artist, it's completely and utterly necessary to fully understand everything that you are signing before you sign anything. The terms and conditions (that all of us skip and accept without reading) are the exact things that can and will hamstring you in your contracts. Getting legal counsel is the number one priority before beginning any contract talks. Have an attorney present to read over every detail in your contract and explain it in a way that you understand what you're signing. Be sure to know what you are signing, because if you don't you will be under the full control of the label with no recourse. There is nothing worse than doing years of hard work to finally reach the point you were aiming for, only to get taken advantage of by what you thought were people who had your best interest in mind, because you didn't read your contract. It's always better to be Geppetto rather than Pinocchio. Remember how long it took him to lose the strings and become a real boy?

For additional information on understanding and signing your contract, see Chapter 14 in the Appendix.

Chapter 15   WORKING WITH YOUR LABEL AND WHAT TO EXPECT

What exactly is the label going to do for you? How will they assist you in both your music creation and promotion? Depending on the language in your contract, the expectations you should have will vary.

Once you have completed contract negotiations and have signed with a major label, it is time to get to work on your first project. Thinking that now that you're signed the label will do everything for you is the wrong mindset to have and will cause you to fail even before you have started. Even though you're signed to the label, you still have to put in the same amount of work, sometimes more, that you did to get this deal. The difference is now instead of working to get the record deal, you're working to keep the record deal. The label will assist you, but you still have to produce what they expect of you or one of two things will happen. One, you will get dropped, meaning you are no longer signed or associated with that label, which is bad but sometimes can be a blessing in disguise compared to the alternative. Or two, you can be shelved, meaning you are no longer a priority on the label, and although you're signed and contractually obligated to that label, they will get around to working with you when they feel like it.

That brings us to album sales. Once your album is released it's expected to generate a certain number of physical sales, digital downloads, viewed streams, that all add up to a calculated number the label has deemed the album should do. Depending on the popularity of the artist, this number can be anywhere from tens of thousands to hundreds of thousands in the first week. First week numbers are what labels look at, what is coveted the most, and where your chart rankings come from. This is when you hear the terms success or flop. A flop is a relative term and will depend on who the artist is and what type of numbers they have generated with past releases. For new artists somewhere around 20,000-100,000 of total sales (physical, digital, streams, etc.) in the first week can be considered a success. Conversely, for an established artist, this could be considered a flop.

What happens if your release is labeled a flop? If this is your first release, your projection track will be slowed by the label and your second release could be put on hold. If you're an established artist, depending on your stature you may be offered a reprieve, or the budget allocated for your next release could decrease drastically. However, if you meet or surpass the expectations of your release, your budget will grow, the label machine behind you will work faster as you become a primary focus of everyone at the label. Don't take this for granted. Even if you're doing well, I've heard cases where label personnel don't work as hard for an artist because they don't like the artist or the artist isn't personable when speaking with the staff. Be friendly with the label personnel because these are the people that ensure everything you do works properly in regard to:

PROMOTIONS, MARKETING PLANS AND BRANDING

A record label provides you a team of experts in promotion, marketing, and artist branding. They know the dos and don'ts and assist you in growing your audience and creating your image.

FINACIAL SUPPORT FOR PROMOTION, VIDEOS, AND PHOTOS

Constructing videos, photos, and other promotional materials can be very expensive if you want it done right. Record labels provide you with the necessary finances for all of this. The label has a built-in crew specifically to streamline these processes at a fraction of the cost.

SYNCHS FOR FILMS/TV

Record labels can function in a similar capacity to publishing companies where film and TV companies will ask for music to sync and license for their projects.

ACCESS TO PROMOTIONAL OUTLETS

Record labels can offer a more professional backing to artists through their extensive relationships and contacts throughout the industry. They can distribute your music in digital and physical formats across the country and get your music in front of people who want to see it faster and with better promotion in a more efficient fashion than you can at the start of your career.

PRODUCTION COSTS

Studio time for recording, mixing, and mastering is not free or cheap if you want it done professionally. The label puts in your contract a production budget that is specifically allocated to record, mix, and master your projects.

BE PART OF A COMMUNITY

Being part of a label is a trickle-down effect. If one artist succeeds, the entire record label benefits. If you sign with a record label, you become associated with the other artists on the label, which allows you to gain the benefits of exposure and credibility from the label's associated acts.

Aside from the A&R, a major reason you have signed with the label is the major label machine that you now have access to. A marketing team, a social media marketing team, distribution, graphics, managers, touring, scheduling, branding, images, finances, events, promotion, and much more that the label team can offer that you as an independent artist don't have access to before. Use them. A story I hear from artists that have signed with major labels is that the label wasn't helping them the way they thought the label should. The first thing I say is, "What exactly did you expect? What expectations did you have of the label going into signing your deal?" I have heard stories that certain artists don't get the same attention as other artists, because the team at the label didn't know or didn't like the artist they were supposed to be working with. Like it or not, people want to be needed, want to feel appreciated, and want to feel like they matter. The team that works at the label and is responsible for your career are just normal everyday people. They just happen to be working at a major record label. While this is your career, this is only their daily 9-5 job. Be sure to interact and be personable with the label team. For example, an artist I used to work with, every time we went to the label office the artist's manager had a gift for the office people at the label. He knew what each of them liked and always made sure they received something when we were coming to the office (food, cupcakes, intimate small gifts). Not saying this will always work but being personable and interacting with the office workers at the label goes a long way. Similar to your surrounding team, or the friends you have had for years, they will do more for you because they like you. Whereas people that may not be too fond of you will take longer to or not complete what you ask of them at all. I saw some of these same office workers put up with a lot more from the artist and manager than they should have because, as they would say, "We like the artist and her manager." These are the people directly responsible for making your career. If you are on their bad side, what is enticing them to work hard for you when they have a list of other artists that they are doing the same job for?

It's in the label's best interest that you succeed. If they thought you would fail, they wouldn't have signed you. They are, however, in the music business, so their sole purpose of signing you is to make money from your music. If you aren't making them money or are causing more trouble than you are worth business-wise, just like in any other business you can be recalled and shut down.

If you are still in the development stages, the label will pass on you and sign a similar artist that doesn't have to be developed. Be self-sustaining so the label doesn't have to worry about holding your hand. It's the label's job to take you to the next level, they don't call it the Major Label Machine, for nothing. These major labels have an enormous number of resources at their disposal that serve the purpose of taking an already established artist and making them an international superstar. Expect the label to assist you in ways that benefit them as a label more so than they benefit you as an artist.

Often independent record labels are the career starters of the music industry. They generally provide smaller deals to up-and-coming artists but are more hands on in the development process to grow the artist into a house hold name. Indie labels have a recognized reputation of having their ear to the streets for upcoming artists and music trends. Indie record labels have garnered this distinction due to their independence from corporate backers. Founded in 1962 by Herb Alpert and Jerry Moss, A&M Records is recognized as one of the most successful indie labels due to signing artists such as Sting, Sheryl Crow, and Joe Cocker.

If an indie company signs you, this means they see you have potential but still need development. These types of companies sign artists with the goal being to develop the artist into a major act, then shopping them to get signed by a major label. Sometimes these production companies act as independent labels and the artists that sign with them get developed and stay signed with these labels. But in most cases the artist signs with the production company because they can develop the artist, then through their major label connections, get the artist signed to a major record label deal.

For songwriters and producers, if you chose to not sign with a label and instead sign with a publishing company, the terms of your deal are going to be different. A typical publishing deal involves assigning the publishing company a portion of the artist's ownership of the songs in exchange for a share of the royalties for the publisher's exploitation of the songs. The publisher also provides co-writing and song pitching opportunities on behalf of the artist by the company's staff members, known as song pluggers. A few advantages of a publishing deal are:

A DRAW

It can be extremely difficult to make enough money to be financially stable when beginning your career as a songwriter, so a monthly draw can be a way to alleviate some of that burden. The typical draw is considered an advance against the writer's share of royalties' payable under the agreement with the publisher. While some draws are enough to allow the writer to write full time, most are enough to make it so the writer only has to have a part-time job, leaving more time for songwriting.

DEMO BUDGET

Publishing companies can provide a budget for studio sessions for the writer to cut demos. This is much like a production budget for an artist signed to a record label.

SONG PLUGGERS

These are publishing company employees specifically charged with finding placement opportunities for your songs. They use their industry relationships to pitch your songs to artists, producers, labels, and other companies looking for demos.

CONNECTIONS AND VALIDATION

Signing with a publishing company as a songwriter provides you with credibility and validation within the industry. This opens doors to meetings, co-writes, placements, and a variety of other industry opportunities.

The thought of being able to write songs for a living while your publishing company takes care of the details seems appealing, but nothing is ever that simple. Music is a business, so remember the publisher is giving you something in exchange for something.

DRAWS AND BUDGETS ARE LOANS

Any money that the publishing company pays out to you in the way of an advance or a budget is money you will have to pay back in the form of recoupable royalties on the sale and placements of your songs. It's important to understand that unlike a bank loan, even after the publisher has recouped the money they allocated for your advance and/or budget, they still own a percentage of the publishing of your songs and will continue to collect royalties. This will continue to hold true for the term length in your contract with the publishing company. In some cases, the publisher can still own full or partial rights to your songs even after your contract is up. There are instances where the recording the publisher splits with you or gave you an advance for is fully the publisher's property, meaning you will receive no master fee payment if the recording is placed in a film or TV (this stipulation doesn't affect the royalty income your contractually entitled too).

PUBLISHER'S PRIORITIES

In most publishing companies there are many more writers than there are pluggers. This means your songs are in a pile of hundreds (or thousands if you include the back-catalogs of the publishing companies) that the song pluggers are obligated to pitch as well.

VALIDATION DOESN'T ALWAYS CUT IT

Working in the industry for many years, I understand the feeling you get when someone in the industry validates your work. However, this isn't always enough of a reason to give up a portion of your publishing rights. Just like any other skill, if you want to be a songwriter you need to work on your craft every day until you're confident your songs are compatible to the songs on the radio. Utilize resources such as song critiques, songwriting organizations, and your peers, to get constructive feedback. Don't jump at the first opportunity to sign with a publisher because they tell you they think your songs are good and/or they think you have potential.

By not putting a publishing deal on a pedestal, you'll put yourself in a better position to succeed. In other words, you don't need a publishing deal to act like you have a publishing deal. If you decide you would rather not sign with a publisher, you have the following options:

ACT AS YOUR OWN PUBLISHER

You don't need to be affiliated with a publishing company to publish your songs. Through a performing rights organization (BMI, ASCAP and SESAC), it's relatively easy to start your own publishing company. You can visit their website to get started.

CREATE A REGULAR WRITING SCHEDULE

If you want to be a songwriter, you have to treat it like any other job and put in the time. Create and regulate specific times each day dedicated to nothing but practicing songwriting. People in corporate jobs can't skip work because they "aren't feeling like it today," and you can't either.

RECORD DEMO SONGS

Schedule studio time with a professional recording studio (or create one in your house, review chapter 1 for details), and when the demo is recorded spend the extra money to make a professional quality version for placement pitching to artists, film, and TV.

SONG PITCHING

As I have mentioned in previous chapters, it doesn't matter how good a songwriter you are or how good your demos are. If no-one hears them it doesn't matter. Much like social media posting and marketing for artists, this part of songwriting is a necessity. You can't become a professional or successful songwriter if you don't spend the time to send your songs out and make industry connections. This is a tough industry to break into, but once the door is cracked, it's easier to push it open.

NETWORKING

Get out into the world and meet people. This means you have to find opportunities to rub elbows with different music industry personnel. A few places and events that make this process easy are: music conferences, songwriter festivals, and events sponsored by organizations such as the Nashville Songwriters Association International (NSAI) or the Songwriter's Guild of America (SGA)

SIGN AN ADMINISTRATION DEAL

Once you begin to have success placing your songs with artists and in other mediums, the minutiae of copyright law, royalty statements, and licensing can begin to get overwhelming.

It's at this point you can consider signing an administration deal with a label or publishing company. An administration deal means instead of giving away 50%-100% of your copyright, you give the copyright administrator 15%-25% to take care of the legal paperwork allowing you to focus on the songwriting.

If you are signing with one of these types of companies expect to get run through the complete gambit of their artist development program. Everything from how to record properly, to songwriting, to sequencing, to vocal coaching, to marketing, videos, photos, graphics, live shows, branding, image, and so many other aspects of what being an artist is. These types of companies are going to build you from the ground up as an artist. This process can take anywhere from six months to a couple of years. I am now working with a few artists who, through the publishing company I work for, have been developing for close to two years, and are just now beginning to release music. Signing with a production and/or publishing company as an artist is a long tumultuous road, and can sometimes be difficult and irritating, but trust me, if you're signed with these types of companies, they have your best interest in mind, and will do everything in their power to ensure you succeed. I would say that if you get sought by one of these types of companies, it's in your best interest to do so, because these companies are not in it to just make a profit off of you. They want to ensure that you succeed because then they succeed, unlike a major label that will discard you for another artist exactly like you if you don't work out to their immediate expectations.

The expectations you as an artist need to have when signing and beginning to work with any music company need to be realistic. As I spoke about being realistic when taking meetings and negotiating your contract, you need to have a similar mindset once you have signed that contract. Having unrealistic expectations of the company you are signing with will have the same effect as having unrealistic expectations of yourself when negotiating your contract. You will do nothing more than shoot yourself in the foot. A favorite television line of mine is from Diddy on "Making the Band" on the season he formed the group Day26: "There is always someone working harder than you. The work is just beginning, because now you have to prove to everyone at the label you are worth keeping on the label. There are thousands of artists working tirelessly to take your spot. There is always someone working to take your spot. There is always someone not taking a nap." Because you signed a deal doesn't mean you have made it and the work is over. Quite the opposite.

Chapter 16 TOURING

It is time for the step most artists look forward to the most, touring. As a new artist, you may not know what to fully expect from tour life. How does touring work? What is your tour going to look like? Who will be a part of your tour? As the average music fan in the public, you may see the glamorous side of touring, the perfect live show production, the stage energy, the roaring fans, the parties, the adventure, but being the artist on these tours is not always everything it looks like on video.

The road can be a difficult but rewarding place. It will reveal how you're built as an artist, provide endless networking, marketing, and growth opportunities, and above all it can be incredibly fun. Touring can take you places you would otherwise never think to travel to. Be prepared for what is to come, and take advantage of everything touring can offer including:

RESILIENCE

Playing live is a great test to see if you're ready for the road or not. It's also a great learning and growth experience.

NETWORKING

Anything can happen on tour. You'll meet lots of other artists, and a few influential people on the way.

OPPORTUNITY

Once you begin to perform shows outside of your local town/city, you'll find there are more fans waiting to discover you and your music.

FUN

Remember why you began your career in music in the first place. Whether it's for the love of music, bonding with fellow artists, or the places you'll discover, you'll have a great time on tour.

Going on tour is a huge ordeal that takes an entire team. More so than your everyday career, touring includes hundreds of people all of whom have specific intricate roles. Just to ensure your tour logistics run smoothly you will need your everyday manager, tour manager, booking agent, tour promoter, local promoter and technicians. Each of these people play an intricate role in operating your tour.

MANAGERS

The manager's role is to build and coordinate the team on all sides of the music industry, and that, of course, includes the concert business. Management usually takes part in the initial route planning, helps pick the touring team, and serves as a bridge between the live entertainment and all other sides of your career.

BOOKING AGENTS

The agent represents you across the live industry. Their goal is to book the tour and sell the shows to the local talent buyers, finding the venue and negotiating the price. The booking deal is usually pretty straightforward: "Artist A, represented by Agent B, commits to play an N-minute show in Venue C on Day X for a $Y." A good agent is able to get details correct so the venue is sold out, no fans are left without a ticket, you get paid fairly, and the promoter doesn't feel cheated. While the deal is relatively simple, it's hard to nail all the details especially given the fact that the shows are usually booked 8 to 24 months in advance, depending on the scope of the venue.

TOUR PROMOTERS/LOCAL PROMOTERS

Once the show is ready, tour promoters, working closely with the booking agent, either rent venues themselves or subcontract (sell) the shows to local promoters (or a mixture of both).

Local promoters are affiliated or connected with local venues and performance spaces. They buy gigs from the agents and/or tour promoters to own the ticket sales. An art director of a small club, a local group of party promoters, a team from a major US festival, all would fall into this category. The role of the agent becomes clear. If promoters are the middlemen on the side of an artist or a concert space, the agent is the middleman between the middlemen, who builds up the network of promoters (on both fronts) and artists, serving as a liaison between all sides.

However, some of the biggest tours today can be put together without the agent's involvement. One of the main shifts in the live business is the consolidation of tour and local promoters under the umbrella of entertainment conglomerates, with the most notable examples being Live Nation and AEG.

Essentially, these companies have grown their operation to the point where they can internalize the entire process. Live Nation, AEG and alike, can now create centralized international tours, offering 360° deals. However, touring under such exclusive promotion remains reserved for top echelon artists, so most of the shows out there are still put together in collaboration between the tour promoters, booking agents, and local partners.

TOUR MANAGERS AND TECHNICIANS

Tour managers that stay on the road with the crew are the oil that makes the wheels of the tour spin. Extremely complex logistics become involved when you begin a nationwide tour, and the travel logistics become exponentially harder to manage as the tour grows to the international level. For top tier acts, staying on the road with the crew, technicians, and 30 trucks' worth of equipment can cost up to $750K per day. The goal of the tour manager is to make sure that the money doesn't go down the drain when the bus breaks down in Nowhere, Oklahoma. Getting the crew from point A to point B seems to be a pretty straightforward job, but in fact the routine of the tour manager is dealing with the unexpected and solving a dozen new problems each day, all while keeping you ready to perform.

Tour managers are also in charge of the technician crew. While the tour technical support often is overlooked, the fact remains that behind every show there's a team that creates an audiovisual experience the audience paid to see. It takes precise details, expertise and hard work to assemble the stage, set up the lights, the sound system, etc. Without a dedicated live show crew, there are no live shows.

With your touring team in place, it's time to construct the logistics of the physical tour. It is not as simple as showing up to the venue, going on stage, and traveling to the next city. There is a lot of planning and scheduling that has to be factored into your tour.

FESTIVALS AND VENUES

Festivals and venues are at the very core of the live business, providing the space and the base infrastructure for the show. There's often a great deal of vested interest between local promoters and performance spaces. That means that there's usually a local promoter attached to the venue, and the same goes for music festivals.

Outdoor events are a distinct part of the live performance landscape. Operated by promotion groups, prominent festivals can introduce artists to new audiences, all while offering a big paycheck. A major festival performance puts the artist on the map, and the promotional effect of the show itself has to be considered. It can become even more important than the immediate monetary gain, especially for independent, up-and-coming artists. This is why the tour routing will generally be structured around a few big music festival dates and then filled up with local dates corresponding to the travel route.

This is a true trust exercise because as an artist you are responsible for the livelihood of your touring team, just as they are responsible for a portion of your livelihood. If one person is out of line the entire team falls apart. There is a reason why we all saw Zach Brown post an emotional video on social media of him crying when he spoke about having to cancel his tour in 2020 during the Covid-19 pandemic and having to let go of his entire touring team that he has been with for over a decade. These people become your extended family, and we all know how it goes when you don't get along with your family.

FINDING TALENT

The first step is for agents and tour promoters to find and sign the performer. This process is similar to the scouting of artists by label or publishing A&Rs, although the criteria is slightly different. For some types of artists (DJs) touring can be relatively huge, while the recording revenues might stay almost non-existent. As an average show has to be booked 9-10 months in advance, they usually sign tour deals around a year prior to the actual performance. The vast majority of concert tours follow the recording releases to build up the momentum and ride the promotion wave. That has one unavoidable implication: tour promoters and agents sign the artist to perform the material, which is not written yet, which can be risky. That is especially true for debut artists, who might not even have a 40-minute set or any solid live performance skills when they get their first touring deal.

TOUR PRODUCTION AND SHOW STRATEGY

Once the artist is on board, it's time to produce the show, define the tour strategy and routing. This is when the tour promoter starts the show and productions preparations which include: constructing the light show and live visual materials, booking rehearsal sessions, and so on. Meanwhile, the artist, manager, agent and tour promoter work out a general timeframe and draft an approximate route of the future tour. They usually do the initial tour planning around priority shows, like major city performances or music festivals, while the rest of the route is defined in broad strokes. Once the initial planning is over, the tour strategy will be defined in terms of "The artist will play a priority city/music festival in a specific area N weeks after the release."

BOOKING THE TOUR SHOWS

Once the initial route is set out, the agent books the tour, pitching the show to local promoters and festivals. Starting with the priority shows and then filling in the details, the tour route gradually takes its last form. The agent negotiates with local promoters to pick out an optimal venue (in terms of volume, style, etc.) to host the show. As Tom Windish, a senior executive of Paradigm Talent Agency explained in an interview with David Weiszfeld of the soundcharts.com blog:

> "Picking the right venue is perhaps the hardest part of booking a tour: the material is not out yet, and there's no way to predict the reception of the release that's almost a year ahead. Go for a small but safe venue and you risk losing potential ticket sales and disappointing the fans; go big, and you might end up in a half-empty room, losing on the investment and leaving every side of the deal disappointed."

The agent has to make tough decisions in an uncertain situation and taking into account the landscape of the venue in some of the regions that means choosing between a venue capacity of 500 and 2,000 for what is reasonably a 1,000-ticket show. The booking contract local promoters, tour promoters, and artists, will split the net profits of the show. Artists might also get a flat fee to ensure they'll make some money, even if all other parties do their job poorly. Usually for a show, if the artist's flat fee is higher, their net profit share will be lower (and vice versa). The structure of the contract splits often reflects the artist's risk appetite. Some artists self-produce the tour, sacrifice the flat fees, and end up getting almost

100% of the net. Others might ask for a higher "safety" fee, which lowers the gross profits of the tour and the artist's personal stake. Booking agents earn a flat percentage on the revenues on top (though they might put their share back in the pot if the tour doesn't turn out a profit).

SELLING TICKETS

Once the tour is booked, it's time to promote and sell the tickets. On paper, the ball is in the promoter's court here, but in reality, they carry the marketing of the tour out in close collaboration between all the sides.

First is the implementation by the tour promoter of the overarching tour marketing coinciding with the record release. The tour marketing campaign uses wide communication channels to promote the tour rather than a particular show.

Second is the regional marketing owned by the local promoters, which aims to boost the sales of a specific show, focusing on narrow communication channels, like radio, and locally targeted digital advertising.

As far as the actual ticketing strategy is concerned, there's no one-size-fits-all solution, so most teams go through many meetings to define it. There are a lot of decisions to be made when settling the details of the ticketing strategy, especially as technology has put new tools into the hands of promoters, but accepted sales processes follow an Announcement → Pre-Sale → General-Sale pattern. First, they announce the tour through the label or artist-owned channels. That announcement is both a chance to communicate the tour to a wide audience and build up your CRM-base by getting fans to leave their contact information to get notified when tickets go on sale. On the live event market, the buying intent might not realize itself on the first day, so having direct contact with fans and growing your CRM-base is a key tool in the hands of the industry.

Then, the pre-sale takes place. First, reaching out directly to fans in the CRM database (artist-fan relationships are one of the most important assets of an artist). A fan pre-sale ensures that engaged followers will get tickets to the show. Pre-sale strategy might also involve sales through "preferred partners," focusing on direct sales through systems like American Express, Pre-Sales in the US, or Spotify, that allow you to reach your fans and followers across the tour route based on their listening habits and geo-location. Finally, to complete the pre-sale, local promoters can use the local communication channels, like the CRM-base of the venue and local airplay.

All the pre-sale strategies have two primary objectives. First, based on the pre-sale figures (and historical concert attendance data), the promoter can roughly tell how the show is going to sell in general and adjust the marketing campaign accordingly. Second, pre-sale through reasonably closed off channels can help to mediate the problem of the secondary ticket market. In fact, most of the ticketing strategies aim to sell as many seats as possible before putting the show on general sale. Ticketing platforms like Songkick, BandsinTown, or Seated, allow promoters to reach the widest audience, but they also put the show at risk of selling out to the scalper bots in a matter of hours.

PREPARATIONS

Carrying out a 100-show tour means getting the artist and their tour team to a hundred different locations across the globe, all while staying on a tight budget and an even tighter schedule, then making sure that every step has the infrastructure to do the actual show. Extensive tours are extremely complicated logistics that require a lot of planning (usually carried out by the tour manager, affiliated with the tour promoters). Plane tickets, car rental, back line equipment shipping is just a fraction of what needs to be taken care of before reaching the venue.

THE DAY OF THE SHOW

The venue is (hopefully) sold out. The material is well-rehearsed. They deliver the equipment to the club, but the show is still to be done. Someone has to set up the sound, check tickets at the door, take care of the security, prepare the guest list, and set up the bar. This routine can seem insignificant, but in fact, a solid on-site setup is a must if you want the audience to enjoy the performance. Surely all of us can remember that one concert with that hour-long queue, delayed performance, and warm beer at the bar. A poor concert organization can ruin the best of shows. Making sure that the concert goes smoothly is a group effort of the tour crew and the local promoter's team, from tour managers and technicians to local sound engineers and the venue staff.

Finally, one year, tens of thousands of miles and thousands of man-hours later, you will go on stage. Then, the team will get back on the road to repeat steps five and six, until they cross the last row of the tour announcement out. You will eventually get back in the studio and start working on new material, while tour promoters and agents will begin planning the next tour. That's tour life.

As an up-and-coming independent artist, you will have the opportunity to perform at a variety of live shows, each of which are run by different promoters. However, not all live shows are equal, and some promoters will attempt to take advantage of naïve artists that don't have a full understanding of the entertainment industry. Your manager will assist with these bookings and ensure you as the artist are put in the best positions to succeed. A few of the initial shows you could perform at as you begin your rise in the music industry are:

EXPOSURE EVENTS[cxviii]

When an artist is just starting out, exposure events are the most common form of gig you will book. These are where you perform for an audience just to gain exposure. There is typically minimal to no financial gain from these events, and you should plan on spending more time and money than you'll get in immediate return. These events are intended for long-term goals like fan growth or refining your live show for the future hope of being invited on a tour or having your own tour. It's the dress-rehearsal where you can work on your artistry in front of an audience.

PAY-TO-PLAY EVENTS/BUY-ON TOURS[cxix]

These are frustrating but are the norm nowadays. For instance, the West Coast venues (California) are almost 100% pay-to-play for anyone who doesn't already have national radio exposure. The scale of pay-to-play depends on a couple of factors. Your resume, your style of music, your type of live show, your geographic locale, etc. Paying a promoter to gain stage time is something you need to carefully calculate. If you're offered the opportunity to open for a well-known artist and it costs you a fee to do so, it may be worth the investment. Selling tickets to perform is another way you can get an opportunity to perform. In this case, you will buy a certain number of tickets from the promoter that you will have to sell. This is a good and bad situation. Good, because you will get to keep a percentage of each ticket you sell, and you will have a certain number of fans at the show specifically for you. Bad because if you don't sell enough tickets, you lose your performance slot, and also the money you spent on the tickets initially. Buy-on tours are also very common. A known tour has a reputation for featuring great headliners, and the size of the audience in each city is large. These large labels purchase slots on these tours for their up-and-coming artists. They own the opening slots before a headliner. This is a lucrative business for tour or event promoters. They know that their stage is valued real-estate and they charge a premium for it. When you see an artist on a tour poster or as an opener for a major headline, someone in their camp paid a premium for that space. Paying to perform is the first of your expenses. Sometimes these pay-to-play events or tours also take a percentage of your merchandise sales. As long as artists will pay this premium, the promoters will continue to require it.

SELF-PROMOTED EVENTS[cxx]

These are events you put on yourself and are solely responsible to promote and host at a venue of your choosing. While everything about the event is under your control, it's not always the best use of your resources. The financial success or failure of the event is squarely on your shoulders, and the overseeing of details that you would ordinarily not be required to care about can be something that interrupts the flow for an artist.

It's important to do some research before accepting a performance slot at a show because not all opportunities are created equal. Some shows may not be a good opportunity for your career based on the venue and/or audience. As a rapper, you wouldn't want to perform at a local family festival centered on soft rock cover bands. As a rock band, you wouldn't want to perform in an intimate lounge setting either. In each scenario the setting, the audience and the logistics don't correlate well with the artist, and while, yes, it may be an opportunity to play live, if it is not the audience that will enjoy your music and performance it may not be worth doing.

It is your manager's job to consider all of this when booking you shows. Your manager and tour manager need to be responsible for the well-being of you, the audience, and the show as a whole. Included in the litany of things they should consider when booking and/or accepting a show date is, set length and line up placement, venue/technical support, stage dimensions, venue capacity, same day events, merchandise location in the venue, media coverage (if any), allowance of video recording, offer sheets, riders, financial exchange, wifi settings and capacity, venue condition, security, and any possible weather-related issues.

A mental lapse on any one of these details could cause for a catastrophic night. There is a reason why Van Halen is famous for their "No Brown M&Ms" rule in the show rider. They knew that if there were brown M&Ms in their dressing room the venue didn't read their show rider and stipulations. If there were brown M&Ms in their dressing room, they wouldn't perform that night because they knew there was a possibility the stage and/or venue could be unsafe for the band and/or the audience. At the apex of their touring, older venues such as Toronto's Maple Leaf Garden, the original Boston Garden, and Chicago Stadium were not built to withstand the massive amounts of stage equipment to accommodate a band of Van Halen's scope. Knowing this, the band implemented this stipulation into their rider to ensure the safety of the band and everyone in attendance. If it wasn't adhered to, the band had the right to walk out on the performance at the full expense of the promoter.

It's important to fully understand the burden and workload that comes with touring. New artists are naïve in their thinking of touring and tour life, and this is a major reason most become jaded during or shortly after their first tour. You and your team have to evaluate every opportunity that is presented to you. Not every opportunity is a good one and having the wherewithal to turn down unpromising opportunities is important for not only your business acumen but more importantly your mental health and wellbeing.

Touring is great for you as the artist, as this is where most of your income is generated. However, the act of touring can be grueling. Yes, you travel across the country and across the world, but the toll it takes and what is expected of you, is not something you can be prepared for until you have gone through it. Everyone is always excited for the tour and is ecstatic when it begins. A few days into the nonstop travel, believe me, everyone's mood changes, and by the end you're ready to go home. How Tech Nine and Strange Music can tour so many days constantly every year to this day is something I can't fathom. Be prepared mentally, physically, and emotionally for the tour life. Take care of yourself and be cognizant of your health, because life on the road (even if you have the luxury of a private plane) is grueling.

Chapter 17   PRESS RUNS

Doing press runs is how you as an artist promote your new or upcoming release depending on when you start your press run. Normally your press run will begin a few weeks to a month before your project release date. This means you will go on the road across the country for different radio interviews, television appearances, podcast interviews, club walkthroughs, and in person appearances at different venues. Most of this will be done in a relatively short time, meaning you will be constantly traveling to different cities each day and night (sometimes multiple cities in the same day). If you have ever been to a meet and greet with an artist before or after a show and the artist seems less than enthused to be there, it's because this is the twentieth stop in 10 days in the 12th state with constant travel and little rest. Remember, as an artist to take care of yourself physically, mentally, and emotionally during these periods in your career. There is an enormous amount of pressure, stress, and expectations of you as an artist, and as we have seen so often over the last few years, artists break down more often because they are not taking care of themselves.

Your press run will comprise a few different aspects, and depending on your popularity can be local, regional, or national. If you're starting with a local press campaign, this will include local radio stations, local pop-up events, local meet and greets, and different appearances around a city. I'm going to use New York (and New Jersey as they are generally connected during an east coast press run) as an example of a local press run. As a New York artist you will start by doing radio promotion, which includes interviews. If you're an established artist, Hot 97, The Breakfast Club, Power 105, and Ebro in the Morning, are all stops on your press run as it pertains to radio stations. If you're a new artist, you will be doing smaller radio shows throughout all five boroughs. Manhattan is where most of the bigger companies are and therefore reserved for the bigger artists (excluding NYU as a college radio station). Doing interviews with these radio shows (sometimes on the same day) will be a way for you to speak about your new release, different aspects of your life, you as an artist and so on, to a large local audience. The shows will play your single and promote that you are coming on the show. In today's media climate, they will also post your interview online to their social media and YouTube channels for additional promotion. From there you will have local meet and greets with fans at different venues, where you will sign autographs and take pictures. In New York there are a litany of venues and locations that you will go to. These will change depending on your brand, but most artists will visit Rucker Park, Times Square, a vast amount of clothing stores in each borough, community run mom & pop shops, and other music/entertainment venues. Be prepared to travel from Brooklyn to the Bronx back to Queens, then finish in Manhattan on the same day. Personally, while traveling with an artist during a single day New York City press run, my team and I traveled from Brooklyn to Manhattan to Queens then back to Manhattan and finished back in Brooklyn.

Last, you will do club walkthroughs, which means you will have a paid appearance at specific clubs and lounges. Normally, you will not show up before midnight, and when you arrive, you will be escorted to your section, get free drinks, and will perform a short music set at the club. In most cases a walkthrough club set means you stand in the DJ booth with a microphone while your song is playing, partially singing along, and partially hyping the crowd. After about an hour at the club, you leave and that is your walkthrough.

Moving to the regional press campaign, you will now travel to a few different states. Most of the time these are within driving distance, but sometimes (due to schedule) you will fly. The same events you did during your local press run will occur (radio interviews, online shows, meet and greets, club walkthrough) for you to gain exposure with a different audience while touching base with your fans in that market. When doing out-of-town press runs, you will do multiple different stops in the same day at a variety of different places throughout an entire city. These press stops will include morning television, afternoon radio shows, evening internet shows and performances, finishing with late night club appearances. Be prepared for 14-16 hour days, especially if you are traveling to that city the same day as these events.

Finally, if you are doing national press runs, you will travel almost nonstop. Each city you go to will have multiple events scheduled for the same day (anywhere from two to eight in the same day, one every hour) then leaving that night to go to a different city. While this is great publicity, if you are not prepared and properly taken care of (by yourself, your team, and your label) you are in for a tough road. In most cases, these national press runs will be accompanied by a show, which means that in one day your schedule could look as follows:

- 9am: Morning radio interview
- 10:30am: second radio interview
- 11am: travel to venue
- 1pm: sound check
- 4pm: Fan Meet and Greet
- 8pm: Show Time
- 12am: Club appearance
- 3am: travel to next city

Granted, not every single day will be this hectic, as not every city will include radio interviews and club appearances. Some cities will have multiple shows so you won't be traveling every day, and occasionally you will have a day or two in between shows and travel, allowing for some downtime before your next show or traveling to your next city.

For the next example, let's assume you are doing a press run while touring, this means not only are you conducting meet and greets and interviews during the day, but you are performing each night. All I have to say is welcome to the life of an artist. During the day you will travel to a variety of radio stations to basically do what amounts to the same interviews, all across the city you are in, then traveling to the venue for sound check, and after that, spending the rest of your day in the dressing room, preparing to perform your hour long show that night. You would think your night is over after that, right? Sorry, you're wrong. After the show you will do a meet and greet with fans who purchased VIP tickets, taking pictures, signing autographs, talking to every fan for what amounts to a few hours, before getting in your travel bus, or van, or plane, to go to the next city to do the same thing all over again. As a fan you may see the tour videos of all the fun antics, laughs, events, parties, and shows that the artist does, but you never truly see the behind the scenes of what the artist is doing prior to and after the shows. The press, the travel, the preparation, it's hours upon hours of work just for the artist (not mentioning the team the artist is traveling with, which can range from a few team members to an entire show staff that is setting up and breaking down all the equipment used for the live show at each venue, packing and unpacking said equipment every night hours before the artist gets to the venue for sound check and hours after the artist leaves, before traveling to the next city). I have been on tour and press runs where I was awake for 72 hours just to ensure everything was operating smoothly so the artist was comfortable and could focus solely on preparing for the show. It's exhausting, and when you hear the war stories artists tell from their tours, they are telling the truth.

Have you ever wondered why after a three-month tour you don't hear from or see that artist for weeks? It's because a majority of the time the artist is completely worn out. On tour, artists and their teams are doing anything and everything to give the fans everything they expected and more. So much so that they end up sick, malnourished, and run down, which is why you are seeing more and more artists nowadays canceling shows and full tour dates because they cannot keep up with the schedule, they've committed themselves to. As an artist you have to be mindful to always take care of yourself while on the road because the toll it takes on you mentally, physically, emotionally, and spiritually is excruciating.

Finally, the third option is doing shows without the press run. Here you are traveling the country from city to city, coast to coast on a few months' extensive tour. You will begin this journey one of two ways, either close to or in the city you live in or on the opposite side of the country. In both cases, your last shows will always be as close to your hometown (or the town you live in) as possible. You will spend one, sometimes two nights (depending on how many shows you have in that city, normally not over two, unless you become Dave Chappelle and get booked out in NYC for months straight) in a single city before traveling to your next stop. As a new act you may not be afforded the luxury of a plane, meaning you are getting a tour bus (if you are lucky) or a sprinter van, piling your entire team in there, and taking a road trip to your destinations. In either case, be prepared to start your show around 9-10-11 pm, be on stage for at least an hour, be in the dressing room after the show for at least another hour, then traveling to the next city. Depending on where you are going, you will arrive very early in the morning, check into a hotel, get a few hours of sleep (if you are lucky) then start your day around nine or ten in the morning that same day for a fan meet and greet at the venue before the show. Once the meet and greet is done, you will have a sound check for your show that night, then be in the green room waiting for your call time. Yes, in the green room you will have food, drinks and other things that you asked for, but sitting around in a green room for hours isn't great, especially coming off little sleep and days of travel.

Touring is fun and getting to travel the country is an amazing experience. Each city has something amazing to offer, and each fan base will have a unique energy during your show. Interacting with the fan base in each city is rewarding, and the treatment from the staff and venues can be fantastic. Having the opportunity to experience each city's food, traditions, and aesthetics are things only experience can attest to as words will not do them justice. Touring is grueling. If you are not prepared for the road and the expectation of doing live shows and events every day and night, it can catch up to you fast. Where some of this responsibility lies with your team, it's ultimately your responsibility to know your own body and your limitations. We hear all the time in sports, athletes need to know their bodies to avoid injury. The same holds true for artists, especially on the road. Because the schedule is so intense it's easy for you and everyone on your team to disregard your health to get the job done. Let me be the first one to tell you, as an assistant manager for an artist during tours, you can go days without proper sleep and meals. There were days I would not eat or sleep before the next stop because of the schedule and making sure the artist was properly taken care of. Your health is the most important thing as an artist, because if you break down mentally, physically or emotionally you will have to cancel shows. There is no shame in telling your team something is wrong or that you need more time to get yourself right. Your team will cancel or move events prior to your show to ensure you are ready to perform. In some cases, they will even reschedule show dates if it's in your best interest.

Chapter 18 SUSTAINING YOUR CAREER

You have put in months, most likely years of time and effort to become the artist you are now. You have done all the recording; you have gotten through the post-production; you have assembled your team; you have done live shows; you have produced and distributed merchandise; you have affiliated yourself with distributors and PROs; you have released your music; you have signed a record deal; you have gone on press runs and tours; and you are constantly working with your label. After all of that, how do you as an artist sustain a successful career in the music industry?

In today's digital and streaming age, it's easier than ever to release music. It's easier than ever to create music. Through social media, it's easy to grow and captivate a fan base. It's easy to stay engaged and communicate with that fan base. If all this is true, why do so many artists come and go? Why do so many artists get signed only to never be heard from again? What are they doing wrong that they can't sustain their career once they have "made it?" It's because they don't know what it takes to sustain their careers. They are not prepared for the artist's life after they have reached the point of being signed and becoming famous. Once you have signed with a major label, that is when the actual work begins.

What are some things that make an artist sustainable? What is it that has made Drake become one of the most popular artists of all time? Why can Eminem and Jay-Z drop projects with little to no roll out, no press, and have millions of fans listen to their album? How has Lil Wayne been able to release five Carter albums along with countless mix tapes, and every time have people waiting on the edge of their seats to listen to them? How are Chance the Rapper, Beyonce, Kendrick Lamar, and The Weeknd able to not be fully active on social media, but still sell millions of copies, go number one, sell out every show in every city, year after year after year? What do these artists have in common? Work ethic and undeniably great music.

Music is subjective, and the music I listen to will differ vastly from the next persons, and what I deem as a great artist, a great song, or a great album, can be considered by another person as utter garbage. I will be the first to say that the new generation of Rap that is out now (the more trap sounding, less lyrical, efx driven, auto tune style) I can't always listen to. It's not for me. That being said, there are millions of people that absolutely love this music and listen to it non-stop. As an A&R and music publisher, I have spent years training my ears to understand why this music is popular and why people (especially the younger generation) love this sound. Keeping everything, I have spoken about thus far in mind, how do you as an artist sustain a career in the music industry?

CREATE MUSIC TO CAPTIVATE AN AUDIENCE

Captivating an audience is the key to a successful music career. "Gone are the days of record labels creating rock stars," says producer Julie Pyle of Jayde Monroe Productions. "To be successful in the industry today, a band must act as a CEO and create a strong and unique brand."[cxxi] It's imperative that you conduct market research on the geographic of your audience, the age demographics of your audience. What are the similar artists and genres they listen to, and what platforms do they use to listen to music.

GIVE THE AUDIENCE SOMETHING TO RELATE TO

To maintain and grow your audience base you have to provide them with a message, a brand and music they relate to.

Mike Varney of Shrapnel Records says: "There is always a curve in each genre of music and you have to be careful not to jump on an existing bandwagon that is phasing out. You take the chance of falling behind the curve, as other bands who are more groundbreaking shape the industry. Hopefully, you can see the curve and naturally create music which will be perceived as fresh and not a rehash of what has been popular in the previous years."[cxxii]

ONLINE AND OFFLINE MUSIC PROMOTION IS ESSENTIAL

It's important to choose the right online and offline promotional channels to reach your audience. An active digital presence and footprint are essential, but you also need to appear on DSPs. Spotify is the leading platform for streaming music, so if you can get onto one curator's playlist, others will follow.

Terrestrial radio still holds an important position in the music industry. Connecting with local DJs and having them spin your record is a great way to broaden your audience and local reach. Once your songs are in the rotation of the local DJs, the bigger market radio stations will pick up your song. Radio spins are good, but live interviews and performances are essential to personalizing yourself. Interviews will help the audience personally relate to you and show them you are more than just another artist making music.

PREPARE FOR A TUMULTUOUS JOURNEY

The music industry is feast or famine, so it's best to pray for the best but prepare for the worst. Be prepared to work for years (sometimes 10-20 years) before getting your first break. Financial burdens can be tough during your journey, but it only takes one song to change your life. Alex Grossi of Quiet Riot says, "If you truly love music and want it badly enough, anything is possible."[cxxiii]

DIVERSITY IS THE KEY TO LONGEVITY

Being diversified in your networking and musical ability is key to creating longevity in your career. It's great to network at music industry events, but this isn't the end all be all for networking in the music industry. Some options are to start giving music lessons, performing at weddings and corporate events, be part of the technical team for local shows, and/or learn to produce and collaborate with other local artists.

BE AN ARTIST YOU WOULD BE PROUD OF

All of us want to be the best versions of ourselves. Unfortunately, the media chooses to focus on the negatives, meaning you need to ensure there is next to nothing negative for them to discuss. It's not always easy but wearing a smile, being genuinely friendly, and acting in a way you can be proud of, is a great start. The music industry and fame in general can be difficult in regard to your privacy and personal life. It's important to try and maintain balance by associating with people and building relationships outside of this industry.

BUILD A TEAM, DON'T TRAVEL THIS JOURNEY ALONE

The favorite term of the music industry is "It isn't what you know but who you know." To succeed in this industry, you can't do it alone. You have to have support around you. It takes a village, and you need the right people to keep the village thriving. Make it a point to hang out with like-minded people, be supportive of other artists, make friends within the industry, and form strong alliances.

DON'T PUBLICALLY COMPLAIN

The music industry has an old saying, "Want an artist to complain? Give them a gig." Working in this industry is a privilege that most people would kill for, and this means that no one wants to hear you complain about minuscule details. You're only allowed to complain if you're fighting for your rights and/or something you truly believe in, and even then, in most cases the people still don't want to hear it. You can voice your opinions about creative matters, explain your vision, and of course share your music, but if you complain about the low hanging fruit issues in the industry (venue management, not being given a shot, or streaming payouts), you will quickly lose the respect of the industry.

It's a sad fact that in today's music industry the labels and companies signing artists aren't necessarily looking for the greatest music or most talented artists to sign and sell. Rather they are looking for great personalities who happen to create good music. This means your personality needs to shine as much if not more than your music. Think of this like a WWE character. People gravitate to their connection to the characteristics and story of the person rather than the actual wrestling. You need to show the label that working with you adds value to their company. Labels don't want to work with an artist that is flaky and inconsistent. You have to be on point because if you're not they will find another artist who is.

Every artist wants to get their foot in the door to the music industry, but the misconception of this is that once you're in the door the work is done. This thought process is the fastest way to get shown out the same door you just entered. To be a successful artist you have to create a strategy to get you in the music business, keeps you there, and ensure you and the people around you thrive. Getting noticed might seem like the hard part, but staying noticed is even harder. Once you get that coveted industry spot, the same hundreds of thousands of artists you were competing with for that spot are now competing with you to take your spot. This means those same artists are now watching and studying you, waiting for you to slip so they can steal your spot. The slightest appearance of relaxation is cause for doubt by your label and creates an opening for the artists waiting in the wings.

Most artist think they are competing with other artists, when the reality is your only competition is yourself. You don't have to be better than the artists competing for your spot. You have to be better than your last effort. If you don't continue to grow and progress in your career in the label's mind, they'll look for a replacement. Understand, the greatest requirement for building a successful career is having the right mindset. Most artists don't know what to expect when coming into the industry and thus don't start out with the correct mindset to set themselves up for success. However, the few who do are split into two categories: those who can maintain that successful mindset, and those who let the success go to their heads. Opportunity isn't given but rather created by those with the right mindset. If you want a successful music career, you must be proactive in creating the opportunity for yourself.

Most artist miss out on career opportunities because they don't pay attention to the little details. Putting all the pieces together is the fastest way to success in developing your career in music. When the pieces don't fit and are disconnected, the machine doesn't work properly and the job doesn't get done. When all the pieces are connected and in proper working order your production rate increases and the chance to achieve your goals skyrockets.

With all that being said, how have artists used these techniques to have sustainable careers that have lasted 15-20 years? The two major points are their unmatched work ethic and their undoubtable incredible music. Yes, each artist has something in particular that separates them from the rest of their peers, but each of these artists has those two details that are unmatched.

Starting with Eminem and Jay-Z, can you name two other rappers that have the knowledge and lyrical prowess that these two have? Not to mention the time both of them spend on each album, let alone each song they record. I have heard stories of Eminem working with Dr. Dre in the studio for hours on the sound of a single hi-hat in one song. Now if you know music, you know what a hi-hat sounds like. You also know that in most cases a lot of them sound the same. So, to spend hours on this one sound, on one song (that may or may not be featured on an album or even be released) shows you how much care is put into his records. Add that precision to his lyrical ability, where he just jots phrases and stanzas down, not for any song but to be used at a later date, (so much so that in an interview with Lil Wayne, he mentioned having to look up his own lyrics on Google to make sure he wasn't using the same lyrics twice) coupled with his off the head freestyle ability that we have all seen over numerous videos and performances, is it any wonder Eminem is considered one of the top Hip-Hop artists and lyricists of all time. Jay-Z is the same way. There is a video of him in the studio with Rick Rubin recording "99 Problems" where Rick says: "I have never seen anything like Jay, he doesn't write anything down, he goes into the booth, feels and understands the record and then records." Artists nowadays say they don't write things down, and it shows with their short lines all followed by some grunt and the same word at the end of every line. Can you tell when Jay-Z or Eminem are rapping off the top of their head? The ability to continually grow as an artist as you grow in age is something most artists don't do well. You will hear a lot of artists as they mature and still try to rap and sound like they did at 21 when they first came out. As Eminem and Jay-Z have matured, so have their lyrics. Jay has gone from rapping about the street life and selling drugs to rapping about the art in his house, his kids, his wife, working with the NFL and owning an NBA team. Eminem has gone from "I don't give a Fuck," to speaking on political issues and the state of the country. Being able to mature with their lyrics and not continuously staying in the same box is an aspect of their musicality that separates them from every other artist and is why both are considered among the top Hip-Hop artists of all time.

How about the next age of artists? Drake and Beyonce have two of the greatest work ethics in the music industry bar none. There's a story of Beyonce working so diligently that she once worked three or more days without realizing she didn't eat. The videos and documentation of the practice and rehearsal Beyonce does for each song, each performance, each show, are unmatched by any artist of this generation, and probably only rivaled by Prince or Michael Jackson. Going from being in a three-girl group to being the undoubtable lead singer and stand out of that group to becoming a worldwide super-mega star, is just the tip of the iceberg to what separates Beyonce from the rest of the artists. The empowerment and embodiment she has shown and given to everything she stands for is why she is the living image of what every artist should strive for. Drake's work ethic is unmatched, but in a unique sense. Starting with a role in a Canadian television show, to getting signed by Lil Wayne, to becoming ambassador to the Toronto Raptors franchise, Drake has continued to rise. Every year since he first came out as a major artist under Young Money, Drake has had a chart-topping release. Whether it be a solo project, multiple features on other projects, or singles/features of his own, there has not been a single year where Drake hasn't had some release land in the top five or top ten on one or multiple charts. Going from being a rapity rapper on songs like "Ransom" and on his first album "Thank Me Later" to becoming the sing-rap melodic hit making genius he is today; Drake has transitioned beautifully and is on a run like no other. So much so that when one of his latest releases didn't land at number one after the first week releases, people were wondering what happened. His Number One album streak on the Billboard 200 chart ended after a decade. Following his ninth consecutive No. One spot with "Care Package," the streak ended with "Dark Lane Demo Tapes." The tape lost to Kenny Chesney's album "Here and Now." "Dark Lane Demo Tapes" moved approximately 223,000 equivalent album units, with Chesney's release scoring 233,000.

Finally, touching on the new age of music, specifically in the Hip-Hop genre, Russ, Chance the Rapper, and Migos all have had a major success of their own because of their work ethic and the new sound they have created. Russ and Chance specifically have independently been working for years, releasing their own music and captivating their own fan base. Russ spent years recording music in his and his friend's basement, releasing music through independent distribution channels, allowing him to fully own his entire catalog, netting him over a million dollars from certain songs each year just from streams. He has been able to become one of the top independent artists of this generation (possibly of all time), growing and sustaining his fan base to ensure longevity of his songs and his catalog. He mentioned in an interview with Joe Budden on "The Pull Up" that due to the way he has released and promoted his music he has songs that were released years ago that have just recently gained traction to the point they are going gold and platinum and have become some of his most famous songs. Chance won a Grammy from his "Coloring Book" mix tape, and additional Grammy nominations for his first official album release in 2019, all while staying independent. Migos changed the soundscape of rap music, ushering in the sound you hear everyone trying to emulate today. These three artists made their names from creating a sound that has changed the landscape of modern rap music and ushered in the next generation of artists, all while creating undeniable hit songs. When you create a sound that every new artist tries to emulate, there's no doubt that you can have a sustainable career.

CONCLUSION

Starting with the recording process through how to successfully sustain your career, the process of becoming a successful artist is a long and tumultuous road. If you are expecting to become an overnight success, this is not the industry for you. Frankly, the thought people have of "one hit single going viral" is not only nearly impossible but a mind frame of an act that has already been lost. If you think you can record a song off your laptop microphone, release it on SoundCloud, spam accounts on social media, and have the next viral hit, I am sorry to break it to you, but you are mistaken. Being an artist in today's music environment is easier than ever, because of the advancement in technology and the ubiquity of social media, but becoming a known artist and sustaining your career is extremely difficult.

Having a proper recording, getting the post-production done properly, understanding how to work and operate a social media page, understanding the different independent distribution channels to release your music on, assembling your team, rehearsing for and performing live shows, producing and selling merchandise, preparing for different label meetings, having the correct representation during your contract negotiations, knowing what to expect after signing your contract, beginning working with your label, what to expect from touring, and finally knowing how to sustain your music career past getting signed, are the knowledge basics you must have when navigating your music career. By no means is the information I have provided the end all be all of becoming an artist. What I have provided is just the start because the music industry is complex and forever changing.

As someone who has spent years working in the music industry in a variety of positions, my goal in writing *The Blueprint* is to shed light on things I see artists need but don't have access to. The information is thorough, but it still leaves you to figure things out on your own. A lot of what is in these steps is trial and error but having a greater understanding of how things work and why they operate as they do can give you a leg up in the game.

ADVICE FROM THE EXPERTS

Helado Negro, United States Artists Fellow in Music Award winner, Grants to Artists award in Music from the Foundation for Contemporary Arts winner, Joyce Foundation award winner:

"My close friend and inspiring creative, Michael Kaufmann, said something about the commerce aspect of art and music that resonated in my mind. He said that experimental economies are maybe the most important development in how to afford making any art. It's where we can create new challenges for personal creativity. Something I've realized that's become so much at my fingertips is being able to sell a digital version of a song directly to people who appreciate the music I make. That's never been available before without being affiliated with another outlet like iTunes or Bandcamp, both of which have amazing benefits and certain built-in infrastructures that are great for long term development. But to be able to put a song up for a week in a limited fashion, while nothing new, can definitely be further explored as a medium, and hopefully develops the idea of music making and sound delivery."[cxxiv]

Jane Penny, Member of Canadian Indie Rock Group *TOPS:*

"Most artists and musicians I know in Canada try to get as many grants as they can. They're so great when you get them, but a lot of bands don't especially new bands as they're based on a lot of arbitrary statistics about the commercial potential of the artist. We've gotten some tour grants, which really helped because on tour we live on a little more than $10 a day, plus whatever we get at the venue. Right now in Canada the government is cutting a lot of arts funding, so I think in the future grants will continue to be crucial but might be harder to get. I didn't make a ton of money in 2014, just enough to keep going. But I feel good about how I spend my time and I feel things growing, more people at shows and we are writing and have a lot of touring planned this year already so that's cool. Money buys space and musical equipment, and I'd like to have more of both of those, but all you really need is your own mind at the end of the day. People confuse wealth with value: if something makes money, they immediately value it, or at least respect it, but a lot of the most lucrative music is, arguably, pretty shit."[cxxv]

Holly Herndo, Composer, musician, and sound artist:

"There is a long legacy of patronage in independent music. Many of the great avant-garde American composers would simply not have been able to operate without state support from Europe, a university, or private money, and the same climate absolutely exists today but is rarely discussed in the open. I've done a lot of projects with arts institutions and did a large project with a Swedish design company last year, and honestly really enjoy challenging myself in these new environments. There are so many aspects of my artistic practice that are applicable to other fields, and it is both a matter of intellectual curiosity and financial security that I cast a wide net. I chose to pursue the academic path and have been fortunate to receive scholarship money to allow for me to get better at what I do in that supportive environment. I wrote my first album between scholarship supported graduate school and working a day job at a children's museum, and now earn money between teaching commitments at Stanford (where I also attend classes), live shows, and myriad commissions from the art and fashion worlds. I am incredibly grateful for these opportunities; however, I also cannot remember a single day in the last five years where I was not working or concerned about money. You have to make your work your life, and although I love what I do, there is nothing casual about the choices that I have made. I have just begun to lecture a class I co-designed for my program, am often grading papers before soundcheck, and am really interested in pursuing teaching as a compliment to my practice. I don't think that it is any surprise that there has been such a stylistic shift back to the club in the advent of the global financial turmoil of the past seven years—as club music is a stable economy with relatively low overheads for the artists involved. The life of a touring club artist can be very stressful, but the numbers work when you are a solo performer with a guaranteed weekend audience at a sizable club that sells drinks at a high markup. Many people can get by working within this system; however, the anxiety is always present that you may be dedicating a large portion of your life to a career path that is ultimately trend based, and may eventually reject you. I think it is incredibly important to be honest about these things, particularly to yourself, as everyone in this field ought to have a plan B in their pocket. It's very hard to support yourself while making music. Cities have become increasingly expensive, and opportunities and attention often gravitate towards impenetrably expensive major cultural centers like New York and London. Finding a day job flexible to the necessity of a touring schedule may require making other professional sacrifices, and with there being no long-term financial securities in a career like music it requires a constant hustle. We live in an era of austerity and precarity, and that requires a pragmatism of sorts. I also think that working outside of your niche may help to foster artwork that is more in tune with the world around it. I want to hear more work about people's daily lives. Your personal experience is of great political and cultural importance."[cxxvi]

White Mystery, Rock Duo:

"The cost of making music differs for each artist, but the best way to make a profit is to work hard, look decent, be polite, and live frugal. Working with brands like Levi's and Red Bull allows White Mystery to play shows for bigger audiences and take on creative projects like releasing a double album while remaining a 100% independent band."[cxxvii]

Brenmar, DJ/Producer:

"I come from a remix background. I've been 'playing' the sampler since I was 15. The remix has been a blessing for me, a saving grace even. It has opened doors and given me opportunities I didn't even know were an option. Taking something and making it your own is truly a skill in and of itself, and very much a skill that is part of the 21st century. All that being said, I don't think there's actually too much money to be made from remixes. Maybe if you're Zedd or something the majors will give you a few Gs for an official remix but, all said and told, you have to look a little deeper to find ways to capitalize off of your remixes. If you find yourself with a hot remix that people are playing out then you need to make sure that remix is on Spotify, iTunes, and all official channels of digital music distribution. Upload that baby to YouTube, enable ads and get those streaming pennies because if your remix makes it into the million plays mark (I know a million) you might actually see some real dough. Then try and channel any buzz into some live gigs that's real money in your pocket that month, not six months to a year later as is the case with digital sales/streaming."[cxxviii]

Cindy Mizelle, (Bruce Springsteen, Whitney Houston, Dave Matthews, Alicia Keys, Rolling Stones) has worked with many legendary artists, and contributed her vocal talents to over 120 albums. She has also written songs for other singers, such as Aretha Franklin. She's toured with "The Boss" as part of the "Seeger Sessions Band" and on the "Wrecking Ball Tour," has this to say in regard to rehearsal and touring:

"In recording sessions, it's rare to get material beforehand. You might even be asked about arrangements when you show up. So, I try to research everything about the artist I'm going to work with. I try to find every version of their songs to see how they're different. That way I'm prepared for whatever comes. Tour rehearsals typically last eight hours or more. You read through the lyrics and get a feel for the music and the show. Then, you'll run through the songs, usually 12 or more with alternative arrangements. You might also script moves for different songs. It takes a lot of concentration and energy. I find it helpful to take notes, so I know what I need to do. There are a lot of things that may not be written down, especially with live shows. Knowing things like the vibe of a song, its personality, and how it's going to be presented are important considerations. That's where live rehearsals can get intense. I've worked with a lot of artists who choreograph their shows. You work it out in rehearsal so that the performance is tight, exciting and entertaining. Luther Vandross and Whitney Houston planned every move on stage. That's what professionals do. When you rehearse properly, you become aware of the dynamics each person brings to the mix. You need to be sensitive to the artist you're supporting and know what they need from you. You need to be a team player. That's where rehearsals pay off. There are so many things to deal with on the road, the itinerary, your hotel information, the sound check, the production…all the little details that are part of a tour. You shouldn't have to think about your performance on stage too. It should be automatic, you know it, you live it, you do it. If you've rehearsed enough, you can enjoy the show along with the audience. If you're on top of it, you can see what's out there and often that will elevate your performance."[cxxix]

Briana Lee, (Katy Perry, Elvis Costello, John Legend, Nick Jonas, Thirty Seconds to Mars) has been featured in Disney's "The Little Mermaid Live" and "La La Land Live" in concert at the Hollywood Bowl. Currently, she's expanding into more roles as a vocal arranger, producer, and vocal contractor for television and other media, has this to say in regard to rehearsal and touring:

"The biggest difference between recording sessions and live rehearsals is what's expected of you. I often go in blind to recording sessions. You don't always get material until you're there. But, for live work, you can do research online and see what they've done before. If you don't practice, you won't learn the material. If I'm doing sessions or prepping for a tour, my world revolves around practice and everything else shuts down. I'll lay out the lyrics on the floor and learn the emotional content of each song as well as the music. Most of the time rehearsing for a live show can take anywhere from two days to a few weeks. It depends on the project and how complex the production is. There is also practice involved, working out arrangements and harmonies, which takes up additional time. It really varies. It depends on the artist and the project. Sometimes there are concrete ideas and other times they don't know what they want. Sometimes they ask me for ideas, so you have to be prepared for anything. You would think that a rock act would be less formal and looser. But Jared Leto is very focused. He knows exactly what he wants. He pays attention to every little detail. He knows how he wants the songs to sound, how he wants to present them on stage, and how the overall production should look. He would be a great musical director; he covers all the bases. There are usually very few surprises during rehearsals because everything is planned out. But Elvis is a free spirit when he performs, sometimes leaving you flying by the seat of your pants. He occasionally would play a song we never rehearsed, just because he felt like it. I learned to get familiar with most of his songs, so I wouldn't let him down. When that happens, you roll with it and try your best. A lot of artists choreograph their show in rehearsals. Not so much for dance moves, but just movement in general and where you need to be on stage. Movement is always a big part of a live performance. If there's no plan or organization, it wastes a lot of time. You need to know what you want to do. If people bring problems or disputes into rehearsal, it can affect everyone."[cxxx]

Larry Butler, (Ry Cooder, Randy Newman, Isaac Hayes, U2, Van Halen, ZZ Top) who specializes in live performance and touring. Started at Warner Bros. Records as the in-house tour manager for WB artists, helping them perfect their live shows. That led to a position as Artist Development Director and VP of Artist Relations. He is also the author of *The Singer/Songwriter Rule Book*, has this to say in regard to rehearsal and touring:

"There is a distinction. Practice is learning the material and running through each song step by step. Rehearsal is preparing for a live show. You should do both enough times so you can play and perform without thinking about it. Rehearsal is putting it all together and making a show of it. In fact, Paul Simon said, 'The show is too important not to rehearse.' You need to be organized and have a plan. Remember a live show is visual so you have to incorporate those elements. Know what you want to do and run through it to make it as entertaining as possible. If you have trouble with that, get someone to help you. Everything you do on stage should be scripted. That's what the pros do. Walking around aimlessly does not engage an audience. If you don't want to choreograph your movements well, then welcome to the world of amateurs. If you want total strangers to appreciate your music, play it live to see what works before you spend the time and money to record it. Sometimes magic happens. Most often that occurs because of rehearsal and experience. Everything clicks and works together. But that only happens after you've rehearsed enough and are aware enough to recognize it. If you're not paying attention to the visual aspects of your performance, it's not a rehearsal it's practice. Sometimes artists forget that people are watching them. It's not about simply playing live; it's about putting on an entertaining show. If you're going to videotape rehearsal, look at the camera as if it's the audience. You should also try to use a room with a mirror, so you can watch yourself."[cxxxi]

Top Music Industry Executives on what their Million-Dollar Man artist creation would look like

Mike Cameron, Co-Owner of Water Music Publishing:

"Beyonce. I think that Beyonce had to have a particular work ethic especially in the time she came out, and I think she has never let up. I think every artist has their limitations, but I think Beyonce is a good poster for anyone that wants to make it."

DJ Doughboy, New Jersey DJ/Producer/Writer:

"If I had the perfect artist, it would be Chris Brown without the hood stuff. It would be young Chris Brown without the trouble. I think Chris Brown is incredible. He can sing, he can write, he can dance, he can act, he has an incredible work ethic, this boy is bad."

Troy Patterson, A&R/Manager/Producer:

"If I could be a million-dollar man an artist it would be Stevie Wonder or Michael Jackson. They are two of the most incredible artists of our lifetime. Some of these artists will have close to that and some of them won't. We are talking about long years of career. Stevie's career is almost four or five decades. When you look at these kinds of artists, that's what I want. That's a legacy."

Don Richardson, A&R/Manager/Singer:

"Amazing work ethic, and that's not only with being an artist, but in working out, conditioning, taking care of their body, going to the doctor. You got to be in tune with yourself, with your body and your mind, and work hard. If you do those things and give 100% every day, you're going to get it. It may not be a million dollars. It may be $300,000 in a year, but you're going to make that for the rest of your life."

APPENDIX

Chapter 10   MERCHANDISE

KUNAKI^{cxxxii}
Kunaki will create retail-ready CDs and DVDs for you to sell online. They can also assist with distribution.

MERCHIFY^{cxxxiii}
Merchify offers on-demand printing for clothing, bags and more. Simply create a product, advertise it on Shopify and once it's sold, they'll produce and ship it for you.

BRAVADO^{cxxxiv}
They have a team of designers who can create your merchandise, as well as good relationships with brick-and-mortar companies. They'll get your merchandise in real stores, selling to fans on the street. Bravado is more suited for larger acts but is certainly worth a look.

DIZZYJAM^{cxxxv}
DizzyJam lets you create a free online store, design merchandise and sell it without any stock or payment concerns. They'll create your merchandise, ship it and then send you the profit.

STICKER GUY
They make custom stickers with UV-Cured inks, scratch-proof, and weatherproof vinyl.

VISTAPRINT
Vistaprint can create any type of marketing promotional material you may need. From business cards, picture printing on clothing, posters, logs, labels and much more.

ZAZZLE
Makes custom guitar picks with a variety of designs and logs for all marketing promotion. In addition, Zazzle creates custom printing for clothing, bags, buttons and more.

MERCH.LY

Merch.ly has the professional services and quality products you need to make custom apparel at a reasonable price. Whether it's shirts, hats, or some of the smaller items, Merch.ly will assist with any and all of your custom apparel needs.

CRAVEDOG

Cravedog offers a wide variety of services; from replicating CDs, DVDs and Blue-ray to pressing Vinyl to Apparel and Promotional Merchandise.

Chapter 11   MUSIC PUBLISHING

BERNE CONVENTION[cxxxvi]

- Signed in 1886. Ratified by nearly 180 countries.
- Establishes minimum standards of protection.
  - Types of works protected.
  - Duration of protection.
  - Scope of exceptions.
  - Limitations.
  - Principles such as "national treatment" (works originating in one signatory country are given the same protection in the other signatory countries as each grant to works of its own nationals).
  - Principles such as "automatic protection" (copyright inheres automatically in a qualifying work upon its fixation in a tangible medium and without any required prior formality).

WIPO COPYRIGHT TREATY[cxxxvii]

- Signed in 1996.
- Makes clear that computer programs and databases are protected by copyright.
- Recognizes that the transmission of works over the Internet and similar networks is an exclusive right within the scope of copyright, originally held by the creator.
- Categorizes as copyright infringements both:
  - The circumvention of technological protection measures attached to works.

- The removal from a work of embedded rights management information.

THE AGREEMENT ON TRADE RELATED ASPECTS OF INTELLECTUAL PROPERTY RIGHTS (TRIPS)[cxxxviii]

- Signed in 1996.
- Administered by the World Trade Organization.
- Includes a number of provisions related to the enforcement of IP rights.
- Says that national laws have to make the effective enforcement of IP rights possible and describes in detail how enforcement should be addressed.

SINGLE SONG AGREEMENT[cxxxix]

This is an agreement between a writer and a music publisher where the writer grants specific rights for one or more songs to the publisher, for a one-time recoupable advance payment by the publisher. The publisher will handle the business aspects of the work and pay royalties to the songwriter. With the exception of print music, the songwriter usually gets a 50% share of the money collected by the publisher. Be careful that the deal does not state a share drawn from a limited list of specified publishers' receipts, like mechanical, synchronization and transcription. This could mean that the publisher can collect from income streams outside of this limited list. A list is ok but end it with a statement like "and all other monies not referred to by this agreement." Ensure that the contract explicitly states that you get a share of publishers' advances and guarantees are specifically for your compositions.

EXCLUSIVE SONGWRITER AGREEMENT (ESWA)[cxl]

The ESWA is a contract normally for staff writers where the song writer grants the entire publisher's share of the income to the music publisher. Any compositions written within a time period specified in the contract belong exclusively to the music publisher. EWSA deals are normally offered to writers with a track record of writing hits, making the publisher feel confident that they will recoup their investment in the writer. The writer negotiates a deal with the publisher for an advance based on future royalties, for all or some of the writer's songs. In exchange, the writer grants exclusive rights to those songs to the publisher. The writer is normally paid on a weekly or quarterly basis. An ESWA can be tied to, or independent of, a record contract.

CO-PUBLISHING AGREEMENT (CO-PUB)[cxli]

The co-publishing deal is the most common form of publishing agreement where the songwriter and the music publisher co-own the copyrights of musical compositions governed by the agreement. A split of the royalties is agreed where the song writer assigns a percentage to the publisher. The split is normally 50/50 with the writer assigning the publisher's share to the publisher and retaining all the writer's share. In a 75/25 co-pub deal the writer keeps 100% of the songwriter's share, and 50% of the publisher's share, which is 75% of the entire copyrights, the remaining 25% is assigned to the publisher. The Net Publishers Share (everything received by the publisher, meaning both the share of income allocated to the publisher and the writer) is gross income and is divided up:

- Administration Fee
- Songwriter royalties
- Expenses

Administration fees, usually between 10% and 20%, are intended to cover indirect expenses such as rent, utilities, staffing costs etc. In reality, this is just a bargaining chip. Expenses are direct costs, specifically related to the song, including copyright registration fees, demo recording costs, collection costs, and lead sheets. Who administers the deal is important, because with only one copyright owner it may be obvious, but when copyright ownership is shared the exact roles and responsibilities need to be defined? The same is true when there are any restrictions placed upon administration, or exceptions. In a true co-administration co-publishing deal, a license is required by both owners in order to use the song. Exceptions can be applied to co-administration co-publishing deals where certain types of licenses can be granted by only one administrator. For example, a recording artist who is likely to have recording contract obligations regarding mechanical licenses, promotional videos etc. usually have exceptions including:

- Controlled Compositions (governed by another deal).
- Statutory Rate Licenses (A large subject that can hide a multitude of sins and overall worth objecting too).
- Print (Exclusivity to print the music by one party or the other).

The co-publishing deals include "duration of rights," meaning eventually the songwriter will get the entirety of their rights back. It might take a while though as the duration of rights is set up on a case-by-case basis, ranging from 2 years to 20 and more. The co-publishing deals are a lot like traditional full-publishing. Publishers will provide an advance (recouped by the songwriter's share until made whole) and actively work the writer's career, (pitching the compositions, maximizing sync opportunities, financing the recording of demo material, scheduling the songwriter to write for prominent recording artists), or the songwriters will commit to the minimum number of songs deliverable under the contract duration. For both co-pub and full-pub deals, the sync fees splits will be defined on a case-by-case basis.

ADMINISTRATION AGREEMENT (Admin)[cxlii]

The administration agreement is an agreement between a songwriter/publisher and an independent administrator, or between a songwriter/publisher and another music publisher. An admin agreement is used when the songwriter self-publishes their work and licenses songs to the music publisher for a fixed term at an agreed split of royalties in a specified territory. The music publisher/independent administrator administers and exploits the copyrights for the copyright owner, be that the songwriter or a separate publisher. Exploitation functions typically include accountant or business manager roles. Admin deals tend to be reserved for only the most popular songwriters, where ownership of the copyright is usually not transferred to the administrator. For example, Jake Gosling and Max Martin don't need the publisher to promote their compositions, they're already big enough to get the representation they need from their publishing. However, they need someone to register their work with all the CMOs around the globe, audit and claim their royalties, look over countless syncs, and many other aspects. The triple-A songwriters usually go for administration deals, keeping full control over their music, while maximizing the incoming royalties. The licensed music publisher gets approximately 10-20% of the gross royalties from the agreed territory during the agreed time period, usually longer than the co-publishing one, stretching up to five years. Admin deals are also used when songwriters are signed to different publishers, or songwriters who do their own publishing or have co-written a piece of work. The same goes for the artists that write music for themselves, focusing entirely on the recording side of the business. If the only person you're writing for is yourself, there's no point in getting a full-blown publishing representation. That is precisely why most of the distribution aggregators, like TuneCore and CDBaby, offer publishing administration deals in addition to distributing their music to the likes of Spotify.

Chapter 14 UNDERSTANDING AND SIGNING YOUR CONTRACT

SPLIT SHEET

An agreement that identifies the ownership percentage each producer and songwriter have in the song. It also includes other information such as each person's specific contribution (lyrics, hook, melody, beats, etc.) and publisher information, as well as if different versions of the song were created. This information will serve as written evidence of copyright ownership and will assure any third parties such as your PRO or a potential publisher that there is no dispute about royalty distribution.

MASTER-USE LICENSE[cxliii]

A master-use license permits the licensee to use a copyrighted sound recording on a new project. Typically, licensees are seeking to use recordings in audiovisual projects, as a sample in a new audio recording, or for distribution. By obtaining a master-use license, the only rights being granted are to the sound recording. This means that any copyrighted composition embodied in the recording must be licensed separately.

PERFORMANCE LICENSE[cxliv]

An agreement, usually between a performing rights organization (PRO) and a music user in the form of a blanket license, allowing the licensee to publicly perform a composition in exchange for a payment.

PRO AFFILIATION[cxlv]

This is the deal that the songwriter signs when they become a member of a PRO. The agreement lasts for a specified amount of time and is exclusive, meaning the writer cannot be signed with more than one PRO at a time.

BOOKING/PERFORMANCE DEAL[cxlvi]

This is the agreement entered into by a concert promoter or venue and an artist or the artist's agent. The artist agent typically has power of attorney, meaning that they can sign the deal that binds the artist to playing at the venue at the specified date and time.

FOREIGN SUB-PUBLISHING AGREEMENT

The foreign sub-publishing agreement is similar to an administration agreement. The only difference is that the publisher is contracting with another publisher in a foreign country to represent its catalogue in that territory. For example, if a US publisher wants to have a publisher in England represent its catalog in the United Kingdom, or if a publisher in France wants its catalog represented in the United States by an American publisher, the agreement is referred to as a sub-publishing agreement. As with the administration agreement, representation is limited to a specified duration (usually not less than three years), and the fees retained by the foreign sub-publisher for its services are negotiable within certain limits.

OFFER[cxlvii]

This is the promise to do something in exchange for something else. Importantly, the offeror must make the offer with the intent that the contract will be a binding agreement if signed. For example, record labels offer artists contracts to record a certain amount of music for a certain amount of time in exchange for an advance and royalties, as well as marketing and promotion.

ACCEPTANCE[cxlviii]

A party can accept an offer by assenting, with intent, to do so. This means that they must make a concrete action to accept, and they must be fully aware of the offer at hand. Acceptance can take many forms: signatures, verbal affirmations, and handshakes can all be valid. It's the most prudent, however, to have any formal agreement memorialized in writing. Note: Email chains can be legally binding offers and acceptances of agreements if the language shows as much.

CONSIDERATION[cxlix]

What each party brings to the table in an agreement must be something of value, and this piece is called the consideration. It can be money, or it can be the simple promise to do (or not do) something. For example, a homeowner could contract with a landscaper to have their lawn mowed once per month in exchange for a sum of money. Conversely, a programmer at a tech company could sign a non-compete contract with their current employer, agreeing not to leave to work for a competitor within a certain time frame.

CAPACITY[cl]

The parties to the agreement must have the capacity to enter into it. For example, a minor under the age of 18 or 21 (depending on the laws governing the contract) may void any contract into which they enter because they are seen in the eyes of the law to be unable to make a rational legal agreement in some scenarios.

INTERPRETATION[cli]

Sometimes the terms of a contract can be ambiguous. In general, courts try to discover the intent behind the agreement. Courts try as much as possible to adhere to what the contract actually says, as opposed to bringing in outside evidence. This is called the four corners principle (named for the four corners of a piece of paper).

DEFINITIONS[clii]

Since contracts are generally interpreted in themselves with as little regard to outside evidence as possible, the definitions of terms within the agreement are important. Many contracts contain a "Definitions" section, which explicitly states what significant words mean with respect to the agreement. Other times, however, terms are simply defined within the flow of the writing or left undefined. It is important to take note of any concrete definitions or ambiguities in any contract.

BREACH[cliii]

When a party fails to fulfill all promises made in an agreement, a breach of contract occurs. Courts may find evidence of either partial or full breaches, depending on the circumstances and terms of the contract.

ASSIGNMENT OF RIGHTS[cliv]

It's the assignment of copyright of music from the writer or singer to the music publisher. If the copyright is infringed, the publisher can take legal action against the writer or singer.

RIGHTS TO RETURN COPYRIGHT[clv]

This is the most complex term of the contract, which abides by the publisher to give back the copyright in case of commercial failure after a certain period of time.

ADVANCE, ROYALTIES, RECOUP[clvi]

It will set the royalty rate, the quantum of any advances, and the definition of royalty base.

JURISDICTION[clvii]

This clause recites the law that governs the contract.

TERRITORY[clviii]

The territory of a contract refers to the legal jurisdictions where the provisions of the contract can apply. In the case of licensing agreements, the territory can apply to the geographic areas where the licensing will be done. For example, a singer-songwriter could have a digital distribution agreement with a record label covering the entire world, and also have an affiliation with SoundExchange solely covering the United States.

GRANT OF RIGHTS[clix]

In any license agreement (master, mechanical performance, synch, etc), the grant of rights clause enables the licensee to use a copyrighted work in some capacity. Under copyright law, any of the six exclusive rights in a copyrighted work may be owned and licensed separately. For example, a PRO may have the exclusive right to perform a work while a distributor may have the exclusive right to distribute it. This is separate from a transfer of ownership in a copyright. An assignment or transfer of copyright involves the author offering up ownership (and all the exclusive rights entailed) to another entity. A licensing deal (i.e., PRO affiliation) is not the same as transferring ownership in perpetuity (i.e., selling a catalogue to a music publisher). This is a critical component to look for in any clause detailing the grant or licensing of copyrights.

TERMINATION RIGHTS[clx]

Under the Copyright Act of 1976, authors of copyrighted works may end outside ownership in their works and have their copyrights reverted to them after 35 years. Termination rights, however, are subject to many conditions and notification must be given well in advance.

CONTROLLED COMPOSITION[clxi]

A controlled composition clause affects the mechanical royalties paid on a composition that is written or co-written by the recording artist. The controlled composition clause in a recording contract places a limit on how much the label is required to pay for songs in which the artist is also the songwriter. Only parties that agree to this stipulation are subject to it. For example, if an artist-writer co-writes a song, the other writers would not be bound to the same clause unless the co-writers explicitly agreed to such.

SECONDARY INCOME[clxii]

A well-negotiated deal will ensure that the artist is entitled to a 50/50 share of any secondary income earned by the label. This could be in the form of advances paid by overseas labels licensing your record, income from compilations, or sync fees that are paid when a sound recording is used in a film or TV commercial or on a computer game.

LEAVING MEMBERS[clxiii]

With a group signed to a label, usually the company will reserve the right to end the contract should a key member of the band leave. The label may also try to obtain a clause allowing them to sign any leaving member as a solo artist and if the group break up before releasing a record, but after spending their advance, they'll probably be sued for breach of contract and return of the monies they've received. Care should be taken not to allow the label to recoup advances paid to leaving members for solo releases against the remaining members' royalties.

RE-RECORDING RESTRICTIONS[clxiv]

This prevents the artist from re-recording their music on another label for a certain number of years following expiry of the contract. Any restriction you agree to should apply for a maximum of five years following the end of the contract and should only ever cover records released.

RESERVE LIMITS[clxv]

The reserve limits exist because retailers insist upon being able to return products they can't sell. The labels shift that risk to the artist by withholding a portion of royalty payments until they can verify the product shipped has been sold. This means the label will set aside a certain amount of money that they will have the right to keep in the event retail stores are unable to sell all of your albums. They use this as an insurance buffer, because the label will have to buy back these unsold albums from the stores and this buyback will be taken out of your profits.

FLAT FEE[clxvi]

A single payment used to buy an artist's ownership or revenue rights on a record. This is either done by considering the record a work for hire, or by a transfer of ownership. In either case, the label does not need to pay any future royalties. This is common practice for remixes, where the labels are owners of the original records and the remixes are technically derivative works. Flat fees $500+ for remixes of small electronic artists to $10,000's for ghost productions.

ACCOUNTING CLAUSE[clxvii]

This relates to the frequency and speed with which the label provides royalty statements and makes payments. Most labels will account twice a year, at the end of June and December, with a 90-day term. Ideally, you want monthly accounting. However, the frequency with which a label can account is tied to the speed of its distribution company. When dealing with majors,

THE BLUEPRINT

ask for a quarterly accounting with a 45-day term to provide statements. With indies, inquire about the speed with which their distributor pays and push for monthly if possible. You will want to add language that relates to the speed with processing of received invoices. Many majors intentionally leave out any language that commits them to paying any invoices within a certain period. Good phrasing is like 'label will make any monies owed to the artist payable within 30 days upon receipt of a valid invoice, to be sent to email@email.com or postal address as specified above'.

AUDITING CLAUSE[clxviii]

Gives the artist the right to check whether the label has paid out the right amount of money and isn't holding anything back. Auditing clauses allow for an audit by a registered accountant of the artist's choice once a year where the difference is paid back and if bigger than 10% the label covers the full costs of the audit. Many major management companies and publishers send over accountants to labels yearly, without it being considered an insult to the audited party.

RIGHTS OF ASSIGNMENT[clxix]

Means the ability for each of the parties to transfer the rights granted in the record deal to another party. Usually, the label will ask to have the right of assignment to subsidiaries, which is ok, if the label guarantees to uphold the terms of the record deal and maintain the best interests of the artist. Also, the agreement should cover incidents such as the label going bankrupt or either of the parties breaching the contract. Language should be added that whenever a party is in breach, the other party has to notify the other, imposing a 30-to-60-day cure period within which the breach may be fixed. In cases of bankruptcy or termination through a non-cured breach, the artist should have all rights returned within the fullest extent possible (respecting licenses that have already occurred, and such). This can be difficult when a label has already granted licenses to others (such as rights to distribute, to include on compilations or syncs to TV), which will then still be valid even if the rights transfer back to you.

203

WORK CITED

"13 Different Places To Submit Your Music!" *Cymatics.fm*, cymatics.fm/blogs/production/13-places-to-submit-your-music.

"16 LinkedIn Statistics That Matter to Marketers in 2019." *Hootsuite*, 22 June 2020, blog.hootsuite.com/linkedin-statistics-business/.

26/11/19, Open Mic UK |. "Recording Contracts: Different Types of Deals Explained Bad 360 Deals." *Open Mic UK*, www.openmicuk.co.uk/advice/recording-contracts-explained/.

"5 Rules for Meeting with A&R." *StudioPros*, studiopros.com/5-rules-for-meeting-with-ar/.

"50 Incredible Instagram Statistics You Need to Know." *Brandwatch*, www.brandwatch.com/blog/instagram-stats/#:~:text=Instagram user statistics,has 1bn monthly active users.&text=Over 60% of users log,aged between 18 and 24.

"60 Incredible and Interesting Twitter Stats and Statistics." *Brandwatch*, www.brandwatch.com/blog/twitter-stats-and-statistics/#:~:text=Twitter user statistics,users write 80% of tweets.

"7 Key Members of Every Artist's Team." *AWAL*, www.awal.com/blog/7-important-members-to-every-artists-team.

"A Guide To Music Merchandise: Rotor Videos ." *Rotor Videos*, rotorvideos.com/blog/finance-creativity-with-music-merchandise.

Aboulhosn, Sarah. "18 Facebook Statistics Every Marketer Should Know in 2020." *Sprout Social*, 17 Aug. 2020, sproutsocial.com/insights/facebook-stats-for-marketers/.

"Advantages to Working with a Record Label." *Funktasy*, 16 Mar. 2020, www.funktasy.com/advantages-working-record-label/.

Barnhart, Brent. "How to Rise Above Social Media Algorithms." *Sprout Social*, 26 Mar. 2020, sproutsocial.com/insights/social-media-algorithms/.

Baur, Bernard. "Rehearse... Don't Regret! Make The Most of Your Rehearsal Time." *Music Connection Magazine*, 27 Aug. 2018, www.musicconnection.com/rehearse-dont-forget/.

"Best Music Streaming Services for Indie Artists: Rotor Videos ." *Rotor Videos*, rotorvideos.com/blog/best-music-streaming-sites-promote-your-tracks.

bradfordswanson Follow. "Subjective Comparison of Vocal Microphones." *SlideShare*, 14 Nov. 2012, www.slideshare.net/bradfordswanson/an-online-resource-for-the-subjective-comparison-of-vocal-microphones-for-slideshare.

Budi Voogt April 12th, et al. "The Truth About Record Deals (And How To Negotiate Them)." *Heroic Academy*, 12 Apr. 2018, heroic.academy/truth-about-record-deals/.

Budi Voogt December 31st, et al. "The Unconventional Guide to Getting Signed by a Record Label." *Heroic Academy*, 31 Dec. 2019, heroic.academy/unconventional-guide-getting-signed-record-label/.

Carmicheal, Kayla. "Paid Social Media: Worth The Investment?" *HubSpot Blog*, blog.hubspot.com/marketing/paid-social-media#:~:text=Paid social media is a,examples of paid social media.

Cyberpr. "3 Social Media Music Marketing Essentials." *Cyber PR Music*, 15 May 2019, www.cyberprmusic.com/social-media-music-marketing/.

"Digital Marketing 101: How To Promote and Market Your Music Online." *TuneCore*, www.tunecore.com/guides/digital-marketing-for-musicians-101.

Evans, Luke. "Music Industry Contracts." *Exploration*, Exploration, 18 Apr. 2019, exploration.io/music-industry-contracts/.

Fitzjohn, Sean, et al. "The Vocal EQ Chart (Vocal Frequency Ranges EQ Tips)." *Producer Hive*, 24 July 2020, producerhive.com/music-production-recording-tips/how-to-use-a-vocal-eq-chart/.

Gardner, Barry. "The Ultimate Vocal Recording Tutorial." *Music & Audio Envato Tuts* , Envato Tuts, 8 May 2013, music.tutsplus.com/tutorials/the-ultimate-vocal-recording-tutorial--audio-17783.

Goldstein, Alice. "10 Essential Tips For a Long and Lucrative Music Career." *Entrepreneur*, 16 June 2017, www.entrepreneur.com/article/295461.

Goldmacher, Cliff. "The Pros & Cons of Signing a Publishing Deal." *BMI.com*. N.p., 25 May 2010. Web. 01 Sept. 2020.

Guest Post on 07/10/2019 in D.I.Y. | Permalink | Comments (0). "Mastering Your Merch: Music Merchandise Strategies." *Hypebot*, 10 July 2019, www.hypebot.com/hypebot/2019/07/mastering-your-merch-music-merchandise-basics.html.

Haskins, Jane. "How to Copyright a Song." *Legalzoom*, 21 Aug. 2020, www.legalzoom.com/articles/how-to-copyright-a-song.

Hess, Patrick. "A Guide for Touring in the Music Industry." *HuffPost*, HuffPost, 7 Dec. 2017, www.huffpost.com/entry/a-guide-for-touring-in-th_b_5644842.

Hooke Audio. "How to Pick A Microphone For a Podcast." *Hooke Audio*, 3 June 2019, hookeaudio.com/blog/podcasting/how-to-pick-a-microphone-for-a-podcast/.

"How Music Publishing Works: Music Publishing Administration 101." *TuneCore*, www.tunecore.com/guides/music-publishing-101.

"How To Balance All The Elements In A Mix." *Mastering The Mix*, 3 Mar. 2020, www.masteringthemix.com/blogs/learn/how-to-balance-all-the-elements-in-a-mix.

"How To Balance All The Elements In A Mix." *Mastering The Mix*, 3 Mar. 2020, www.masteringthemix.com/blogs/learn/how-to-balance-all-the-elements-in-a-mix.

"How to Get Your Music in 150 Digital Stores Worldwide." *TuneCore*, www.tunecore.com/digital-music-stores.

"How to Promote Your Music: The Essential Guide." *LANDR Blog*, 21 Feb. 2020, blog.landr.com/how-to-promote-your-music/.

Ingvaldsen, Torsten. "Drake's Decade-Long No. 1 Streak Ends With 'Dark Lane Demo Tapes'." *HYPEBEAST*, HYPEBEAST, 11 May 2020, hypebeast.com/2020/5/drake-dark-lane-demo-tapes-billboard-200-chart-debut-no-2.

IV, G.W. Childs. "5 Rehearsal Tips For Better Live Gigs." *Ask.Audio*, Ask.Audio, 18 Apr. 2017, ask.audio/articles/5-rehearsal-tips-for-better-live-gigs.

Jamie, et al. "Creating a Winning Team to Support Your Artist or Band." *SmartistU*, 13 Nov. 2018, smartistu.com/creating-a-winning-team-to-support-your-artist-or-band.

Kaminsky, Michelle. "8 Basic Facts Every Musician Should Know About Copyright Law." *Legalzoom*, 4 Aug. 2020, www.legalzoom.com/articles/8-basic-facts-every-musician-should-know-about-copyright-law.

Katz, Frances. "Music Publishing Tips: Split Sheets and Lyric Sheets." *SongTrust*, blog.songtrust.com/understanding-split-sheets-and-lyric-sheets.

Keerthy NarayananFollowMixing and Mastering Engineer at HomeGrown MixesMusic Arranger on the Grammy Winning Album Winds of Samsara et al. "Why Most Musicians Fail To Grow, Expand & Sustain A Successful Career In Music Over The Long Term." *LinkedIn*, www.linkedin.com/pulse/why-most-musicians-fail-grow-expand-sustain-career-music-narayan/.

Kusek, Dave. "The Musician's Essential Guide to Merch: What to Get, How Much to Charge, and Where to Buy." *Sonicbids Blog - Music Career Advice and Gigs*, blog.sonicbids.com/the-musicians-essential-merch-guide-what-to-get-how-much-to-charge-where-to-buy.

Legaspi, Althea. "Blurred Lines' Copyright Suit Against Robin Thicke, Pharrell Ends in $5M Judgment." *Rolling Stone*, Rolling Stone, 13 Dec. 2018, www.rollingstone.com/music/music-news/robin-thicke-pharrell-williams-blurred-lines-copyright-suit-final-5-million-dollar-judgment-768508/.

Lent, Jordan. "The 10 Best Cheap Studio Monitors Under $200 Budget [year]." *Consordini.com*. 15 May 2020. Web.

Lombardi/, Posted By : Dan. "Should I Build A Home Studio Or Pay For Studio Time To Record?" *5PiECE Music*, 26 Jan. 2019, www.5piecemusic.com/build-home-studio-pay-studio-time-record/.

Majewski, Greg, et al. "What Is Music Mastering and Why Do I Need It?" *DIY Musician Blog*, 13 July 2020, diymusician.cdbaby.com/musician-tips/what-is-music-mastering/.

Majewski, Greg, et al. "Here's Why You Need a Professional Mixing Engineer." *DIY Musician Blog*, 13 July 2020, diymusician.cdbaby.com/musician-tips/4-reasons-you-should-hire-a-professional-mixing-engineer/.

Majewski, Greg, et al. "Building a Great Team to Support Your Music Career." *DIY Musician Blog*, 13 July 2020, diymusician.cdbaby.com/musician-tips/building-a-great-team-to-support-your-music-career/.

"Major Label Contract Clause Critique | Future of Music Coalition." *Future of Music Coalition*, Future of Music Coalition, futureofmusic.org/article/article/major-label-contract-clause-critique.

McDonald, Heather. "360 Deals in the Music and the Associated Controversy." *The Balance Careers*, www.thebalancecareers.com/how-360-deals-in-the-music-industry-work-2460343.

McDonald, Heather. "Why Record Labels Have Such Tremendous Influence on the Music Industry." *The Balance Careers*, www.thebalancecareers.com/what-is-a-record-label-2460614.

McGuire, Patrick. "7 Top Marketing Strategies for Musicians." *Bandzoogle Blog*, Bandzoogle, 26 Aug. 2020, bandzoogle.com/blog/7-top-marketing-strategies-for-musicians.

"Mixing Vocals : The Ultimate Guide to EQ'ing Vocals." *Behind The Mixer*, 19 May 2018, www.behindthemixer.com/mixing-vocals-the-ultimate-guide-to-eqing-vocals/.

"Mixing Your Music: The Easy Guide to Sounding Like a Pro." *LANDR*, www.landr.com/how-to-mix.

Moorwood, Victoria. "Juice WRLD Hit with $15 Million Copyright Infringement Lawsuit over 'Lucid Dreams.'" *REVOLT*, REVOLT, 22 Oct. 2019, www.revolt.tv/2019/10/22/20926678/juice-wrld-lucid-dreams-lawsuit.

Muller, Marissa G. "10 Ways To Fund Your Music Career." *The FADER*, The FADER, 7 Nov. 2017, www.thefader.com/2015/02/03/10-ways-to-fund-your-music-career.

Music Gateway. "ASCAP vs BMI vs SESAC - How To Get Your Royalties." *Music Gateway*, 22 Aug. 2019, www.musicgateway.com/blog/how-to/ascap-vs-bmi-vs-sesac.

Music Gateway. "DIY Touring: Your Guide To Making A Music Tour Happen." *Music Gateway*, 22 Aug. 2019, www.musicgateway.com/blog/how-to/diy-touring-guide-to-making-music-tour-happen.

"Music Industry Contracts: All You Should Know." *Simple Music Contracts*, www.simplemusiccontracts.com/contracts.

"Music Publishing-101." *CD Baby*. N.p., n.d. Web.
"Music Production 101: The 4 Basic Steps to Recording a Song." *Ehomerecordingstudio*, 1 Oct. 2018, ehomerecordingstudio.com/how-to-record-a-song/.

Newartistmodel. "How to Promote Your Music & Grow Your Fanbase." *New Artist Model*, Newartistmodel Http://Newartistmodel.com/Wp-Content/Uploads/2013/12/logo_transparent.Png, 15 Aug. 2020, newartistmodel.com/promote-your-music/.

Newartistmodel. "Build a Team for Music Success." *New Artist Model*, Newartistmodel Http://Newartistmodel.com/Wp-Content/Uploads/2013/12/logo_transparent.Png, 14 Jan. 2020, newartistmodel.com/build-team-music-success/.

Post, Guest. "Best Cheap Microphones for Musicians on a Budget: 2020 Reviews." *Acoustic Bridge*, 24 July 2020, acousticbridge.com/best-cheap-microphones/.

"Production Rehearsal." *Bobby Owsinski's Music Production Blog*, 24 Oct. 2019, bobbyowsinskiblog.com/2019/11/06/production-rehearsal/professional.

Rob MayzesAudio. "The 3 Key Phases for Recording Vocals Like a Pro." *Musician on a Mission*, 30 May 2020, www.musicianonamission.com/recording-vocals-how-to-record-vocals/professional.

Rob MayzesAudio. "Vocal Compression: Learn How to Mix Like the Pros." *Musician on a Mission*, 9 June 2020, www.musicianonamission.com/vocal-compression-how-to-compress-vocals/

"Q. Do I Need to Use Professional Mastering?" *Soundonsound*, 1 Sept. 2020, www.soundonsound.com/sound-advice/q-do-i-need-use-professional-mastering.

Smith, Craig, et al. "15 Interesting Tidal Statistics and Facts." *Expandedramblings*, 11 July 2020, expandedramblings.com/index.php/tidal-statistics/.

Smith, Craig, et al. "20 Amazing IHeartRadio Statistics." *DMR*, 11 July 2020, expandedramblings.com/index.php/iheartradio-statistics/.

Songstuff. "Music Publishing Contracts." *Songstuff*, 7 Apr. 2016, www.songstuff.com/music-business/article/music_publishing_contracts/.

"Songwriter and Music Publisher Agreements." *Www.ascap.com*, www.ascap.com/help/music-business-101/200809.

"Spotify Usage and Revenue Statistics (2020)." *Business of Apps*, 30 July 2020, www.businessofapps.com/data/spotify-statistics/.

Staff, ForTunes. "5 Hard Facts about Your A&R Meetings." *ForTunes Blog*, 21 July 2020, blog.fortunes.io/5-hard-facts-about-your-ar-meeting/.

"Submit Music To A&R's: 7 Key Tips." *Omari MC*, www.omarimc.com/submit-music-to-ars-7-key-tips/.

"The 9 Home Recording Studio Essentials for Beginners." *Ehomerecordingstudio*, 1 Feb. 2019, ehomerecordingstudio.com/home-recording-studio-essentials/.

The Do's and Don'ts of Music Merchandising – News – Spotify for Artists, artists.spotify.com/blog/the-dos-and-donts-of-music-merchandising.

The Harry Fox Agency, www.harryfox.com/#/faq.

Thomas Sontag is A&R at Turbo Recordings and Multi Culti. "Demo Submission: How to Send Music to Record Labels." *LANDR Blog*, 13 Mar. 2020, blog.landr.com/dos-and-donts-of-demo-submission-how-to-get-your/.

Thorne, Desi. "Music Licensing 101: What Is a Performing Rights Organization?" *Bandzoogle Blog*, Bandzoogle, 13 Feb. 2019, bandzoogle.com/blog/music-licensing-101-what-is-a-performing-rights-organization.

Ucaya. "Market Intelligence for the Music Industry." *Soundcharts*, soundcharts.com/blog/music-distribution.

Ucaya. "Market Intelligence for the Music Industry." *Soundcharts*, soundcharts.com/blog/how-the-music-publishing-works.

Ucaya. "Market Intelligence for the Music Industry." *Soundcharts*, soundcharts.com/blog/mechanics-of-touring.

Watson, Amy. "Topic: Pandora." *Statista*, www.statista.com/topics/1349/pandora/#:~:text=Pandora is America's leading online,million U.S. dollars from subscriptions.

Watson, Amy. "IHeartRadio Listenership per Week in the U.S. 2019." *Statista*, 3 Dec. 2019, www.statista.com/statistics/294635/iheartradio-listenership-in-the-us/#:~:text=In 2019, eight percent of,publishers in the United States.

"What Is Global Copyright? International Copyright Basics." *RightsDirect*, www.rightsdirect.com/international-copyright-basics/.

"What to Expect in a Label Meeting." *Spinnup*, 11 Apr. 2020, spinnup.com/uc/blog/what-to-expect-in-a-label-meeting/#:~:text=Take your music on USB,than wonderful for showcasing music.

White, Paul. "Vocal Recording & Production Masterclass." *Soundonsound*, 1 Sept. 2020, www.soundonsound.com/techniques/vocal-recording-production-masterclass.

"YouTube Revenue and Usage Statistics (2020)." *Business of Apps*, 28 Aug. 2020, www.businessofapps.com/data/youtube-statistics/.

Perez, Sarah. "TikTok Announces a Deal with UnitedMasters, Its First Music Distribution Partnership." *TechCrunch*, TechCrunch, 17 Aug. 2020, techcrunch.com/2020/08/17/tiktok-announces-a-deal-with-unitedmasters-its-first-music-distribution-partnership/.

Perez, Sarah. "TikTok Strikes New Licensing Agreement with Sony Music." *TechCrunch*, TechCrunch, 2 Nov. 2020, techcrunch.com/2020/11/02/tiktok-strikes-new-licensing-agreement-with-sony-music/.

Harris, Josh, and Sam Haveson. "Fleets: a New Way to Join the Conversation." Twitter, Twitter, 17 Nov. 2020, blog.twitter.com/en_us/topics/product/2020/introducing-fleets-new-way-to-join-the-conversation.html.

Herman, Jenn. "Instagram Reels: What Marketers Need to Know." Social Media Examiner | Social Media Marketing, 24 Nov. 2020, www.socialmediaexaminer.com/instagram-reels-what-marketers-need-to-know/.

Schrodt, Paul. "The 10 Biggest Record Deals of All Time, Ranked." Business Insider, Business Insider, 24 May 2016, www.businessinsider.com/biggest-record-deals-2016-5#9-whitney-houston--100-million-2001-2.

"ATH-M20x." *Audio*, www.audio-technica.com/en-us/ath-m20x.

"Bluebird SL." *Blue*, www.bluemic.com/en-us/products/bluebird-sl/.

"K240 STUDIO." *Professional Studio Headphones*, www.akg.com/Headphones/Professional%20Headphones/K240-Studio.html.

"NT1-A 1' Cardioid Condenser Microphone." *RØDE Microphones*, www.rode.com/microphones/nt1-a.

"The X1 S." *SE Electronics*, www.seelectronics.com/se-x1s-microphone.

ASMGPublishing. "Payment Plan." *Tumblr*, asmgpublishing.com/management.

Budi Voogt April 12th, et al. "The Truth About Record Deals (And How To Negotiate Them)." *Heroic Academy*, 12 Apr. 2018, heroic.academy/truth-about-record-deals/.

Evans, Luke. "Music Industry Contracts." *Exploration*, Exploration, 5 Apr. 2021, exploration.io/music-industry-contracts/.

"EXCLUSIVE MANAGEMENT AGREEMENT." *Law Insider*, www.lawinsider.com/contracts/fXoxRrDkout.

"Finance-Creativity-with-Music-Merchandise." *Rotorvideos*, rotorvideos.com/blog/finance-creativity-with-music-merchandise.

"Future of Music Coalition." *Major Label Contract Clause Critique | Future of Music Coalition*, futureofmusic.org/article/article/major-label-contract-clause-critique.

Hess, Patrick. "A Guide for Touring in the Music Industry." *HuffPost*, HuffPost, 7 Dec. 2017, www.huffpost.com/entry/a-guide-for-touring-in-th_b_5644842.

"Music-Industry-Contracts." *Doitemedia*, doitemedia.com/2021/05/15/music-industry-contracts/.

Songstuff. "Music Publishing Contracts." *Songstuff*, 7 Apr. 2016, www.songstuff.com/music-business/article/music_publishing_contracts/.

"What Is Global Copyright? International Copyright Basics." *RightsDirect*, 23 Dec. 2020, www.rightsdirect.com/international-copyright-basics/.

"30 Days of Free Uploads to Spotify." *Get Your Music to Millions of Listeners*, www.recordunion.com/.

ASMGPublishing. "Payment Plan." *Tumblr*, asmgpublishing.com/management.

aswad, jem. "TikTok Strikes Licensing Deal With Sony Music Entertainment." *Yahoo!*, Yahoo!, www.yahoo.com/entertainment/tiktok-strikes-licensing-deal-sony-161423808.html.

Baur, Bernard. "Rehearse... Don't Regret! Make The Most of Your Rehearsal Time." *Music Connection Magazine*, 27 Aug. 2018, www.musicconnection.com/rehearse-dont-forget/.

"Best Music Streaming Services for Indie Artists: Rotor Videos 🎬." *Rotor Videos*, rotorvideos.com/blog/best-music-streaming-sites-promote-your-tracks.

"Bluebird SL." *Blue*, www.bluemic.com/en-us/products/bluebird-sl/.

bridge, acoustic. "Best Cheap Microphones for Musicians on a Budget: 2020 Reviews." *Acoustic Bridge*, 2021, acousticbridge.com/best-cheap-microphones/#:~:text=Condenser%20microphones%20create%20sound%20with,and%20the%20backplate%20stays%20still.&text=Condenser%20mics%20need%20a%20power,batteries.

Budi Voogt April 12th, et al. "The Truth About Record Deals (And How To Negotiate Them)." *Heroic Academy*, 12 Apr. 2018, heroic.academy/truth-about-record-deals/.

by DoiteMedia, Published. "Music Industry Contracts." *Doite Media*, doitemedia.com/2021/05/15/music-industry-contracts/.

CD Baby, cdbaby.com/.

Coleman, Basha. "Paid Social Media: Worth The Investment?" *HubSpot Blog*, 6 Apr. 2021, blog.hubspot.com/marketing/paid-social-media.

"DistroKid Is the Easiest Way for Musicians to Get Their Music into Spotify, ITunes, Apple Music, Amazon, TikTok, Google Play, and More." *DistroKid*, distrokid.com/.

Evans, Luke. "Music Industry Contracts." *Exploration*, Exploration, 5 Apr. 2021, exploration.io/music-industry-contracts/.

"EXCLUSIVE MANAGEMENT AGREEMENT." *Law Insider*, www.lawinsider.com/contracts/fXoxRrDkout.

"Focusrite Scarlett 2i2 3rd Generation Recording Bundle." *Sweetwater*, www.sweetwater.com/store/detail/Scarlet2i2SG3--focusrite-scarlett-2i2-studio-3rd-gen-recording-bundle?mrkgadid=3331460994&mrkgcl=28&mrkgen=gtext&mrkgbflag=0&mrkgcat=studio&recording=&acctid=21700000001645388&dskeywordid=43700046746307397&lid=43700046746307397&ds_s_kwgid=58700005287203675&device=c&network=g&matchtype=b&adpos=largenumber&locationid=9003474&creative=377026426769&targetid=kwd-301030327111&campaignid=1671271322&awsearchcpc=1&gclid=Cj0KCQjw5auGBhDEARIsAFyNm9FccckXlWhFOOYJ3W7pmd5dmxZTtIPV2Ab2UHdIyw0399pBZGTVVAkaAnldEALw_wcB&gclsrc=aw.ds.

"Future of Music Coalition." *Major Label Contract Clause Critique | Future of Music Coalition*, futureofmusic.org/article/article/major-label-contract-clause-critique.

Goldstein, Alice. "10 Essential Tips For a Long and Lucrative Music Career." *Entrepreneur*, 16 June 2017, www.entrepreneur.com/article/295461.

"A Guide To Music Merchandise: Rotor Videos 🎬." *Rotor Videos*, rotorvideos.com/blog/finance-creativity-with-music-merchandise.

hess, patrick. "A Guide for Touring in the Music Industry..." *Creative Guitar Studio*, creativeguitarstudio.blogspot.com/2014/08/a-guide-for-touring-in-music-industry.html.

"JBL 305P MkII." *Powered 5" (10.16 Cm) Two-Way Studio Monitor*, www.jbl.com/studio-monitors/305PMKII-.html.

Legaspi, Althea. "'Blurred Lines' Copyright Suit Against Robin Thicke, Pharrell Ends in $5M Judgment." *Rolling Stone*, Rolling Stone, 13 Dec. 2018, www.rollingstone.com/music/music-news/robin-thicke-pharrell-williams-blurred-lines-copyright-suit-final-5-million-dollar-judgment-768508/.

"LinkedIn Statistics & Facts." *LinkedIn Marketing for Lead Generation*, 3 May 2020, link4leads.com/linkedin-statistics-facts/.

"Manley Reference Cardioid Large-Diaphragm Tube Condener Microphone and Core Channel Strip Bundle." *Sweetwater*, www.sweetwater.com/store/detail/ManBun--manley-reference-cardioid-microphone-and-core-channel-strip-bundle.

"Mixing Vocals : The Ultimate Guide to EQ'ing Vocals." *Behind The Mixer*, 19 May 2018, www.behindthemixer.com/mixing-vocals-the-ultimate-guide-to-eqing-vocals/.

Moorwood, Victoria. "Juice WRLD Hit with $15 Million Copyright Infringement Lawsuit over 'Lucid Dreams.'" *REVOLT*, REVOLT, 22 Oct. 2019, www.revolt.tv/2019/10/22/20926678/juice-wrld-lucid-dreams-lawsuit.

Muller, Marissa G. "10 Ways To Fund Your Music Career." *The FADER*, The FADER, 7 Nov. 2017, www.thefader.com/2015/02/03/10-ways-to-fund-your-music-career.

"Music Copyrights 101 - Protect and Copyright Your Music." *United States*, 20 Nov. 2019, www.tunecore.com/guides/copyrights-101).

Music Gateway. "ASCAP vs BMI vs SESAC - How To Get Your Royalties." *Music Gateway*, 22 Aug. 2019, www.musicgateway.com/blog/how-to/ascap-vs-bmi-vs-sesac.

"Music Services and Brand Opportunities for Artists." *UnitedMasters*, unitedmasters.com/.

Music, Kobalt. *AWAL*, www.awal.com/.

"A New Music Distribution Platform for Independent Artists." *Level*, levelmusic.com/.

"PreSonus AudioBox ITwo Studio - 2x2 USB/IPad Recording System." *Sweetwater*, www.sweetwater.com/store/detail/AudioBxi2Stu--presonus-audiobox-itwo-studio-2x2-usb-ipad-recording-system.

"Release Your Music with Ditto." *Ditto Music Distribution*, dittomusic.com/en/?utm_source=google&utm_medium=cpc&utm_campaign=USA_%7C_Brand_%7C_Ditto&utm_adgroup=USA_%7C_Brand_%7C_Ditto_Music&gclid=CjwKCAjwiLGGBhAqEiwAgq3q_qqbNzraJf-JaFLYWUXLOZRmAWW9As9BF9h7Fxs8B1lo5JQvVPni3RoCMYUQAvD_BwE.

"ROKIT 5 G4." *KRK SYSTEMS - ROKIT 5 G4 Professional Bi-Amp Studio Monitors Speaker*, www.krkmusic.com/Studio-Monitors/ROKIT-5-G4?gclid=CjwKCAjwiLGGBhAqEiwAgq3q_pjXSEXgAslGYBvcR65kJw-CSvbNnqSE2S_6zmYIeOGigCmaiaMBmhoCAKQQAvD_BwE.

"SM27." *Professional Large Diaphragm Condenser Microphone*, www.shure.com/en-US/products/microphones/sm27.

smith, kit. "50 Incredible Instagram Statistics You Need to Know." *Brandwatch*, www.brandwatch.com/blog/instagram-stats/.

Songstuff. "Music Publishing Contracts." *Songstuff*, 7 Apr. 2016, www.songstuff.com/music-business/article/music_publishing_contracts/).

Spinnup, spinnup.com/.

"Spotify Revenue and Usage Statistics (2021)." *Business of Apps*, 2 Apr. 2021, www.businessofapps.com/data/spotify-statistics/.

"TikTok Announces a Deal with UnitedMasters, Its First Music Distribution Partnership." *Yahoo! Finance*, Yahoo!, au.finance.yahoo.com/news/tiktok-announces-deal-unitedmasters-first-143349364.html.

"Townsend Labs Sphere L22 and Apollo Twin X DUO Heritage Edition Vocal Recording Bundle." *Sweetwater*, www.sweetwater.com/store/detail/L22-TXDHE--townsend-labs-sphere-l22-and-apollo-twin-by-duo-heritage-edition-vocal-recording-bundle.

"TuneCore: Sell Your Music Online - Digital Music Distribution." *United States*, 7 June 2021, www.tunecore.com/?ref=c_9003682&cmp=e_&utm_content=257744318877_&utm_term=tunecore&utm_source=google&utm_medium=cpc&utm_campaign=us_b_tem o&gclid=CjwKCAjwiLGGBhAqEiwAgq3q_pNOIMy0OLou_8bRYNi05wDuXrOKy afhijhrHD5SZnvS6DYBvgZMfRoCAHcQAvD_BwE.

Ucaya. "Market Intelligence for the Music Industry." *Soundcharts*, soundcharts.com/blog/how-the-music-publishing-works.

VAVER, DAVID. "PRINCIPLES OF COPYRIGHT." *Wip*, www.wipo.int/edocs/pubdocs/fr/copyright/844/wipo_pub_844.pdf.

"What Do Ai Need As A Beginner Artist ?: #1 Beginner Artist Guide." *WHITEBOIBEATS.COM*, www.whiteboibeats.com/blog/beginner-artist-guide#/.

"What Is Global Copyright? International Copyright Basics." *RightsDirect*, 23 Dec. 2020, www.rightsdirect.com/international-copyright-basics/.

"The X1 S." *SE Electronics*, www.seelectronics.com/se-x1s-microphone.

"YouTube Revenue and Usage Statistics (2021)." *Business of Apps*, 14 May 2021, www.businessofapps.com/data/youtube-statistics/#1.

ABOUT THE AUTHOR

Frank Demilt is a 27-year-old graduate of the Ithaca College Roy Park School of Communications. With 8 years in the music industry, he has collaborated with numerous Grammy-award & Emmy-award nominated/winning artists and producers. Now working as the head of artist development/A&R for the award-winning publishing company Water Music, he is grooming the next generation of artists for success in the business. *The Blueprint* is Frank's first book.

ENDNOTES

i https://www.sweetwater.com/store/detail/AudioBxi2Stu--presonus-audiobox-itwo-studio-2x2-usb-ipad-recording-system

ii https://www.sweetwater.com/store/detail/Scarlet2i2SG3--focusrite-scarlett-2i2-studio-3rd-gen-recording-bundle?mrkgadid=3331460994&mrkgcl=28&mrkgen=gtext&mrkgbflag=0&mrkgcat=studio&recording=&acctid=21700000001645388&dskeywordid=43700046746307397&lid=43700046746307397&ds_s_kwgid=58700005287203675&device=c&network=g&matchtype=b&adpos=largenumber&locationid=9003474&creative=377026426769&targetid=kwd-301030327111&campaignid=1671271322&awsearchcpc=1&gclid=Cj0KCQjw5auGBhDEARIsAFyNm9FccckXlWhFOOYJ3W7pmd5dmxZTtIPV2Ab2UHdIyw0399pBZGTVVAkaAnldEALw_wcB&gclsrc=aw.ds

iii Dwrl.utexas.edu

iv https://acousticbridge.com/best-cheap-microphones/#:~:text=Condenser%20microphones%20create%20sound%20with,and%20the%20backplate%20stays%20still.&text=Condenser%20mics%20need%20a%20power,batteries

v https://acousticbridge.com/best-cheap-microphones/#:~:text=Condenser%20microphones%20create%20sound%20with,and%20the%20backplate%20stays%20still.&text=Condenser%20mics%20need%20a%20power,batteries

vi https://acousticbridge.com/best-cheap-microphones/#:~:text=Condenser%20microphones%20create%20sound%20with,and%20the%20backplate%20stays%20still.&text=Condenser%20mics%20need%20a%20power,batteries

vii https://www.bluemic.com/en-us/products/bluebird-sl/

viii https://www.shure.com/en-US/products/microphones/sm27

ix https://www.seelectronics.com/se-x1s-microphone

x https://www.recordingbase.com/near-field-vs-far-field/

xi https://www.recordingbase.com/near-field-vs-far-field/

xii https://www.krkmusic.com/Studio-Monitors/ROKIT-5-G4?gclid=CjwKCAjwiLGGBhAqEiwAgq3q_pjXSEXgAslGYBvcR65kJw-CSvbNnqSE2S_6zmYIeOGigCmaiaMBmhoCAKQQAvD_BwE

xiii https://www.jbl.com/studio-monitors/305PMKII-.html

xiv https://www.sweetwater.com/store/detail/L22-TXDHE--townsend-labs-sphere-l22-and-apollo-twin-by-duo-heritage-edition-vocal-recording-bundle

xv https://www.sweetwater.com/store/detail/ManBun--manley-reference-cardioid-microphone-and-core-channel-strip-bundle

xvi Musicianonamission.com

xvii https://www.behindthemixer.com/mixing-vocals-the-ultimate-guide-to-eqing-vocals/

xviii Producerhive.com

xix https://www.behindthemixer.com/mixing-vocals-the-ultimate-guide-to-eqing-vocals/

xx Musicmixpro.co.uk

xxi https://www.behindthemixer.com/mixing-vocals-the-ultimate-guide-to-eqing-vocals/

xxii https://www.behindthemixer.com/mixing-vocals-the-ultimate-guide-to-eqing-vocals/

xxiii https://www.behindthemixer.com/mixing-vocals-the-ultimate-guide-to-eqing-vocals/

xxiv https://www.behindthemixer.com/mixing-vocals-the-ultimate-guide-to-eqing-vocals/

xxv https://www.behindthemixer.com/mixing-vocals-the-ultimate-guide-to-eqing-vocals/

xxvi https://www.behindthemixer.com/mixing-vocals-the-ultimate-guide-to-eqing-vocals/

xxvii https://www.behindthemixer.com/mixing-vocals-the-ultimate-guide-to-eqing-vocals/

xxviii https://www.behindthemixer.com/mixing-vocals-the-ultimate-guide-to-eqing-vocals/

xxix Masteringthemix.com

xxx https://www.musicgateway.com/blog/how-to/ascap-vs-bmi-vs-sesac

xxxi https://www.musicgateway.com/blog/how-to/ascap-vs-bmi-vs-sesac

xxxii https://www.musicgateway.com/blog/how-to/ascap-vs-bmi-vs-sesac

xxxiii https://www.tunecore.com/guides/copyrights-101

xxxiv https://www.whiteboibeats.com/blog/beginner-artist-guide#/

xxxv https://www.whiteboibeats.com/blog/beginner-artist-guide#/

xxxvi https://www.whiteboibeats.com/blog/beginner-artist-guide#/

xxxvii https://www.whiteboibeats.com/blog/beginner-artist-guide#/

xxxviii https://www.whiteboibeats.com/blog/beginner-artist-guide#/

xxxix https://www.whiteboibeats.com/blog/beginner-artist-guide#/

xl https://www.legalzoom.com/articles/8-basic-facts-every-musician-should-know-about-copyright-law

xli https://www.legalzoom.com/articles/8-basic-facts-every-musician-should-know-about-copyright-law

xlii https://www.legalzoom.com/articles/8-basic-facts-every-musician-should-know-about-copyright-law

xliii https://www.legalzoom.com/articles/8-basic-facts-every-musician-should-know-about-copyright-law

xliv https://www.legalzoom.com/articles/8-basic-facts-every-musician-should-know-about-copyright-law

xlv https://www.legalzoom.com/articles/8-basic-facts-every-musician-should-know-about-copyright-law

xlvi https://www.legalzoom.com/articles/8-basic-facts-every-musician-should-know-about-copyright-law

xlvii https://www.legalzoom.com/articles/8-basic-facts-every-musician-should-know-about-copyright-law

xlviii https://www.wipo.int/edocs/pubdocs/fr/copyright/844/wipo_pub_844.pdf

xlix https://distrokid.com/

l https://cdbaby.com/

li https://www.tunecore.com/?ref=c_9003682&cmp=e_&utm_content=257744318877_&utm_term=tunecore&utm_source=google&utm_medium=cpc&utm_campaign=us_b_temo&gclid=CjwKCAjwiLGGBhAqEiwAgq3q_pNOIMy0OLou_8bRYNi05wDuXrOKyafhijhrHD5SZnvS6DYBvgZMfRoCAHcQAvD_BwE

lii https://www.awal.com/

liii https://unitedmasters.com/

liv https://dittomusic.com/en/?utm_source=google&utm_medium=cpc&utm_campaign=USA_%7C_Brand_%7C_Ditto&utm_adgroup=USA_%7C_Brand_%7C_Ditto_Music&gclid=CjwKCAjwiLGGBhAqEiwAgq3q_qqbNzraJf-JaFLYWUXLOZRmAWW9As9BF9h7Fxs8B1lo5JQvVPni3RoCMYUQAvD_BwE

lv https://www.recordunion.com/

lvi https://spinnup.com/

lvii https://levelmusic.com/

lviii https://www.businessofapps.com/data/youtube-statistics/#1

lix https://www.businessofapps.com/data/spotify-statistics/

lx https://rotorvideos.com/blog/best-music-streaming-sites-promote-your-tracks

lxi https://rotorvideos.com/blog/best-music-streaming-sites-promote-your-tracks

lxii https://rotorvideos.com/blog/best-music-streaming-sites-promote-your-tracks

lxiii https://rotorvideos.com/blog/best-music-streaming-sites-promote-your-tracks

lxiv https://rotorvideos.com/blog/best-music-streaming-sites-promote-your-tracks

lxv https://rotorvideos.com/blog/best-music-streaming-sites-promote-your-tracks

lxvi https://rotorvideos.com/blog/best-music-streaming-sites-promote-your-tracks

lxvii https://rotorvideos.com/blog/best-music-streaming-sites-promote-your-tracks

lxviii https://rotorvideos.com/blog/best-music-streaming-sites-promote-your-tracks

lxix https://rotorvideos.com/blog/best-music-streaming-sites-promote-your-tracks

lxx https://rotorvideos.com/blog/best-music-streaming-sites-promote-your-tracks

lxxi https://rotorvideos.com/blog/best-music-streaming-sites-promote-your-tracks

lxxii https://www.brandwatch.com/blog/instagram-stats/

lxxiii https://www.keystoneclick.com/resource-library/blog/facebook-who-uses-it-what-motivates-them-and-what-content-engages-them

lxxiv https://blog.twitter.com/en_us/topics/product/2020/introducing-fleets-new-way-to-join-the-conversation

lxxv https://au.finance.yahoo.com/news/tiktok-announces-deal-unitedmasters-first-143349364.html

lxxvi https://www.yahoo.com/entertainment/tiktok-strikes-licensing-deal-sony-161423808.html

lxxvii https://link4leads.com/statistics_facts/linkedin-has-675-million-monthly-users/

lxxviii https://blog.hubspot.com/marketing/paid-social-media

lxxix https://blog.hubspot.com/marketing/paid-social-media

lxxx https://blog.hubspot.com/marketing/paid-social-media

lxxxi https://blog.hubspot.com/marketing/paid-social-media

lxxxii https://rotorvideos.com/blog/finance-creativity-with-music-merchandise

lxxxiii https://rotorvideos.com/blog/finance-creativity-with-music-merchandise

lxxxiv https://rotorvideos.com/blog/finance-creativity-with-music-merchandise

lxxxv https://rotorvideos.com/blog/finance-creativity-with-music-merchandise

lxxxvi https://rotorvideos.com/blog/finance-creativity-with-music-merchandise

lxxxvii https://rotorvideos.com/blog/finance-creativity-with-music-merchandise

lxxxviii https://soundcharts.com/blog/how-the-music-publishing-works

lxxxix https://www.rollingstone.com/music/music-news/robin-thicke-pharrell-williams-blurred-lines-copyright-suit-final-5-million-dollar-judgment-768508/

xc https://www.rollingstone.com/music/music-news/robin-thicke-pharrell-williams-blurred-lines-copyright-suit-final-5-million-dollar-judgment-768508/

xci https://doitemedia.com/2021/05/15/music-industry-contracts/

xcii https://doitemedia.com/2021/05/15/music-industry-contracts/

xciii https://doitemedia.com/2021/05/15/music-industry-contracts/

xciv https://doitemedia.com/2021/05/15/music-industry-contracts/

xcv https://doitemedia.com/2021/05/15/music-industry-contracts/

xcvi https://doitemedia.com/2021/05/15/music-industry-contracts/

xcvii https://doitemedia.com/2021/05/15/music-industry-contracts/

xcviii https://doitemedia.com/2021/05/15/music-industry-contracts/

xcix https://www.lawinsider.com/contracts/fXoxRrDkout

c https://sloppyvinyl.com/2020/06/20/understanding-your-contracts/

ci https://sloppyvinyl.com/2020/06/20/understanding-your-contracts/

cii https://sloppyvinyl.com/2020/06/20/understanding-your-contracts/

ciii https://exploration.io/music-industry-contracts/

civ https://exploration.io/music-industry-contracts/

cv https://exploration.io/music-industry-contracts/

cvi https://exploration.io/music-industry-contracts/

cvii https://exploration.io/music-industry-contracts/

cviii https://exploration.io/music-industry-contracts/

cix https://exploration.io/music-industry-contracts/

cx https://exploration.io/music-industry-contracts/

cxi https://exploration.io/music-industry-contracts/

cxii https://exploration.io/music-industry-contracts/

cxiii https://exploration.io/music-industry-contracts/

cxiv https://exploration.io/music-industry-contracts/

cxv https://heroic.academy/truth-about-record-deals/

cxvi https://heroic.academy/truth-about-record-deals/

cxvii https://heroic.academy/truth-about-record-deals/

cxviii http://creativeguitarstudio.blogspot.com/2014/08/a-guide-for-touring-in-music-industry.html

cxix http://creativeguitarstudio.blogspot.com/2014/08/a-guide-for-touring-in-music-industry.html
cxx http://creativeguitarstudio.blogspot.com/2014/08/a-guide-for-touring-in-music-industry.html
cxxi https://www.entrepreneur.com/article/295461
cxxii https://www.entrepreneur.com/article/295461
cxxiii https://www.entrepreneur.com/article/295461
cxxiv https://www.thefader.com/2015/02/03/10-ways-to-fund-your-music-career
cxxv https://www.thefader.com/2015/02/03/10-ways-to-fund-your-music-career
cxxvi https://www.thefader.com/2015/02/03/10-ways-to-fund-your-music-career
cxxvii https://www.thefader.com/2015/02/03/10-ways-to-fund-your-music-career
cxxviii https://www.thefader.com/2015/02/03/10-ways-to-fund-your-music-career
cxxix https://www.musicconnection.com/rehearse-dont-forget/
cxxx https://www.musicconnection.com/rehearse-dont-forget/
cxxxi https://www.musicconnection.com/rehearse-dont-forget/
cxxxii https://rotorvideos.com/blog/finance-creativity-with-music-merchandise
cxxxiii https://rotorvideos.com/blog/finance-creativity-with-music-merchandise
cxxxiv https://rotorvideos.com/blog/finance-creativity-with-music-merchandise
cxxxv https://rotorvideos.com/blog/finance-creativity-with-music-merchandise
cxxxvi https://www.rightsdirect.com/international-copyright-basics/
cxxxvii https://www.rightsdirect.com/international-copyright-basics/
cxxxviii https://www.rightsdirect.com/international-copyright-basics/
cxxxix https://www.songstuff.com/music-business/article/music_publishing_contracts/
cxl https://www.songstuff.com/music-business/article/music_publishing_contracts/
cxli https://www.songstuff.com/music-business/article/music_publishing_contracts/
cxlii https://www.songstuff.com/music-business/article/music_publishing_contracts/
cxliii https://exploration.io/music-industry-contracts/
cxliv https://exploration.io/music-industry-contracts/
cxlv https://exploration.io/music-industry-contracts/
cxlvi https://exploration.io/music-industry-contracts/
cxlvii https://doitemedia.com/2021/05/15/music-industry-contracts/
cxlviii https://exploration.io/music-industry-contracts/
cxlix https://doitemedia.com/2021/05/15/music-industry-contracts/
cl https://doitemedia.com/2021/05/15/music-industry-contracts/
cli https://doitemedia.com/2021/05/15/music-industry-contracts/
clii https://exploration.io/music-industry-contracts/
cliii https://exploration.io/music-industry-contracts/
cliv https://exploration.io/music-industry-contracts/
clv https://sloppyvinyl.com/2020/06/20/understanding-your-contracts/
clvi https://doitemedia.com/2021/05/15/music-industry-contracts/
clvii https://doitemedia.com/2021/05/15/music-industry-contracts/
clviii https://doitemedia.com/2021/05/15/music-industry-contracts/
clix https://exploration.io/music-industry-contracts/
clx https://doitemedia.com/2021/05/15/music-industry-contracts/
clxi https://doitemedia.com/2021/05/15/music-industry-contracts/
clxii https://sloppyvinyl.com/2020/06/20/understanding-your-contracts/
clxiii https://sloppyvinyl.com/2020/06/20/understanding-your-contracts/
clxiv https://sloppyvinyl.com/2020/06/20/understanding-your-contracts/
clxv https://heroic.academy/truth-about-record-deals/
clxvi https://heroic.academy/truth-about-record-deals/
clxvii https://heroic.academy/truth-about-record-deals/

clxviii https://heroic.academy/truth-about-record-deals/
clxix https://heroic.academy/truth-about-record-deals/